Understanding JPA 2.2

Java Persistence API

Antonio Goncalves

2021-05-03

Table of Contents

Understanding JPA 2.2

agoncal.fascicle@gmail.com

The distribution of the book is made through Amazon KDP (Kindle Direct Publishing).[1]

Any source code referenced by the author in this text is available to readers at https://github.com/agoncal/agoncal-fascicle-jpa/tree/2.2. This source code is available for reproduction and distribution as it uses an MIT licence.[2]

- www.antoniogoncalves.org
- agoncal.teachable.com
- www.amazon.com/author/agoncal

You can find two different formats of this fascicle:

- eBook (PDF/EPUB): https://agoncal.teachable.com/p/ebook-understanding-jpa
- Paper book: https://www.amazon.com/Understanding-JPA-2-2-Persistence-fascicle/dp/1093918977 (ISBN: 9781093918977)

Version Date: 2021-05-03

To my wonderful kids, Eloise, Ligia and Ennio, who are the best thing life has given me.

Foreword

Lots of Java applications use an *Object-Relational Mapping* (ORM) framework, like Hibernate ORM or EclipseLink, to read data from and to write it to a relational database. As a reader of this fascicle, you might already know that both frameworks implement the Java Persistence API (JPA) specification and that the popular Spring Data JPA project integrates them into the Spring ecosystem. But don't worry if you've never heard about the JPA specification. If that's the case, I want to congratulate you on your decision to learn about it.

JPA is one of the most popular specifications in the Java world. It defines an easy-to-use way to map database records to Java objects and to update the database records based on the changes you performed on these Java objects. It also specifies a query language that you can use to define database queries based on your Java classes. All of these powerful features are relatively easy to use if you know the basic concepts of JPA. That's why Hibernate ORM and other JPA implementations have become so popular and are used in most enterprise Java applications.

So, it should be evident that, as a professional Java developer or somebody who aspires to become one, you should have a solid understanding of JPA's general concepts and capabilities.

When Antonio asked me to write this foreword, I more than happily agreed to do it. I still remember reading his blog articles at the relative beginning of my career as a Java developer in the mid-2000s. That makes writing this foreword something special. His ability to explain complex features in an easily understandable way still amazes me, and it made me a long-time reader and follower of his work.

I obviously wasn't the only one who liked his style of teaching and writing. In 2007, he wrote and published his first book about Java EE 5. And that was just the beginning. During the following years, he wrote 3 additional books and recorded 7 video courses teaching Java developers various Java EE specifications, like JPA or Bean Validation. He also worked as an expert group member on various Java EE specifications and co-created the Devoxx France and the Voxxed Days Microservices conferences. Antonio is clearly a prolific member of the Java EE community, and that's just one of the reasons why he became a Java Champion.

Several years into my career, after I learned as much about JPA and Hibernate ORM as I could, and after I became a freelance consultant and trainer specialised in solving Java persistence problems, I finally met Antonio at a speaker's dinner in Prague. And let me tell you, he not only has an impressive knowledge about Java EE technologies and knows how to share it with other developers, but he is also a great guy who's fun to hang out with. This was just one of the various reasons why I happily agreed to proofread this fascicle and to write this foreword.

But let's get back to this fascicle.

The JPA specification defines a vast feature set that makes working with a relational database simple and complex at the same time. It only takes a few annotations to implement robust and efficient mappings. You can then focus on your business code, and the JPA implementation takes care of all the nitty-gritty details.

But it only works that way if you're familiar with the general concepts of the specification. You need to know how the internal life cycle model works, which annotations you need to use and all the defaults that your JPA implementation applies.

Antonio does a great job explaining all of it in this fascicle. He first shows you the necessary configuration parameters and mapping annotations that you need in order to start implementing your first persistence layer. After that, Antonio explains the different query capabilities defined by the JPA specification before he dives into its more advanced features, like life cycle events and caching.

And after you've learned about all the features specified by the JPA specification, you should pay special attention to Chapter 10. There, Antonio shows you how to use your new knowledge to implement and test a small application so that you are well prepared to use JPA in your own projects.

Thorben Janssen
Independent Consultant and Trainer
https://thoughts-on-java.org

[1] KDP https://kdp.amazon.com

[2] MIT licence https://opensource.org/licenses/MIT

About the Author

Antonio Goncalves is a senior software architect living in Paris. Having been focused on Java development since the late 1990s, his career has taken him to many different countries and companies where he now works as a recognised consultant. As a former employee of BEA Systems (acquired by Oracle), he developed a very early expertise on distributed systems. He is particularly fond of open source and is a member of the OSSGTP (Open Source Solution Get Together Paris). Antonio loves to create bonds with the community. So, he created the Paris Java User Group in 2008 and co-created Devoxx France in 2012 and Voxxed Microservices in 2018.[3]

Antonio wrote his first book on Java EE 5, in French, in 2007. He then joined the JCP to become an Expert Member of various JSRs (Java EE 8, Java EE 7, Java EE 6, CDI 2.0, JPA 2.0, and EJB 3.1) and wrote *Beginning Java EE 7* and *Beginning Java EE 8* with Apress.[4] Still hooked on sharing his knowledge, Antonio Goncalves decided to then self-publish his later fascicles.

For the last few years, Antonio has given talks at international conferences, mainly on Java, distributed systems and microservices, including JavaOne, Devoxx, GeeCon, The Server Side Symposium, Jazoon, and many Java User Groups. He has also written numerous technical papers and articles for IT websites (DevX) and IT magazines (Java Magazine, Programmez, Linux Magazine). Since 2009, he has been part of the French Java podcast called Les Cast Codeurs.[5]

In recognition of his expertise and all of his work for the Java community, Antonio has been elected **Java Champion**.[6]

Antonio is a graduate of the Conservatoire National des Arts et Métiers in Paris (with an engineering degree in IT), Brighton University (with an MSc in object-oriented design), Universidad del Pais Vasco in Spain, and UFSCar University in Brazil (MPhil in Distributed Systems). He also taught for more than 10 years at the Conservatoire National des Arts et Métiers where he previously studied.

Follow Antonio on Twitter (@agoncal) and on his blog (www.antoniogoncalves.org).

[3] Devoxx France https://devoxx.fr

[4] Amazon https://www.amazon.com/author/agoncal

[5] Les Cast Codeurs https://lescastcodeurs.com

[6] Java Champions https://developer.oracle.com/javachampions

Acknowledgments

In your hands, you have a technical fascicle that comes from my history of writing, learning and sharing. When writing, you need a dose of curiosity, a glimpse of discipline, an inch of concentration, and a huge amount of craziness. And of course, you need to be surrounded by people who help you in any possible way (so you don't get totally crazy). And this is the space to thank them.

First of all, I really want to thank my proofreading team. After the process of writing, I was constantly in contact with Thorben, Youness, Aurelie and Aymeric who reviewed the book and gave me precious advice. I have to say, it was a real pleasure to work with such knowledgeable developers.

It is a great honour to have **Thorben Janssen** writing the foreword of this book. Thorben is an independent consultant and trainer specialised in solving Java persistence problems with JPA and Hibernate. He is also the author of Amazon's bestselling book Hibernate Tips - More than 70 solutions to common Hibernate problems. Thorben has been working with Java and Java EE for almost 20 years and is a member of the CDI 2.0 expert group (JSR 365). He writes about JPA, Hibernate ORM and other persistence-related topics on his blog.[7]

Youness Teimouri is a Senior Software Java Developer with over a decade of experience in Java development. He has utilised Java stack to grow numerous companies in a variety of industries such as Telecoms, Mobile Banking, ERP and Field Service Management systems. He has co-authored and contributed to some papers on Cloud-Computing and some of my previous books. Youness is fascinated by the endless possibilities of Java in different industries and enjoys mentoring junior developers, inspiring them to develop their own Java skill-set. He lives in Canada.[8]

Aurélie Vache is a Cloud Developer (& DevOps) at Continental Intelligent Transportation Systems in Toulouse, France.[9] She has been working as a developer for more than 10 years. Formerly a Java/Java EE developer, then Web, Full-Stack, and Lead developer, she is now a Cloud developer and doing DevOps on connected and autonomous vehicles projects. Go, Docker, Kubernetes, Istio, Jenkins, Terraform ... are part of her everyday life. She is a swiss-knife. As a leader in Duchess France, an association that promotes female developers and women in IT, she is strongly involved with their coaching initiative #AdoptADuchess that helps junior developers and people in reconversion.[10] She is also one of DevFest Toulouse organisers, a member of the Toulouse Data Science (TDS) core team, and a mentor at Simplon and Elles Bougent. She loves writing technical articles.

Aymeric Beaumet is a Senior Software Engineer from Paris, France. His primary professional focus is on back end architecture and development but he is also curious to explore a wide range of computer science topics in his free time like machine learning or home automation. His previous experiences are as diverse as working for early startups to working for companies like Microsoft. He now works at PayFit as a Performance Engineer, focusing on scalability, availability and language theory. He likes to assist the Node.js, JS, TS, Golang and Rust Paris meetups; he is also a volunteer at the Devoxx France conference; you might meet him there!

Thanks to my proofreader, **Gary Branigan**, who added a Shakespearean touch to the fascicle.

Integrating JPA with CDI and JTA is a bit of work. I would like to thank Gunnar Morling for his help in integrating all these technologies so they can be easily tested.

I could not have written this fascicle without the help and support of the Java community: blogs, articles, mailing lists, forums, tweets etc.

The fascicle you have in your hands uses a rich Asciidoctor 2.0.14 toolchain, making it possible to create PDF, EPUB and MOBI files. I am really grateful to the entire Asciidoctor community, and to Dan Allen and Marat Radchenko in particular, who helped me in sorting out a few things so that the end result looks so great.[11] PlantUML is an amazing tool with a very rich syntax for drawing diagrams... and sometimes, you need a bit of help. So, thanks to the PlantUML community.[12] As for the text editor used to write this fascicle, you might have guessed: it's an IDE! Thank you JetBrains for providing me with a free licence for your excellent IntelliJ IDEA.[13]

Living in Paris, I also have to thank all the bars who have given me shelter so that I could write while drinking coffee and talking to people: La Fontaine, Le Chat Bossu, La Grille, La Liberté and Bottle Shop.

As you might have guessed, I have a passion for IT. But I have other passions such as science, art, philosophy, cooking... and music (I even play jazz guitar). I cannot work without listening to music, so while I was writing this fascicle, I spent most of my time listing to the best radio ever: FIP.[14] Thank you FIP.

And a big kiss to my wonderful kids, Eloise, Ligia and Ennio. They are the best present life has given me.

Thank you all!

[7] Thorben Janssen blog https://thoughts-on-java.org

[8] Youness Teimouri http://www.youness-teimouri.com

[9] @aurelievache https://twitter.com/aurelievache

[10] Duchess France http://www.duchess-france.org

[11] Asciidoctor http://asciidoctor.org

[12] PlantUML http://plantuml.com

[13] IntelliJ IDEA https://www.jetbrains.com/idea

[14] FIP https://www.fip.fr

Introduction

In the late 90s, I was working on J2EE 1.2: the very first release of the *Java Enterprise Edition*. It was also the time where companies started to realise the potential of the Internet for their business. For a few months, I worked for a famous English airline company setting up their e-commerce website. Yes, it was a time where you would usually buy a flight or train ticket at a travel agency. This revolutionary move (buying flights online) came at a technical cost: a cluster for static content (HTML, CSS, images), a cluster for the web tier (Servlets and JSPs), a cluster for Stateless EJBs, a cluster for Entity Beans, and a cluster for the database. And as you can imagine, load balancing, failover and sticky sessions for every tier were loaded with application servers. This e-commerce website went live… and it worked!

Then came Struts, Spring and Hibernate. Full J2EE application servers shrank down to servlet containers such as Tomcat or Jetty. We could see things moving, such as architectures becoming stateless, failover being abandoned, migrations from SOAP to REST and mobile devices taking over web crawling. Then came the *Internet of Things* (IoT), the cloud, microservices, *Function as a Service* (FaaS), and it never stops moving. Other things didn't change, like the good old *Gang of Four* design patterns, architecture design patterns, unit testing frameworks and building tools. We reinvented some wheels and gave them different names, but we also learnt dozens of new promising programming languages (running on top of the JVM or not) and agile techniques. Thanks to these evolutions that I have witnessed, today you can sit down, read this fascicle and write some code.

Where Does This Fascicle Come From?

Involved in J2EE since 1998, I followed its evolution and joined the Java EE expert group from version 6 to version 8. During that time, I wrote a book in French called "*Java EE 5*".[15] The book was published by a French editor and got noticed. I was then contacted by Apress, an American editor, to work on an English version. I liked the challenge. So, I changed the structure of the book, updated it, translated it, and I ended up with a "*Beginning Java EE 6*" book. A few years later, Java EE 7 was released, so I updated my book, added a few extra chapters, and ended up with a "*Beginning Java EE 7*" that was 500 pages long.[16]. This process of writing got a bit painful (some text editors shouldn't be used to write books), inflexible (it's hard to update a paper book frequently) and I also had some arguments with my editor.[17]

Parallel to that, the history of Java EE 8 was also somewhat painful and long.[18] I was still part of the Expert Group, but nobody really knew why the experts' mailing list was so quiet. No real exchange, no real vision, no real challenges. That's when I decided not to work on a Java EE 8 book. But the community said otherwise. I started receiving emails about updating my book. I used to always meet someone at a conference going "*Hey, Antonio, when is your next book coming out?*" My answer was "*No way!*"

I decided to take stock. What was holding me back from writing? Clearly it was my editor and Java EE 8. So, I decided to get rid of both. I extracted the chapters I wanted from my Java EE 7 book and updated them. That's where the idea of writing "*fascicles*", instead of an entire book, came from. Then, I looked at self-publishing, and here I am at Amazon Kindle Publishing.[19]

Java Persistence API took up three chapters of my "Beginning Java EE 7" and was more than one hundred pages long. It was about Java Persistence API 2.0. Since then, this specification has evolved towards a version 2.2 and is used in many different frameworks. I even created an entire online course for PluralSight.[20] And today, I still use JPA extensively in my projects.

I hope you'll find this fascicle useful.

Who Is This Fascicle For?

Java Persistence API has its genesis in the Hibernate community. It was then specified in the JCP and became part of the Java EE platform.

So, this fascicle is for the Java community as a whole. If you come from Java EE, you will be, of course, very familiar with JPA. But this fascicle is also meant to be used by the Spring community. Spring has embraced JPA since the beginning. So, all of the explanations and examples you'll see in this fascicle work out of the box with Spring, Java EE and other Java technologies.

And of course, Java Persistence API works on plain vanilla Java SE, so any Java developer can benefit from it. The only requirement to follow and understand this fascicle is to know Java and have some knowledge of relational database.

How Is This Fascicle Structured?

This fascicle concentrates on JPA 2.2. Its structure will help you to discover this technology as well as helping you to further dive into it if you already have some experience of it.

This fascicle starts with Chapter 1, *First Step with JPA* by showing a few lines of JPA code. That's because, as developers, we like to read code first when learning a new technology.

Chapter 2, *Understanding Java Persistence API* briefly presents Java Persistence API, the problems it addresses and explains the common concerns discussed throughout the fascicle. This chapter also looks at the standardisation side of this technology and where it comes from.

Chapter 3, *Getting Started* is all about showing some basic code of Java Persistence API and introducing its main APIs and deployment descriptors.

Chapter 4, *Mapping Entities* introduces object to relational mapping (i.e. mapping Java objects to a relational database) and shows how we can use annotation and XML to map JPA entities to a relational database.

Once entities are mapped, Chapter 5, *Managing Entities* will show you how to manage these entities: how to persist, remove, or find entities from a relational database.

CRUD operations on entities are not enough. Chapter 6, *Querying Entities* explains how to use the powerful Java Persistence Query Language so you can query entities following different criteria.

Entities have a complex life cycle that is explained in Chapter 7, *Callbacks and Listeners*. This chapter also covers callbacks and listeners.

Chapter 8, *Advanced Topics* covers some advanced topics such as caching and concurrency access.

Chapter 9, *Integrating JPA with Other Technologies* shows how to integrate Java Persistence API with other technologies such as Bean Validation, CDI, JTA and Spring.

In Chapter 10, *Putting It All Together*, you'll build a more complex application with most of the concepts that have been introduced throughout this fascicle.

Chapter 11, *Summary* wraps up with a summary of what you've learnt in this fascicle.

Appendix A, *Setting up the Development Environment on macOS* highlights the tools used throughout the fascicle and how to install them.

JPA 2.2 has a long history of specifications behind it. Appendix B, *Java Persistence API Specification Versions* lists all the revisions of this specification.

Appendix C points to some external references which are worth reading if you want to know more about JPA.

This is not the only fascicle I have written. You'll find a description of the other fascicles I wrote and online courses I created in Appendix D:

- *Understanding Bean Validation 2.0*
- *Understanding JPA 2.2*
- *Understanding Quarkus 2.x*
- *Practising Quarkus 2.x*

Conventions

This fascicle uses a diverse range of languages, mostly Java, but also JSON, XML, YAML or shell scripts. Each code example is displayed appropriately and appears in `fixed-width font`. All the included code comes from a public Git repository and is continuously tested. Therefore, you shouldn't have any problem with code that is not syntactically correct. In some cases, the original source code has been specially formatted to fit within the available page space, with additional line breaks or modified indentation. To increase readability, some examples omit code where it is seen as unnecessary. But always remember that you can find the entire code online at https://github.com/agoncal/agoncal-fascicle-jpa/tree/2.2.

Italics are used to *highlight an important word for the first time*, or to give the definition of an abbreviation or *acronym*. Bold is **rarely used**.

Some useful information.

Something you really should do if you want the code to work properly.

Warns you of a possible technical problem.

The Sample Application

Throughout the book, you will see snippets of code all belonging to the Vintage Store application. I created this application for my very first book, and I still use it as an example. This application is an e-commerce website allowing users to browse a catalogue of vintage stuff (vinyl, tapes, books and CDs). Using a shopping cart, they can add or remove items as they browse the catalogue and then check out so that they can pay and obtain a purchase order. The application has external interactions with a bank system to validate credit card numbers.

The actors interacting with the system are:

- *Employees* of the company who need to manage both the catalogue of items and the customers' details. They can also browse the purchase orders.
- *Users* who are anonymous persons visiting the website and who are consulting the catalogue of books and CDs. If they want to buy an item, they need to create an account to become customers.
- *Customers* who can login to the system, browse the catalogue, update their account details, and buy items online.
- The external *Bank* to which the system delegates credit card validations.

Figure 1 depicts the use case diagram which describes the system's actors and functionalities.

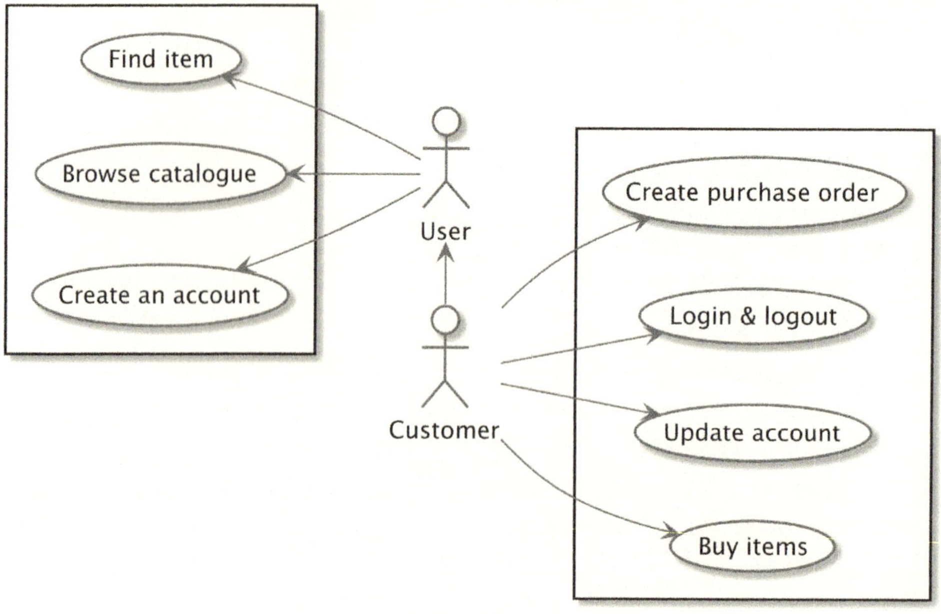

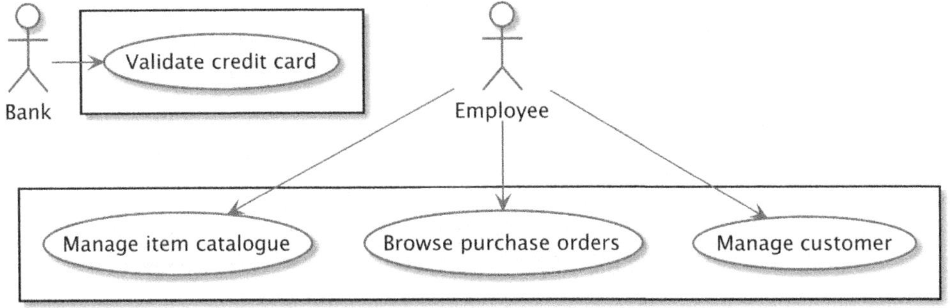

Figure 1. Use case diagram of the Vintage Store application

The Vintage Store application manipulates a few domain objects that are described in Figure 2. Vinyl, tapes, books and CDs, of course, but also chapters, authors, purchase orders, invoices and shopping carts. Don't spend too much time on this diagram for now as you will come across most of these objects throughout this fascicle.

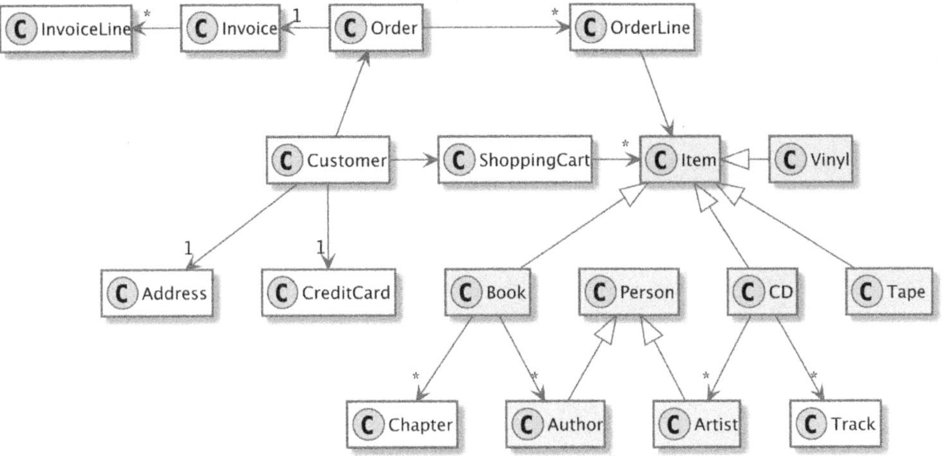

Figure 2. Class diagram of the Vintage Store application

The code you'll see in this fascicle gets its inspiration from the Vintage Store application, but it's not the original application per-se. You can download the code of the original application if you want, but it's not necessary in order to follow the code of this fascicle.[21]

Downloading and Running the Code

The source code of the examples in the fascicle is available from a public Git repository and can be cloned, downloaded or browsed online at https://github.com/agoncal/agoncal-fascicle-jpa/tree/2.2. The code has been developed and tested on the macOS platform but should also work on Windows or Linux. The examples used in this fascicle are designed to be compiled with Java 11, to be built with Maven 3.6.x and to be tested with JUnit 5.x and to store data in an H2 database. Appendix A shows you how to install all of these software packages which will be used in most of the chapters to build, run and test the code.

Getting Help

Having trouble with the code, the content or the structure of the fascicle? Didn't understand something? Not clear enough? I am here to help! Do not hesitate to report issues or any questions at https://github.com/agoncal/agoncal-fascicle-jpa/issues. I'll do my best to answer them. This will also allow me to improve the content of this fascicle, and upload a new version through Amazon Kindle Publishing.

Contacting the Author

If you have any questions about the content of this fascicle, please use the instructions above and use the GitHub issue tracker. But if you feel like contacting me, drop me an email at agoncal.fascicle@gmail.com or a tweet at @agoncal. You can also visit my blog at:

- www.antoniogoncalves.org
- agoncal.teachable.com

[15] Autonio's books http://amazon.com/author/agoncal

[16] My Java EE Books https://antoniogoncalves.org/category/books

[17] The Uncensored Java EE 7 Book https://antoniogoncalves.org/2014/09/16/the-uncensored-java-ee-7-book

[18] Opening Up Java EE https://blogs.oracle.com/theaquarium/opening-up-ee-update

[19] Amazon Kindle Publishing https://kdp.amazon.com

[20] Java Persistence API course on PluralSight https://www.pluralsight.com/courses/java-persistence-api-21

[21] Code of the Vintage Store application https://github.com/agoncal/agoncal-application-cdbookstore

Chapter 1. First Step with JPA

If you are reading this fascicle, it's because you are a developer. And like most developers, when you learn a new technology or framework, you like to see some code first. So here is the very first step with JPA.

Listing 1 shows a Java class representing the author of a book. An author has a first name, a last name, a biography and an email address. Because it is supposed to be persisted into a relational database, it also has an identifier.

Listing 1. Java Class with JPA Annotations

```
@Entity
public class Author {

  @Id
  @GeneratedValue
  private Long id;
  @Column(nullable = false, length = 50)
  private String firstName;
  private String lastName;
  @Column(length = 2000)
  private String bio;
  private String email;

  // Constructors, getters, setters
}
```

If you look more carefully at Listing 1, you can see a few annotations: `@Entity`, `@Id`, `@GeneratedValue` and `@Column`. What do you think they do? Let me give you a hint. In Listing 2 we give the author a first name and a last name, and after saving the `author` object into the database, we make sure the `id` is not null. This means that the author has been persisted into a relational database, and that something has generated a primary key as an identifier.

Listing 2. The Author Is Persisted into a Relational Database

```
Author author = new Author().firstName("Adams").lastName("Douglas");
assertNull(author.getId(), "Id should be null");

tx.begin();
em.persist(author);
tx.commit();

assertNotNull(author.getId(), "Id should not be null");
```

Look at what happens in Listing 3. This time, we give the author a null first name, and when we persist it, at commit time, a `RollbackException` is thrown because the database column doesn't accept null values.

Listing 3. Rollback Because the Firstname of the Author Is Null

```
Author author = new Author().firstName(null);

tx.begin();
em.persist(author);
assertThrows(RollbackException.class, () -> tx.commit());
```

You didn't understand all the code? You did understand it but you feel there is more to it than that? The fascicle you have in your hands is all about JPA. Thanks to the chapters that follow, you will understand the basics of this technology and will have plenty of examples so that you can dive into more complex topics.

Chapter 2. Understanding Java Persistence API

In the previous *First Step with JPA* chapter, you've already seen some code. But before going further into more code, we need to step back and define some concepts. This *Understanding* chapter gives you some terminology that will be used in the rest of the fascicle so you don't get lost.

Applications are made up of business logic, interaction with other systems, user interfaces etc. and data. Most of the data that our applications manipulate have to be stored in datastores, retrieved, processed and analysed. Datastores are important: they store business data, act as a central point between applications, and can even sometimes process data themselves (e.g. relational databases have triggers and stored procedures). They can take several forms, from relational databases to schemaless databases. But relational databases are what are important to us when talking about JPA.

When developing an application in an object-oriented programming language such as Java, this data can be represented using objects. Objects encapsulate state and behaviour in a nice way, but this state is only accessible when the *Java Virtual Machine* (JVM) is running: if the JVM stops or the garbage collector cleans its memory content, objects disappear, as well as their state. Some objects need to be persistent and, by persistent, I mean objects that are deliberately stored in a permanent datastore so that their state can be reused later.

Object-Relational Mapping tools have been created in several languages in order to bridge objects and relational databases. *Java Persistence API* (JPA) is the standard Java framework to achieve this object-relational mapping. It relies on JDBC and transaction management.

2.1. Understanding JDBC

JDBC stands for *Java DataBase Connectivity*.[22] It is a Java-based technology providing methods for querying and updating data for relational databases. It arrived in the JDK 1.1 in 1997 and today, JDBC 4.2 is part of the JDK 1.8. This old API is very robust and used in many projects and frameworks. However, JDBC is a low-level API and it ends up being quite verbose: it takes several lines of code just to bind an object to an SQL (*Structured Query Language*) query.[23]

For example, take the code in Listing 4 that inserts a new book into the `BOOK` table. With JDBC, we need to create an SQL query to insert data. This query follows the SQL syntax and inserts data into the columns of `BOOK`. We do the mapping programmatically between each attribute of the `Book` class, and the `BOOK` table. The way the mapping works is that we bind the book identifier, as a `Long`, to the first argument of the query. The book title is mapped as a String, to the second argument of the query, the description to the third argument, and so on and so forth. Once the mapping is finished, we execute the query and the data is inserted into the database.

Listing 4. Using JDBC to Insert a New Row in the BOOK Table

```
String query = "INSERT INTO BOOK (ID, TITLE, DESCRIPTION, PRICE, ISBN) VALUES (?, ?,
?, ?, ?)";

try (PreparedStatement stmt = getConnection().prepareStatement(query)) {

  stmt.setLong(1, book.getId());
  stmt.setString(2, book.getTitle());
  stmt.setString(3, book.getDescription());
  stmt.setFloat(4, book.getPrice());
  stmt.setString(5, book.getIsbn());

  stmt.executeUpdate();
}
```

There are a few things that are wrong with the code shown in Listing 4. First of all, SQL is a different language and Java developers might not be confident with it. Once SQL is mastered, the statements are not easy to refactor. If the database structure changes, or the object evolves, we need to manually update each SQL statement. That's because the structure of the DB is closely related to the object, there is no abstraction between both. This programmatic mapping makes the code really verbose, making it harder to read and harder to maintain. Object-Relational Mapping tools solve these problems by bringing some abstraction.

2.2. Understanding Transactions

Transaction management is an important matter for enterprises. It allows applications to have consistent data and to process that data in a reliable manner. Transaction management is a low-level concern that a business developer shouldn't have to code. That's why JTA (*Java Transaction API*) provides these services in a very simple way: either programmatically with a high level of abstraction or declaratively using metadata.

A *transaction* is used to ensure that the data is kept in a consistent state. It represents a logical group of operations that must be performed as a single unit, also known as a *unit of work*. These operations can involve persisting data in one or several databases, sending messages to a MOM (*Message-Oriented Middleware*), or invoking web services. Companies rely on transactions every day for their banking and e-commerce applications or business-to-business interactions with partners.

These indivisible business operations are performed either sequentially or in parallel over a relatively short period of time. Every operation must succeed for the transaction to succeed (we say that the transaction is *committed*). If one of the operations fails, the transaction fails as well (the transaction is rolled back). In terms of code, this is what it looks like:

```
entityManager.getTransaction().begin();
entityManager.getTransaction().commit();
entityManager.getTransaction().rollback();
```

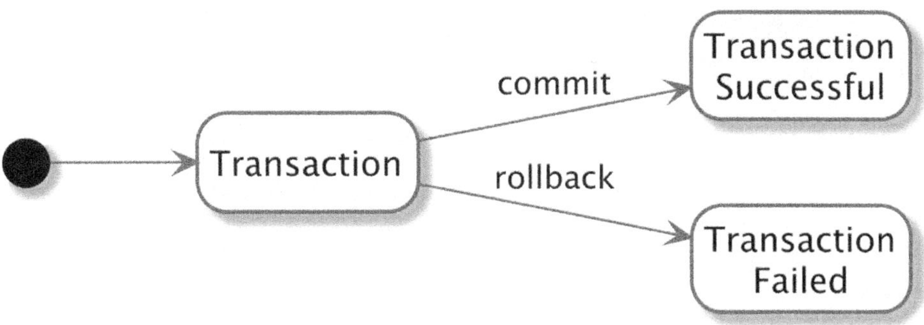

Figure 3. Transaction Management

Transactions must guarantee a degree of reliability and robustness and follow the ACID properties. ACID refers to the four properties that define a reliable transaction: *Atomicity*, *Consistency*, *Isolation*, and *Durability* (described in Table 1).

Table 1. ACID Properties

Property	Description
Atomicity	A transaction is composed of one or more operations grouped in a unit of work. At the conclusion of the transaction, either these operations are all performed successfully (a commit) or none of them is performed at all (a rollback) if something unexpected or irrecoverable happens.
Consistency	At the conclusion of the transaction, the data are left in a consistent state.
Isolation	The intermediate state of a transaction is not visible to external applications.
Durability	Once the transaction is committed, the changes made to the data are visible to other applications.

To explain these properties, I'll take the classic example of a bank transfer: you need to debit your savings account to credit your current account.

When you transfer money from one account to the other, you can imagine a sequence of database accesses: the savings account is debited using an SQL update statement, the current account is credited using a different update statement, and a log is created in a different table to keep track of the transfer. These operations have to be done in the same unit of work (*Atomicity*) because you don't want the debit to occur but not the credit. From the perspective of an external application querying the accounts, only when both operations have been successfully performed are they visible (*Isolation*). With isolation, the external application cannot see the interim state when one account has been debited and the other is still not credited (if it could, it would think the customer has less money than they really do). *Consistency* is when transaction operations (either with a commit or a rollback) are performed within the constraints of the database (such as primary keys, relationships, or fields). Once the transfer is completed, the data can be accessed from other applications (*Durability*).

2.3. Understanding Object-Relational Mapping

Relational databases store data in tables made of rows and columns. Data is identified by primary keys, which are special columns (or a combination of columns) designated to uniquely identify each table record. The relationships between tables are based on foreign keys and join tables with integrity constraints.

All this vocabulary is completely unknown in an object-oriented language such as Java. In Java, we manipulate objects that are instances of classes. Objects inherit from others, have references to collections of other objects, and sometimes recursively point to themselves. We have concrete classes, abstract classes, interfaces, enumerations, annotations, methods, attributes, and so on.

As seen in Figure 4, the principle of *Object-Relational Mapping* (ORM) is to bring the world of relational databases and objects together. ORMs are external tools that give an object-oriented view of relational data, and vice versa.

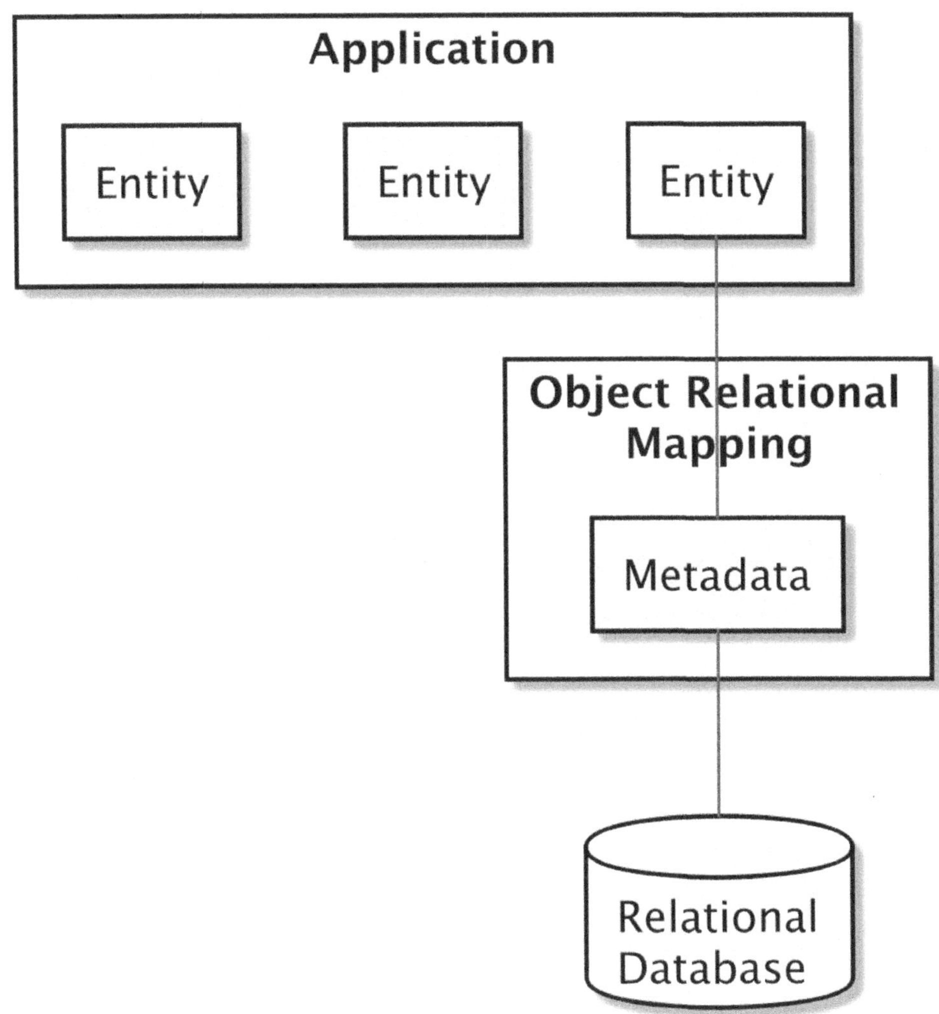

Figure 4. Mapping objects to a relational database

2.3.1. Relational Databases

The relational model organises data into one or more tables made of columns and rows, with a unique key identifying each row. Rows are also called records or tuples. Generally, each table represents one entity type (such as a book, author or purchase order). The rows represent instances of that type of entity (such as the book "*H2G2*" or "*Design Patterns*") with the columns representing values attributed to that instance (such as the title of the book or the price).

How would you store data representing a book in a relational database? Listing 5 shows an SQL script that creates such a table.

Listing 5. SQL Script Creating a BOOK Table Structure

```
CREATE TABLE BOOK
(
  ID            BIGINT NOT NULL,
  DESCRIPTION   VARCHAR,
  ILLUSTRATIONS BOOLEAN,
  ISBN          VARCHAR,
  NBOFPAGES     INTEGER,
  PRICE         DOUBLE,
  TITLE         VARCHAR,
  PRIMARY KEY (ID)
)
```

A *Data Definition Language* (DDL, or data description language) uses a syntax for defining database structures. The table `BOOK` is where we will find all the books of our application. Each book is identified by a unique primary key column (`PRIMARY KEY (ID)`) and each attribute is stored in a column (e.g. `TITLE`, `PRICE`, `ISBN` etc.). A column in a table has a type (e.g. `VARCHAR`, `INTEGER`, `BOOLEAN` etc.) and can accept null values or not (`NOT NULL`).

A new era of NoSQL (Not Only SQL) databases (or schemaless) has emerged with different storage structures: key-values, column, document, or graph. At the moment, JPA is not able to map entities to these structures. Hibernate OGM is an open source framework that attempts to address mapping objects to non-relational databases.[24] EclipseLink also has some extensions to map NoSQL structures.[25] Hibernate OGM or EclipseLink extensions are beyond the scope of this fascicle, but you should have a look at them if you plan to use NoSQL databases.

2.3.2. Entities

When talking about mapping objects to a relational database, persisting objects, or querying objects, the term *entity* should be used rather than *object*. Objects are instances that just live in memory. Entities are objects that live for a short time in memory and persistently in a relational database. They have the ability to be mapped to a database; they can be concrete or abstract; and they support inheritance, relationships, and so on.

In the JPA persistence model, an entity is a *Plain Old Java Object* (POJO). This means an entity is declared, instantiated and used just like any other Java class. An entity usually has attributes (its state), can have business methods (its behaviour), constructors, getters and setters. Listing 6 shows a simple entity.

Listing 6. Simple Example of a Book Entity

```
@Entity
public class Book {

  @Id
  @GeneratedValue
  private Long id;
  private String title;
  private Float price;
  private String description;
  private String isbn;
  private Integer nbOfPages;
  private Boolean illustrations;

  // Constructors, getters, setters
}
```

The example in Listing 6 represents a Book entity from which I've omitted the getters and the setters for clarity. As you can see, except for some annotations, this entity looks exactly like any Java class: it has several attributes (id, title, price etc.) of different types (Long, String, Float, Integer, and Boolean), a default constructor, and getters and setters for each attribute. So how does this map to a table? The answer is: thanks to mapping.

2.3.3. Mapping Entities

The principle of *Object-Relational Mapping* (ORM) is to delegate the task of creating a correspondence between objects and tables, to external tools or frameworks (in our case, JPA). The world of classes, objects, and attributes can then be mapped to relational databases which are made up of tables containing rows and columns. Mapping gives an object-oriented view to developers who can transparently use entities instead of tables. And how does JPA map objects to a database? This is done through *metadata*.

Associated with every entity are metadata that describe the mapping. The metadata enable the persistence provider to recognise an entity and to interpret the mapping. The metadata can be written in two different formats:

- *Annotations*: The code of the entity is directly annotated with all sorts of annotations.
- *XML descriptors*: Instead of (or in addition to) annotations, we can use XML descriptors. The mapping is defined in an external XML file that will be deployed with the entities.

These entities, once mapped, can be managed by JPA. You can persist an entity in the database, remove it, and query it. An ORM lets you manipulate entities while, under the covers, the database is being accessed.

The Book entity (shown in Listing 6) uses JPA annotations so the persistence provider can synchronise the data between the attributes of the Book entity and the columns of the BOOK table. Therefore, if the attribute isbn is updated by the application, the ISBN column will be synchronised (see Figure 5). As you will see in Chapter 5, this synchronisation can be automatic or programmatic depending on the life cycle of the entity.

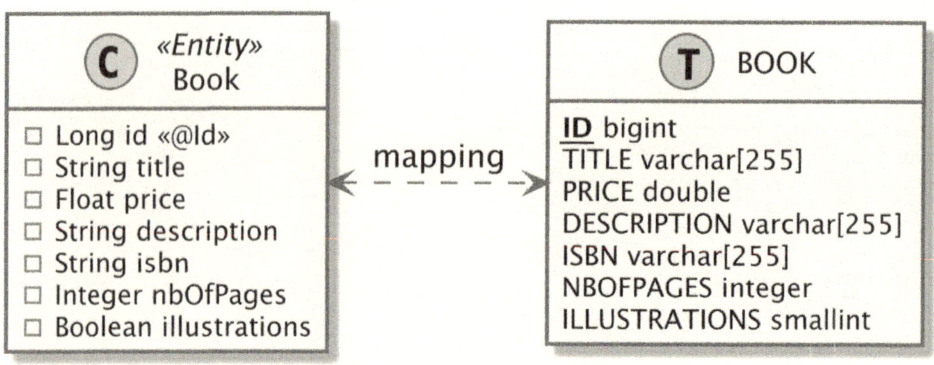

Figure 5. Data synchronisation between the entity and the table

As shown in the DDL in Listing 5, the `Book` entity is mapped to a `BOOK` table, and each column is named after the attribute of the class (e.g. the `isbn` attribute of type `String` is mapped to a column named `ISBN` of type `VARCHAR`).

In this fascicle, I use CamelCase for Java code (e.g. `Book` entity, `isbn` attribute) and UpperCase for SQL script (e.g. `BOOK` table, `ISBN` column). But you need to be careful when picking up a specific case as some databases are case-sensitive.

Without JPA and metadata, the `Book` entity in Listing 6 would be treated just like a POJO. If you manually tried to map a POJO with JPA, then it would be ignored by JPA which would throw an exception. So you need to tell JPA that it deals with an *entity*, not an object, by using the `@Entity` annotation. It is the same for the identifier. You need a way to tell the persistence provider that the `id` attribute has to be mapped to a primary key, so you annotate it with `@Id`. The value of this identifier is automatically generated by the persistence provider, using the optional `@GeneratedValue` annotation. This type of decision characterises the configuration by exception approach (a.k.a. *configuring a component is the exception*), in which annotations are not required for the more common cases and are only used as metadata to be understood by an external provider.

2.3.4. Managing Entities

JPA allows us to map entities to a table and also to query them using different criteria. JPA's power is that it offers the ability to query entities and their relationships in an object-oriented way without the developer having to use the foreign keys or columns of the underlying database. The central piece of the API responsible for orchestrating entities is the `javax.persistence.EntityManager`. Its role is to manage entities, read from and write to a given database, and allow simple CRUD (create, read, update, and delete) operations on entities as well as complex queries using JPQL (*Java Persistence Query Language*). In a technical sense, the entity manager is just an interface whose implementation is done by the persistence provider. At its core, the entity manager delegates all the low-level calls to JDBC bringing the developer a higher-level of abstraction.

In Figure 6, you can see how the `EntityManager` interface can be used by a class (here `Main`) to manipulate entities (in this case, Book). With methods such as persist() and find(), the entity manager hides the JDBC calls to the database as well as the INSERT or SELECT SQL (*Structured Query Language*) statements.

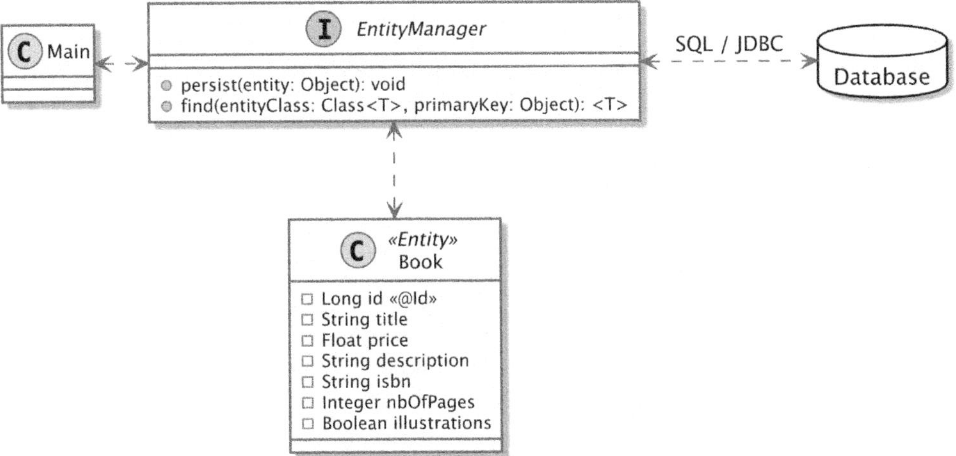

Figure 6. The entity manager interacts with the entity and the underlying database

The JPA implementation (i.e. the persistence provider) used for this fascicle is EclipseLink 2.7.x.[26]

2.4. JPA Overview

In the Java world, there are several frameworks and specifications to achieve object-relational mapping, such as Hibernate, TopLink, or *Java Data Objects* (JDO), but *Java Persistence API* (JPA) is the preferred technology.

Java Persistence API (JPA) is a Java specification that manages objects stored in a relational database.[27] JPA gives the developer an object-oriented view in order to transparently use entities instead of tables. It also comes with a query language (*Java Persistence Query Language*, or JPQL), allowing complex queries over objects.

JPA is just a specification that is part of Java EE and is governed by the JCP (*Java Community Process*). It is then implemented by frameworks such as EclipseLink, Hibernate ORM or OpenJPA.

2.4.1. A Brief History of Java Persistence API

ORM solutions have been around for a long time, even before Java. Products such as TopLink originally started with Smalltalk in 1994 before switching to Java.[28] Commercial ORM products like TopLink have been available since the earliest days of the Java language. They were successful but were never standardised for the Java platform. A similar approach to ORM was standardised in the form of JDO (*Java Data Objects*), which failed to gain any significant market penetration.[29]

In 1998, EJB (*Enterprise JavaBeans*) 1.0 was created and later shipped with J2EE (*Java Enterprise Edition*) 1.2. It was a heavyweight, distributed component used for transactional business logic.

Entity Bean CMP (*Container-Managed Persistence*) was introduced as optional in EJB 1.0, became mandatory in EJB 1.1, and was enhanced through versions up to EJB 2.1 (J2EE 1.4).[30] Persistence could only be done inside the container through a complex mechanism of instantiation using home, local, or remote interfaces. The capabilities of ORM were also very limited, as inheritance was difficult to map.

Parallel to the J2EE world was a popular open source solution that led to some surprising changes in the direction of persistence: Hibernate ORM, which brought back a lightweight, object-oriented persistent model.[31]

After years of complaints about Entity CMP 2. x components and, in acknowledgment of the success and simplicity of open source frameworks such as Hibernate, the persistence model of the Enterprise Edition was completely rearchitected in Java EE 5. JPA 1.0 was created with a very lightweight approach that adopted many Hibernate ORM design principles. The JPA 1.0 specification was bundled with EJB 3.0 (JSR 220).[32] In 2009, JPA 2.0 (JSR 317) was released with Java EE 6 and brought new APIs, extended JPQL, and added new functionalities such as a second-level cache, pessimistic locking, or the criteria API.[33] In 2013, with Java EE 7, JPA 2.1 followed the path of ease of development and brought new features such as schema generation, converters or CDI supports in JSR 338.[34] Today JPA is on its version 2.2 that was shipped at the same time as Java EE 8.[35]

2.4.2. JCP and Eclipse Foundation

The JCP (*Java Community Process*) is an open organisation, created in 1998 by Sun Microsystems, that is involved in the definition of future versions and features of the Java platform.[36] When the need for standardising an existing component or API is identified, the initiator (a.k.a. specification lead) creates a JSR (*Java Specification Request*) and forms a group of experts. This group, made up of company representatives, organisations, universities, and private individuals, is responsible for the development of the JSR and has to deliver:

- One or more specifications that explain the details and define the fundamentals of the JSR,
- A *Reference Implementation* (RI), which is an actual implementation of the specification, and
- A *Technology Compatibility Kit* (TCK), which is a set of tests every implementation needs to pass before claiming to conform to the specification.

Once approved by the *Executive Committee* (EC), the specification is released to the community for other projects to implement.

This is exactly the standardisation process that followed JPA 2.2. It has been standardised under JSR 338, has a reference implementation (EclipseLink) and has a TCK.[37]

In 2017, most Java EE specifications were moved from the JCP to the Eclipse Foundation (including the JPA specification).[38]

The *Eclipse Foundation* is an independent, non-profit entity that acts as a steward for the Eclipse open source software development community.[39] The Foundation focuses on key services such as: intellectual property management, ecosystem development, development process, and IT infrastructure. It was created by IBM in 2001 and is now supported by a consortium of several software vendors (Red Hat, Huawei, Bosch, Fujitsu, SAP, Oracle, etc.).

2.4.3. Java EE and Jakarta EE

Even if Java Persistence API does not rely on Java EE, it is strongly correlated with this platform. So, it is worth mentioning Java EE in a JPA fascicle.

Created in 1998, Java EE (*Java Enterprise Edition*) can be seen as an extension of the *Java Standard Edition* (Java SE).[40] It is a set of specifications intended for enterprise applications in order to facilitate the development of distributed, transactional, and secure applications. It is developed using the *Java Community Process*, with contributions from industry experts and commercial and open source organisations.[41]

In 2017, with version 8 of the platform, Java EE was donated to the Eclipse Foundation and renamed *Jakarta EE*.[42] Jakarta EE is the name of the platform governed by the Jakarta EE Working Group.[43] The first version is Jakarta EE 8, which is based on the Java EE 8 technologies. Future versions will not be driven by the JCP but through the open *Eclipse Foundation*.

2.4.4. What's New in JPA 2.2?

JPA 2.2 is described under the 338 and was released in 2017.[44] It was shipped with Java EE 8 but it was just a *maintenance release*, meaning that it uses the same JSR as JPA 2.1 (still the JSR 338). A maintenance release means that a specification doesn't evolve much, and therefore doesn't need a new JSR. The changes made to JPA 2.2 were mostly to support Java SE 8:

- Adds support for Java SE 8 Lambdas and Streams.
- Adds `@Repeatable` meta-annotation to JPA annotations.
- Support for CDI injection into `AttributeConverter` classes.
- Support for the mapping of the new `java.time` types (e.g. `LocalDate`, `LocalTime` etc.).[45]
- Adds default `Stream getResultStream()` method to `Query` and `TypedQuery` interfaces.

Most of these novelties will be discussed in the chapters that follow.

Appendix B lists all the revisions and major changes of the Java Persistence API specification.

2.4.5. Implementations

EclipseLink is the open source reference implementation of JPA.[46] The project was based on the TopLink product from which Oracle contributed the source code to create the EclipseLink project. Today, EclipseLink 2.7.x implements JPA 2.2. It also adds specific features as it also supports XML persistence through Java XML Binding (JAXB) and through other means such as Service Data Objects (SDOs). It provides support not only for ORM but also for object XML mapping (OXM), object persistence to enterprise information systems (EIS) using Java EE Connector Architecture (JCA), and database web services.

The code in this fascicle uses the standard JPA APIs. As for the implementation, it uses EclipseLink.

At the time of writing this fascicle, EclipseLink is not the only JPA 2.2 compliant implementation, there are others. Hibernate ORM is the famous JPA implementation from Red Hat.[47] It is used in all the Red Hat products including the JBoss Application Server or Wildfly. OpenJPA is the Apache implementation and will soon implement JPA 2.2.[48]

As you can see, despite the reference implementation (EclipseLink), you have several implementations to choose from.

[22] JDBC https://en.wikipedia.org/wiki/Java_Database_Connectivity

[23] SQL https://fr.wikipedia.org/wiki/Structured_Query_Language

[24] Hibernate OGM http://hibernate.org/ogm

[25] EclipseLink NoSQL extension https://wiki.eclipse.org/EclipseLink/Examples/JPA/NoSQL

[26] EclipseLink http://www.eclipse.org/eclipselink

[27] JPA https://jcp.org/en/jsr/detail?id=338

[28] Toplink http://www.oracle.com/technetwork/middleware/toplink

[29] JDO https://jcp.org/en/jsr/detail?id=243

[30] EJB 2.1 https://jcp.org/en/jsr/detail?id=153

[31] Hibernate http://hibernate.org

[32] JSR 220 https://jcp.org/en/jsr/detail?id=220

[33] JSR 317 https://jcp.org/en/jsr/detail?id=317

[34] JSR 338 https://jcp.org/en/jsr/detail?id=338

[35] Java EE 8 https://jcp.org/en/jsr/detail?id=366

[36] JCP https://jcp.org

[37] JPA https://jcp.org/en/jsr/detail?id=338

[38] Eclipse Foundation https://www.eclipse.org/org/foundation

[39] Eclipse Foundation https://www.eclipse.org/org/foundation

[40] Jakarta EE https://en.wikipedia.org/wiki/Jakarta_EE

[41] JCP https://jcp.org

[42] Eclipse Foundation https://www.eclipse.org/org/foundation/

[43] Jakarta EE https://jakarta.ee

[44] JSR 338 https://jcp.org/en/jsr/detail?id=338

[45] JSR 310 https://jcp.org/en/jsr/detail?id=310

[46] EclipseLink http://www.eclipse.org/eclipselink

[47] Hibernate ORM http://hibernate.org/orm

[48] OpenJPA http://openjpa.apache.org

Chapter 3. Getting Started

In the previous chapter, you learnt about persistence and why object-relational mapping tools are important in bringing objects with relational databases together. You've also looked at what Java Persistence API is and where it comes from. Time to see some code.

To get started with a new technology, there is nothing better than a simple "*Hello World*" kind of example. In this *Getting Started* chapter, you will be developing your very first Java Persistence API sample application. It is a simple application made up of only a few classes with not much technical complexity. The idea is to develop something simple to understand and to set up so that you are sure you have the basis to follow the chapters coming up.

Make sure your development environment is set up to execute the code in this chapter. You can go to Appendix A to check that you have all the required tools installed, in particular JDK 11.0.10 or higher, Maven 3.6.x or higher and H2. The code in this chapter can be found at https://github.com/agoncal/agoncal-fascicle-jpa/tree/2.2/getting-started

3.1. Developing Your First JPA Application

Let's develop a simple application that highlights some of the key features of JPA. In this chapter, we'll use a Maven directory structure with an `Artist` class and an `ArtistTest` test class that are persisted in an H2 in-memory database (see Appendix A for more information on H2):

- `pom.xml`: At the root of the project, we find the Maven `pom.xml` file defining all the dependencies.
- `Artist.java`: The artist class with a set of attributes annotated with JPA mapping annotations.
- `ArtistTest.java`: The test class with a set of test cases persisting and querying the `Artist` entity.
- `persistence.xml`: The mandatory deployment descriptor for JPA.

The Maven directory structure ensures we put the business code under `src/main/java` while the test code goes under `src/test/java`. Notice that the deployment descriptor XML file is located under `src/main/resources` (`META-INF` is an internal Java meta directory).

```
.
├── src
│   ├── main
│   │   ├── java
│   │   │   └── org/agoncal/fascicle/jpa/gettingstarted
│   │   │       └── Artist.java
│   │   └── resources
│   │       └── META-INF
│   │           └── persistence.xml
│   └── test
│       └── java
│           └── org/agoncal/fascicle/jpa/gettingstarted
│               └── ArtistTest.java
└── pom.xml
```

We use Maven to build this project because it is the most commonly used build system these days.[49] Plus, we can use Maven in the command line and most IDEs support it.

3.1.1. Setting up the Maven Dependencies

We need to start by creating a `pom.xml` file. The `pom.xml` is the fundamental unit of work in Maven that will be used to build our project. I am breaking down the `pom.xml` file in several parts so you can understand better. First, Listing 7 shows the header of the `pom.xml` with just the `groupId` and `artifactId`.

Listing 7. Header of the pom.xml

```
<project xmlns:xsi="http://www.w3.org/2001/XMLSchema-instance"
         xmlns="http://maven.apache.org/POM/4.0.0"
         xsi:schemaLocation="http://maven.apache.org/POM/4.0.0
http://maven.apache.org/xsd/maven-4.0.0.xsd">
  <modelVersion>4.0.0</modelVersion>

  <groupId>org.agoncal.fascicle.jpa</groupId>
  <artifactId>getting-started</artifactId>
  <version>2.2</version>

  <properties>
    <maven.compiler.source>11</maven.compiler.source>
    <maven.compiler.target>11</maven.compiler.target>
    <project.build.sourceEncoding>UTF-8</project.build.sourceEncoding>
    <project.reporting.outputEncoding>UTF-8</project.reporting.outputEncoding>
  </properties>
```

Listing 8 gives us all the required dependencies to compile and execute the code. Basically, the only JPA dependencies we need here are the ones from EclipseLink (by pulling the reference implementation `org.eclipse.persistence:org.eclipse.persistence.jpa`) as well as the H2 database (`com.h2database:h2`) used by the deployment descriptor to pick up the H2 JDBC driver.

Listing 8. JPA Dependencies

```
  <dependencies>
    <dependency>
      <groupId>org.eclipse.persistence</groupId>
      <artifactId>org.eclipse.persistence.jpa</artifactId>
      <version>2.7.8</version>
    </dependency>
    <dependency>
      <groupId>com.h2database</groupId>
      <artifactId>h2</artifactId>
      <version>1.4.200</version>
    </dependency>
```

We use JUnit 5.x to run our tests.[50] As shown in Listing 9, we need to include the `org.junit.jupiter` dependency whose scope is set to `test` and to setup the `maven-surefire-plugin`. The Surefire plugin is used during the test phase of Maven to execute the unit tests of the application. This way, a simple `mvn test` command will execute the tests.

Listing 9. Test Dependencies

```
    <dependency>
      <groupId>org.junit.jupiter</groupId>
      <artifactId>junit-jupiter-engine</artifactId>
      <version>5.7.1</version>
      <scope>test</scope>
    </dependency>
  </dependencies>

  <build>
    <plugins>
      <plugin>
        <groupId>org.apache.maven.plugins</groupId>
        <artifactId>maven-surefire-plugin</artifactId>
        <version>3.0.0-M5</version>
      </plugin>
    </plugins>
  </build>
</project>
```

At this point, you can import the Maven project into an IDE (most modern Java IDEs include built-in support for Maven).

If you run `mvn dependency:tree`, you will see in Listing 10 that several dependencies were not explicitly defined in the `pom.xml` in Listing 8. That's because Maven transitively pulls all the needed dependencies automatically. That's why we end up with the JPA API (`org.eclipse.persistence:javax.persistence`), for example.

Listing 10. Maven Dependencies Tree

```
+- org.eclipse.persistence:org.eclipse.persistence.jpa:jar:2.7.3:compile
|  +- org.eclipse.persistence:javax.persistence:jar:2.2.1:compile
|  +- org.eclipse.persistence:org.eclipse.persistence.asm:jar:2.7.3:compile
|  +- org.eclipse.persistence:org.eclipse.persistence.antlr:jar:2.7.3:compile
|  +- javax.json:javax.json-api:jar:1.1.2:compile
|  +- org.eclipse.persistence:org.eclipse.persistence.jpa.jpql:jar:2.7.3:compile
|  \- org.eclipse.persistence:org.eclipse.persistence.core:jar:2.7.3:compile
+- com.h2database:h2:jar:1.4.197:compile
\- org.junit.jupiter:junit-jupiter-engine:jar:5.3.2:test
   +- org.apiguardian:apiguardian-api:jar:1.0.0:test
   +- org.junit.platform:junit-platform-engine:jar:1.3.2:test
   |  +- org.junit.platform:junit-platform-commons:jar:1.3.2:test
   |  \- org.opentest4j:opentest4j:jar:1.1.1:test
   \- org.junit.jupiter:junit-jupiter-api:jar:5.3.2:test
```

Appendix A has an entire chapter on Maven, explaining the scopes (runtime, test etc.) and the goals you can use on a `pom.xml`. Please refer to it if you need more in-depth information on Maven.

3.1.2. Mapping the Entity

Let's dive into an example to see how to map an entity into a relational database. In Listing 11, we have an `Artist` class with several attributes. An artist who appears on a CD album has a first name, a last name, an email address, a biography and a date of birth. This code is very straightforward. The `Artist` class does not extend any class nor does it implement any interface. It has a default constructor, getters and setters. The only difference with plain Java code and this class, is the usage of annotations on these attributes.

Listing 11. The Artist Class Annotated with Mapping Annotations

```
@Entity
public class Artist {

  @Id
  @GeneratedValue
  private Long id;
  @Column(nullable = false)
  private String firstName;
  @Column(nullable = false)
  private String lastName;
  private String email;
  @Column(length = 2000)
  private String bio;
  private LocalDate dateOfBirth;

  // Constructors, getters, setters
}
```

The `@Id`, `@GeneratedValue` and `@Column` annotations are used to declare the object-relational mapping which should be applied to the attributes of an `Artist` instance:

- The artist attribute `id` is mapped to the primary key column of the `ARTIST` table and its value is automatically generated by the JPA provider,
- The artist first name and last name must not be null,
- The `email` property has no mapping annotation (so the default mapping will be used, as you'll see in Chapter 4),
- The biography can be null, but if it's not, its size must be less than 2000 characters long, and
- The date of birth uses the `java.time.LocalDate` format.

This code is very straightforward to read. The JPA annotations bring semantic to these attributes ("the `lastname` attribute is not just mapped to a `VARCHAR` column, it has to be mapped a to a `VARCHAR` column that cannot be null") as well as a runtime API to validate the values of these attributes.

3.1.3. Managing the Entity

We use the `javax.persistence.EntityManager` API to manipulate the entity and see the mapping in action. To demonstrate this, let's have a look at a simple unit test: `ArtistTest`.

In Listing 12 we define three attributes (`EntityManagerFactory emf`, `EntityManager em` and `EntityTransaction tx`) that are initialised once (thanks to the JUnit `@BeforeAll` annotation) in the `init()` method. The `@BeforeAll` and `@AfterAll` JUnit annotations allow executions of some code before and after a test is executed. The `init()` method uses the `Persistence` class to get an instance of an `EntityManagerFactory` that refers to a persistence unit called `vintageStorePU`, which I'll describe later. This factory creates an instance of an `EntityManager` (the `em` variable) from which we retrieve an `EntityTransaction`. The `EntityManager` and `EntityManagerFactory` are closed at the end of the test case in the `close()` method. That's the perfect place to create and close an `EntityManager` instance and get a transaction.

Listing 12. Test Class Initialising the JPA Provider

```
public class ArtistTest {

  private static EntityManagerFactory emf;
  private static EntityManager em;
  private static EntityTransaction tx;

  @BeforeAll
  static void init() {
    emf = Persistence.createEntityManagerFactory("cdbookstorePU");
    em = emf.createEntityManager();
    tx = em.getTransaction();
  }

  @AfterAll
  static void close() {
    if (em != null) em.close();
    if (emf != null) emf.close();
  }
```

Now, let's use the `EntityManager` API to persist, find and remove an artist from the database. In Listing 13, we create an instance of an artist with a first name, a last name but no id (the id is null). The `EntityManager.persist()` method persists the artist object into a relational database. Once the transaction is committed, we check that an identifier has been generated and the `id` is not null anymore. In order to complete our test, we want to assert it has been persisted. To that end, we look for the artist by its identifier using the `EntityManager.find()` method and we make sure there is one in the database. Then, with `EntityManager.remove()` we delete the created artist from the database. This time, the `EntityManager.find()` method returns zero artist (as it has just been removed).

Listing 13. Test Case Managing the Artist

```
Artist artist = new Artist().firstName("Adams").lastName("Douglas");
assertNull(artist.getId(), "Id should be null");

tx.begin();
em.persist(artist);
tx.commit();
assertNotNull(artist.getId(), "Id should not be null");

assertNotNull(em.find(Artist.class, artist.getId()), "Artist should have been
persisted in DB");

tx.begin();
em.remove(artist);
tx.commit();

assertNull(em.find(Artist.class, artist.getId()), "Artist should have been removed
from DB");
```

In Listing 14, we create an `artist` object with a `null` first name. The `@Column(nullable = false)` mapping annotation on the `firstName` attribute makes sure it cannot be null. Therefore, when we try to persist the invalid artist into the database, the JPA provider throws a `RollbackException`.

Listing 14. Rollback Because the Firstname of the Author Is Null

```
Artist artist = new Artist().firstName(null);
tx.begin();
em.persist(artist);
assertThrows(RollbackException.class, () -> tx.commit());
```

3.1.4. Querying the Entity

But persisting, finding by identifier or removing an entity from the database are not the only entity manipulations we can do with JPA. In fact, JPA comes with a query language called JPQL (*Java Persistence Query Language*). Listing 15 shows how we use the query mechanism.

Listing 15. Querying the Artist Entity

```
assertEquals(0, em.createQuery("select a from Artist a").getResultList().size());

Artist douglas = new Artist().firstName("Adams").lastName("Douglas");
Artist lovecraft = new Artist().firstName("Howard").lastName("Lovecraft");
tx.begin();
em.persist(douglas);
em.persist(lovecraft);
tx.commit();

assertEquals(2, em.createQuery("select a from Artist a").getResultList().size());
assertEquals(1, em.createQuery("select a from Artist a where a.firstName = 'Adams' ")
.getResultList().size());
```

In Listing 15 we first make sure that, before doing any operation, the database is empty. This is done by querying the number of artists and making sure the result is equal to zero. Then, we persist two artists into the database and issue the same query: the result is now two. As you can see in the last query, we look for an artist whose first name is `Adams` and the result is one. This is just a glimpse at JPQL. Don't worry, Chapter 6 is all about it.

3.1.5. Deployment Descriptor

Which JDBC driver should we use? How should we connect to the database? What's the name of the database? This information is missing from our previous code.

In Listing 12 we initialise the `EntityManagerFactory` with the String `vintageStorePU`. `vintageStorePU` is the name of the persistence unit defined in Listing 16. This XML file, required by the JPA specification, is important as it links the JPA provider (EclipseLink in our case) to the database (H2). It contains all the necessary information to connect to the `vintageStoreDB` database such as the URL or JDBC driver. First, the `<provider>` element defines the persistence provider, in our case, EclipseLink. Then, the persistence unit lists all the entities that should be managed by the entity manager. Here, the `<class>` tag tells the persistence provider to manage the `Artist` class.

Listing 16. JPA Deployment Descriptor

```
<persistence xmlns:xsi="http://www.w3.org/2001/XMLSchema-instance"
             xmlns="http://xmlns.jcp.org/xml/ns/persistence"
             xsi:schemaLocation="http://xmlns.jcp.org/xml/ns/persistence
http://xmlns.jcp.org/xml/ns/persistence/persistence_2_2.xsd"
             version="2.2">
  <persistence-unit name="cdbookstorePU" transaction-type="RESOURCE_LOCAL">
    <provider>org.eclipse.persistence.jpa.PersistenceProvider</provider>
    <class>org.agoncal.fascicle.jpa.gettingstarted.Artist</class>
    <properties>
      <property name="javax.persistence.jdbc.driver" value="org.h2.Driver"/>
      <property name="javax.persistence.jdbc.url" value=
"jdbc:h2:tcp://localhost/~/cdbookstoreDB"/>
      <property name="javax.persistence.schema-generation.database.action" value=
"drop-and-create"/>
      <property name="javax.persistence.schema-generation.scripts.action" value="drop-
and-create"/>
      <property name="javax.persistence.schema-generation.scripts.create-target"
value="cdbookstoreCreate.ddl"/>
      <property name="javax.persistence.schema-generation.scripts.drop-target" value=
"cdbookstoreDrop.ddl"/>
    </properties>
  </persistence-unit>
</persistence>
```

In JPA, the deployment descriptor file is called `persistence.xml`. It also defines all sorts of properties such as the database schema-generation mode: for example, `drop-and-create` means that tables will be dropped and then created.

Notice the `<provider>` tag in Listing 16. It gives the JPA implementation used to run the code. In our case, it's EclipseLink, that's why the value is `org.eclipse.persistence.jpa.PersistenceProvider`. So, to switch implementations (e.g. using Hibernate ORM or Open JPA instead of EclipseLink, it's just a matter of changing the class name. For example, if we wanted to run our code with Hibernate, it would just be a matter of changing the implementation class like this:

```
<persistence-unit name="vintageStorePU" transaction-type="RESOURCE_LOCAL">
  <provider>org.hibernate.jpa.HibernatePersistenceProvider</provider>
```

3.1.6. Running the Tests

We have the `Artist` class, its test case (`ArtistTest`), the deployment descriptor `persistence.xml` and the `pom.xml`. Now it is the time to run the tests. Depending on the IDE you use, executing the tests can be as simple as clicking on a button.

But thanks to Maven, we can execute them on a command line using the `mvn test` command. It is enough to compile the classes and run the tests. But unfortunately, all the tests will fail and you note the exception below:

```
Internal Exception: org.h2.jdbc.JdbcSQLException:
   Connection is broken: "java.net.ConnectException:
      Connection refused (Connection refused): localhost"
```

That's because the H2 database is not up and running. So, make sure H2 is installed (see Appendix A), execute it (with the `h2` command) and run the tests again (`mvn test`). You should see the following output:

```
[INFO] ------------------------
[INFO] Building Getting Started
[INFO] ------------------------
[INFO]
[INFO] --- maven-compiler-plugin:3.7.0:compile (default-compile)
[INFO]
[INFO] --- maven-surefire-plugin:2.22.1:test (default-test)
[INFO]
[INFO] ----------
[INFO]  T E S T S
[INFO] ----------
[INFO] Running org.agoncal.fascicle.jpa.gettingstarted.ArtistTest
[INFO] Tests run: 3, Failures: 0, Errors: 0, Skipped: 0, Time elapsed: 1.031 s
[INFO]
[INFO] Results:
[INFO]
[INFO] Tests run: 3, Failures: 0, Errors: 0, Skipped: 0
[INFO]
[INFO] -------------
[INFO] BUILD SUCCESS
[INFO] -------------
```

What's really important is the result: 3 tests were run and all of them passed. If you have the same output, it means your environment is up and running and that you are ready for more JPA code.

3.1.7. Checking the Database

Thanks to the `javax.persistence.schema-generation.database.action` property in the `persistence.xml` file (see Listing 16), the database was created automatically once the tests were executed. To visualise its content, we can use the H2 console. When you executed the `h2` command, a browser page opened with the URL http://localhost:8082 displaying the H2 console. This console lets you access the `vintageStoreDB` database using a browser interface. You can now enter any SQL statement to visualise the data. For example, enter `SELECT * FROM ARTIST` in Figure 7 to display the content of the table `ARTIST`.

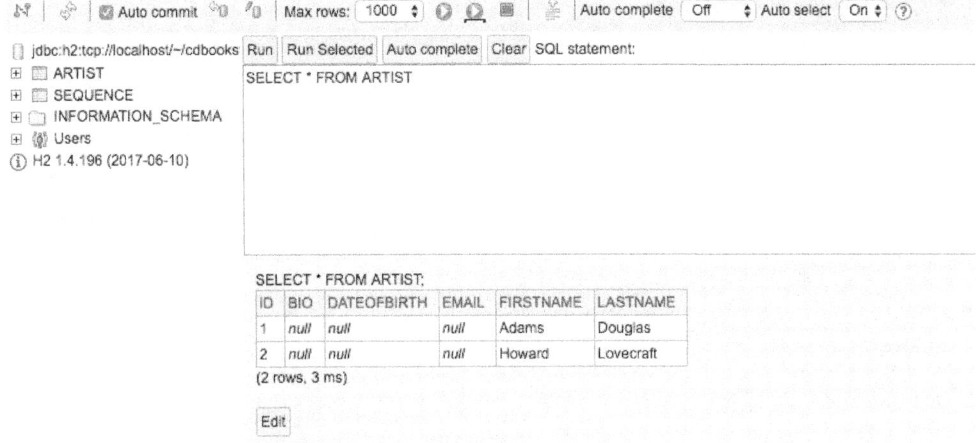

Figure 7. H2 console executing a select statement

To get the structure of the `Artist` table, execute the statement `SHOW COLUMNS FROM ARTIST` as seen in Figure 8.

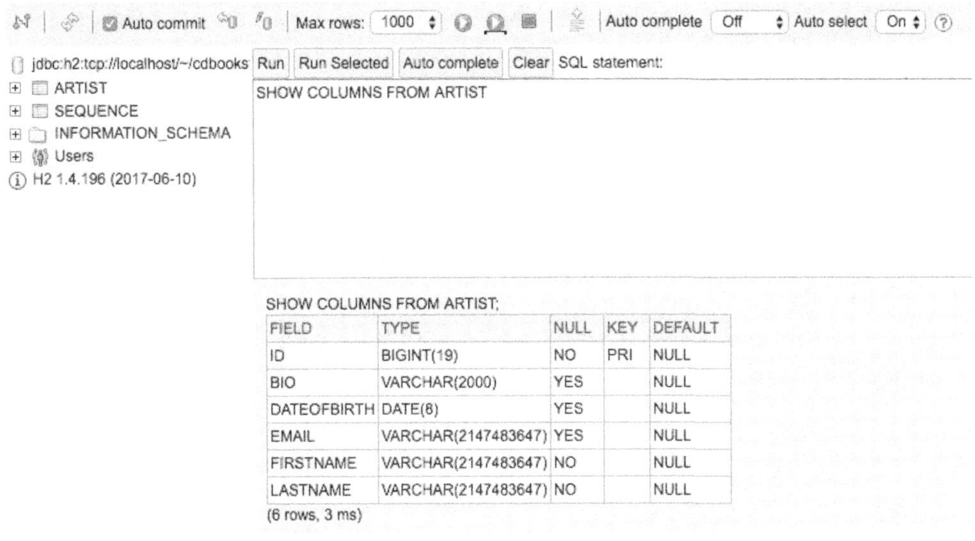

Figure 8. H2 console showing the database structure

3.1.8. Generating the Database Schema

Thanks to the `javax.persistence.schema-generation.scripts.action` property in the `persistence.xml` file (see Listing 16), the database DDL script can be generated. For that, JPA has an API and a standard mechanism to generate the database schema from the entities and the persistence unit. This feature is very convenient when you are in development mode.

Listing 17. API Generating the Database Schema

```
public class SchemaGenerator {

  public static void main(String[] args) {

    Persistence.generateSchema("cdbookstorePU", null);
  }
}
```

As you can see in Listing 17, a simple API call with the name of the persistence unit, and JPA generates the database schema shown in Listing 18.

Listing 18. Script Creating the ARTIST Table Structure

```
CREATE TABLE ARTIST
(
  ID          BIGINT  NOT NULL,
  BIO         VARCHAR(2000),
  DATEOFBIRTH DATE,
  EMAIL       VARCHAR,
  FIRSTNAME   VARCHAR NOT NULL,
  LASTNAME    VARCHAR NOT NULL,
  PRIMARY KEY (ID)
)
```

3.2. A Closer Look at JPA

Now that you've run your first test, let's have a closer look at Java Persistence API. This will give you some terminology that will be used in the chapters that follow.

3.2.1. JPA Packages

The Java Persistence API APIs are all defined under the `javax.persistence` package. Table 2 lists the main subpackages defined in JPA 2.2 (under the root `javax.persistence` package).

Table 2. Main javax.persistence Subpackages

Subpackage	Description
root	Root package of the JPA APIs
`criteria`	Java Persistence Criteria API, allowing the writing of queries in an object-oriented way
`metamodel`	Java Persistence Metamodel API, bringing type safety to the queries
`spi`	Internal SPIs (*Service Provider Interfaces*) implemented by the provider

3.2.2. Main JPA APIs

The class diagram in Figure 9 highlights the main JPA APIs.

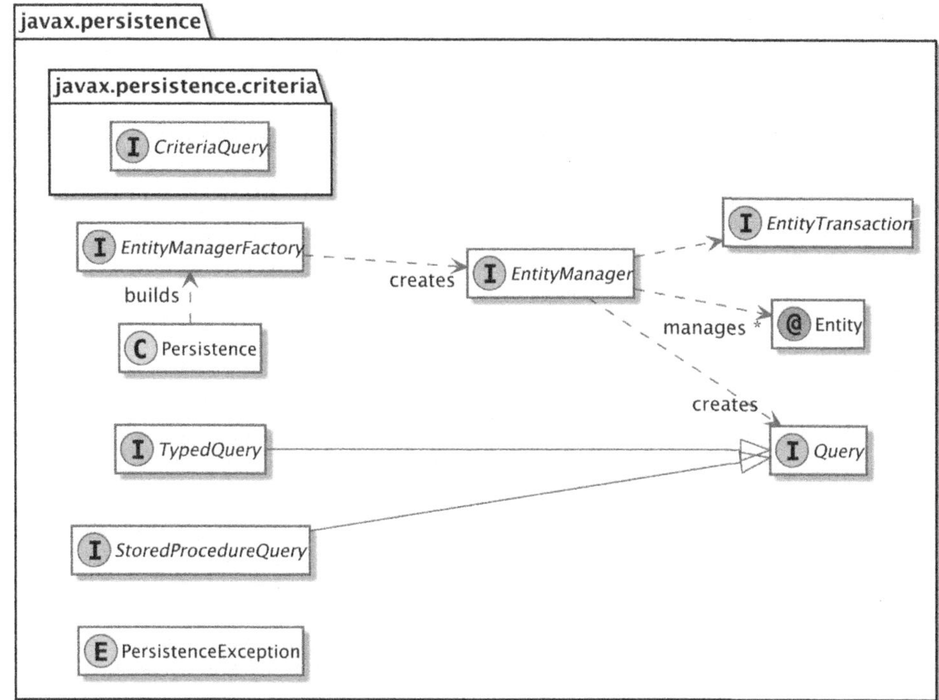

Figure 9. Main JPA APIs

Of course, there are many more APIs in JPA as you will see in the chapters that follow. But Table 3 lists the main ones.

Table 3. Main JPA APIs

API	Description
`Persistence`	Entry point for JPA also used to build an `EntityManagerFactory`
`EntityManagerFactory`	This interface acts as a factory for returning initialised `EntityManager` instances
`EntityManager`	This is the primary JPA interface used by applications to manage persistent objects
`EntityTransaction`	This interface allows operations on persistent objects to be grouped into units of work that either completely succeed or completely fail, leaving the datastore in its original state
`Query` and `TypedQuery`	Set of interfaces allowing the querying of persistent objects that meet certain criteria
`CriteriaQuery`	API to create queries

API	Description
`StoredProcedureQuery`	API to execute stored procedure
`PersistenceException`	Thrown by the persistence provider when a problem occurs

3.2.3. Main JPA Annotations

Along with APIs, JPA comes with a set of annotations. Table 4 lists a subset of the most commonly used annotations.

Table 4. Main JPA Annotations

Annotation	Description
`@Entity`	POJOs become persistent objects when annotated with `@Entity`
`@Column`	Specifies the mapped column for a persistent property (name, length, unique, etc.)
`@GeneratedValue`	Defines the value generation policy of primary keys
`@Id`	Specifies the primary key of an entity
`@Table`	Specifies the primary table for the annotated entity
`@Transient`	Specifies that the property is not persistent
`@OneToOne`, `@OneToMany`, `@ManyToOne`, `@ManyToMany`	Relation multiplicity

This was just a quick introduction of JPA main packages, APIs and annotations. This fascicle will dig into more details in the coming chapters.

3.2.4. Anatomy of an Entity

As seen in Listing 11, for a class to be an entity it has to be annotated with `@javax.persistence.Entity`, which allows the persistence provider to recognise it as a persistent class and not just as a simple POJO. Then, the annotation `@javax.persistence.Id` defines the unique identifier of this object. Because JPA is about mapping objects to relational tables, objects need an Id that will be mapped to a primary key. An entity can also have business methods and does not need to implement any interface or extend any class. In fact, to be an entity, a class must follow these rules.

- The entity class must be annotated with `@javax.persistence.Entity` (or denoted in the XML descriptor as an entity).
- The `@javax.persistence.Id` annotation must be used to denote at least one primary key.
- The entity class must have a no-arg constructor that has to be public or protected. The entity class may have other constructors as well.
- The entity class must be a top-level class. An enum or interface cannot be designated as an entity.

- The entity class must not be final. No methods or persistent instance variables of the entity class may be final.
- If an entity instance has to be passed by value as a detached object (e.g. through a remote interface), the entity class must implement the `Serializable` interface. But that is not required by JPA.

3.2.5. Entity Life Cycle

Entities are just POJOs. But POJOs are not entities. This means that entities have a life cycle, as shown in Figure 10. When the entity manager manages a POJO, it becomes managed, and therefore has a persistence identity (a key that uniquely identifies an instance equivalent to a primary key). We call that an entity. When an entity is not managed (i.e. it is detached from the entity manager), it can be used like any other POJO.

When you create an instance of the `Book` entity with the `new` operator, the object exists in memory, and JPA knows nothing about it (it can even end up being garbage collected). When it becomes managed by the entity manager, the entity synchronises its state with the `BOOK` table. Calling the `EntityManager.remove()` method deletes the data from the database, but the Java object continues living in memory until it gets garbage collected.

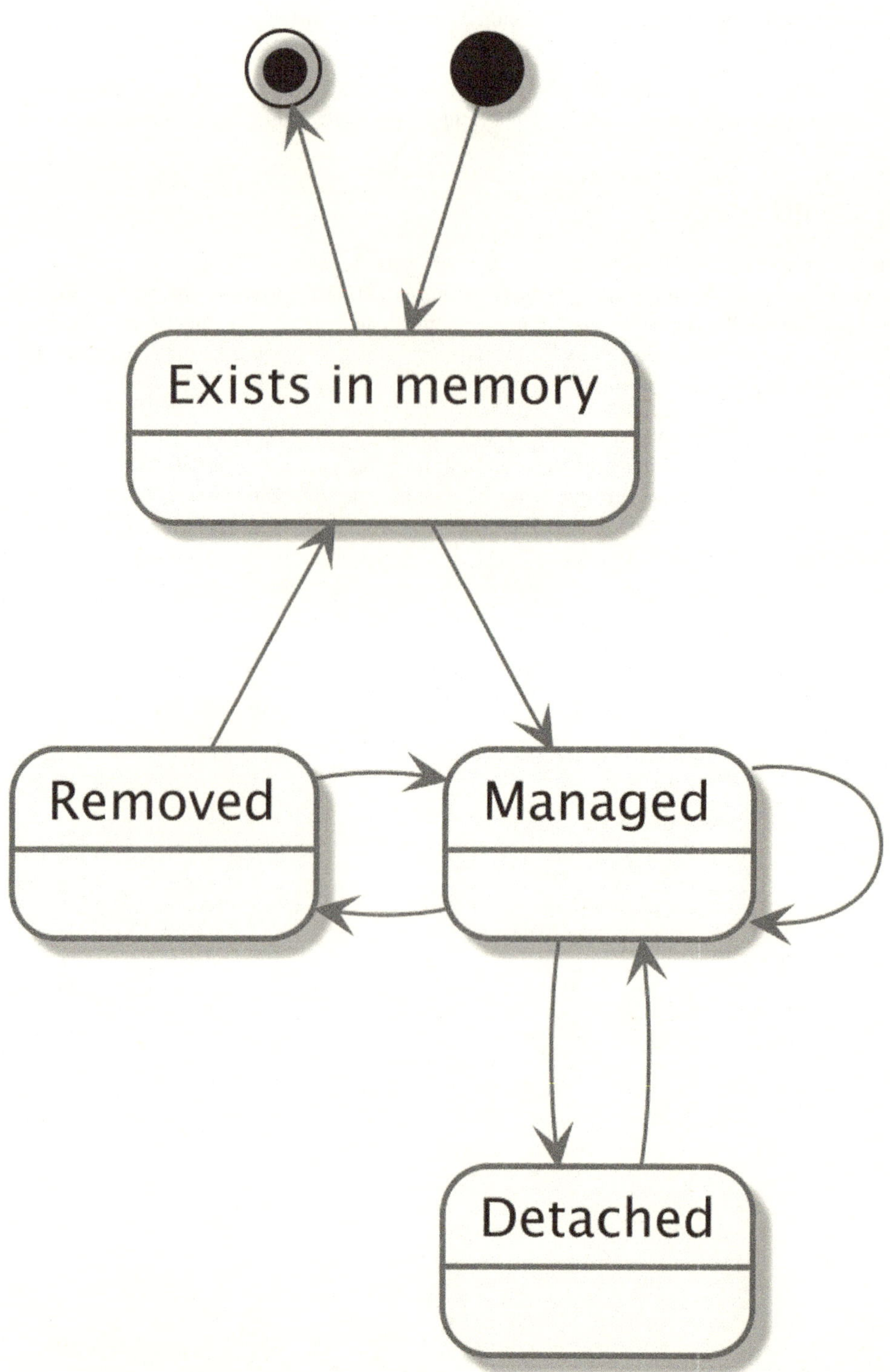

Figure 10. The life cycle of an entity

The operations carried out on entities fall into four categories - persisting, updating, removing, and loading - which correspond to the database operations of inserting, updating, deleting, and selecting, respectively. JPA allows you to hook business logic to the entity when these events occur. These hooks can be set on entity methods (a.k.a. callback methods) or in external classes (a.k.a. listeners). You can think of callback methods and listeners as analogous triggers in a relational database. More on callback methods and listeners in Chapter 7.

3.2.6. Deployment Descriptors

Like several Java technologies, JPA comes with a set of APIs but also some deployment descriptors. A *Deployment Descriptor* (DD) refers to a configuration file that is deployed with the code and configures or overrides parts of the code.

As shown in the diagram in Figure 11, JPA comes with two kinds of XML descriptors:

- `META-INF/persistence.xml`: This mandatory file is used to customise the configuration of the default `EntityManagerFactory`. It can also aggregate zero or many mapping XML descriptors.
- Mapping descriptor: Up to now, we've seen annotations, but JPA also lets you declare mapping via XML. This file describes the object-relational mapping and closely matches the annotations declaration approach.

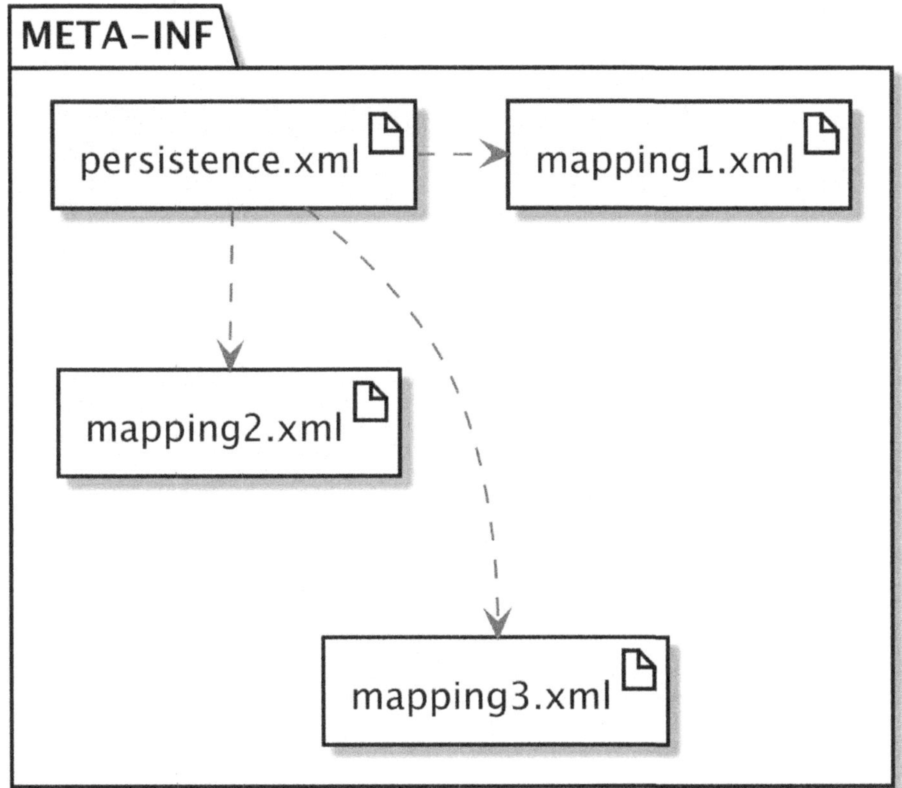

Figure 11. JPA deployment descriptors

Notice that the deployment descriptors are located under the META-INF directory of the application.

Persistence Unit

The persistence.xml deployment descriptor is mandatory and is specified in Listing 19.

Listing 19. persistence.xml

```
<persistence>
  <persistence-unit name="" transaction-type="">
    <description/>
    <provider/>
    <jta-data-source/>
    <non-jta-data-source/>
    <mapping-file/>
    <jar-file/>
    <class/>
    <exclude-unlisted-classes/>
    <shared-cache-mode/>
    <validation-mode/>

    <properties>
      <property name="javax.persistence.lock.timeout" value=""/>
      <property name="javax.persistence.query.timeout" value=""/>
      <property name="javax.persistence.validation.group.pre-persist" value=""/>
      <property name="javax.persistence.validation.group.pre-update" value=""/>
      <property name="javax.persistence.validation.group.pre-remove" value=""/>

      <property name="javax.persistence.jdbc.driver" value=""/>
      <property name="javax.persistence.jdbc.url" value=""/>
      <property name="javax.persistence.jdbc.user" value=""/>
      <property name="javax.persistence.jdbc.password" value=""/>

      <property name="javax.persistence.schema-generation.database.action" value=""/>
      <property name="javax.persistence.schema-generation.scripts.action" value=""/>
      <property name="javax.persistence.schema-generation.scripts.create-target"
value=""/>
      <property name="javax.persistence.schema-generation.scripts.drop-target" value=
""/>
    </properties>
  </persistence-unit>
</persistence>
```

The root element of the persistence.xml file in Listing 19 is the persistence element. This element consists of one or more persistence-unit elements which consist of the name and transaction-type attributes and the following sub-elements:

- description: Provides optional descriptive information.
- provider: Specifies the name of the persistence provider's javax.persistence.spi.PersistenceProvider class.

- `jta-data-source`, `non-jta-data-source`: In a managed environment (Java EE or Spring), these elements are used to specify the JNDI name of the JTA and/or non-JTA datasource to be used by the persistence provider.
- `mapping-file`, `jar-file`, `class`, `exclude-unlisted-classes`: Entities, embeddables, mapped superclasses and converter classes must be implicitly or explicitly denoted as managed persistence classes.
- `shared-cache-mode`: Determines whether second-level caching is in effect for the persistence unit.
- `validation-mode`: Determines whether automatic life cycle event time validation is in effect.
- `properties`: Used to specify both standard and vendor-specific properties and hints that apply to the persistence unit and its configuration:
    - `javax.persistence.lock.timeout`: Milliseconds for pessimistic lock timeout.
    - `javax.persistence.query.timeout`: Milliseconds for query timeout.
    - `javax.persistence.validation.group.pre-persist`, `update`, `remove`: Groups targeted for validation once the pre-persist, pre-update and pre-remove events take place.
    - `javax.persistence.jdbc.driver`: Fully qualified name of the driver class.
    - `javax.persistence.jdbc.url`: Driver-specific URL.
    - `javax.persistence.jdbc.user`: Username used by database connection.
    - `javax.persistence.jdbc.password`: Password for database connection.
    - `javax.persistence.schema-generation.database.action`: Action to be taken by the persistence provider with regard to the database generation (`none`, `create`, `drop-and-create`, `drop`).
    - `javax.persistence.schema-generation.scripts.action`: Action to be taken by the persistence provider with regard to the DDL schema generation (`none`, `create`, `drop-and-create`, `drop`).
    - `javax.persistence.schema-generation.scripts.create-target`, `drop-target`: If scripts are to be generated, the target locations for writing the create and drop scripts.

Mapping Descriptor

The XML mapping descriptor serves as both an alternative to, and an overriding mechanism for, mapping annotations. It is optional and only taken into account by the JPA provider if specified on the `persistence.xml` (with the `mapping-file` element). Listing 20 specifies the structure of the mapping descriptor XML file.

Listing 20. Mapping Descriptor

```
<entity-mappings>
  <description/>
  <access/>
  <catalog/>
  <package/>
  <persistence-unit-metadata/>
  <sequence-generator name=""/>
  <table-generator name=""/>
  <sql-result-set-mapping name=""/>
  <entity class=""/>
  <embeddable class=""/>
  <mapped-superclass class=""/>
  <converter class=""/>
  <named-native-query name="">
    <query/>
  </named-native-query>
  <named-query name="">
    <query/>
  </named-query>
  <named-stored-procedure-query name="" procedure-name=""/>
</entity-mappings>
```

More on mapping descriptors in Chapter 4.

Now that you know the basis of object-relational mapping, have run a "*Hello World*" example, and know a bit more terminology, let's use the following chapters to dig more into JPA.

[49] Maven https://maven.apache.org

[50] JUnit http://junit.org

Chapter 4. Mapping Entities

In the previous chapter, I went through the basics of object-relational mapping (ORM), which is basically mapping entities to tables and attributes to columns. I also introduced configuration by exception which allows the JPA provider to map an entity to a database table using all the defaults. But defaults are not always suitable, especially if you map your domain model to an existing database. JPA comes with a rich set of metadata so you can customise the mapping.

In this chapter, I cover elementary mapping as well as more complex mappings such as relationships, composition, and inheritance. A domain model is made up of objects interacting with each other. Objects and databases have different ways to store relationship information (references in objects and foreign keys in databases). Inheritance is not a feature that relational databases naturally have, and therefore the mapping is not as obvious. In this chapter, I go into some detail and show examples that demonstrate how to map attributes, relationships, and inheritance from a domain model to a database.

The code in this chapter can be found at https://github.com/agoncal/agoncal-fascicle-jpa/tree/2.2/mapping

4.1. Default Mapping

Default mapping rules are an important part of the principle known as *configuration by exception*. Java EE 5 introduced this idea (sometimes referred to as *programming by exception* or *convention over configuration*) and it is still heavily used today, especially in JPA. This means, unless specified differently, the provider should apply the default rules. In other words, having to supply a configuration is the exception to the rule. This allows you to write the minimum amount of code to get your application running, relying on the provider's defaults. If you don't want the provider to apply the default rules, you can customise the mapping to your own needs using metadata.

This means that, for all the other attributes, the following default mapping rules will apply:

- The entity name is mapped to a relational table name (e.g. the `Book` entity is mapped to a `BOOK` table). If you want to map it to another table, you will need to use the `@Table` annotation, as you'll see later in the "Elementary Mapping" section.
- Attribute names are mapped to a column name (e.g. the `id` attribute, or the `getId()` method, is mapped to an `ID` column). If you want to change this default mapping, you will need to use the `@Column` annotation.
- JDBC rules apply for mapping Java primitives to relational data types. A `String` will be mapped to `VARCHAR`, a `Long` to a `BIGINT`, a `Boolean` to a `SMALLINT`, and so on. The default size of a column mapped from a `String` is 255 (a `String` is mapped to a `VARCHAR(255)`). But keep in mind that the default mapping rules are different from one database to another. For example, a `String` is mapped to a `VARCHAR` in H2 and a `VARCHAR2` in Oracle. An `Integer` is mapped to an `INTEGER` in H2 and a `NUMBER` in Oracle. The information of the underlying database is provided in the `persistence.xml` file, which you'll see later.

4.2. Elementary Mapping

There are significant differences in the way Java handles data compared to the way a relational database handles data. In Java, we use classes to describe both attributes for holding data and methods to access and manipulate that data. Once we define a class, we can create as many instances as we need with the `new` keyword. In a relational database, data is stored in non-object structures (columns and rows), and dynamic behaviour is stored functionally as table triggers and stored procedures that are not bound tightly to the data structures, as they are with objects. Sometimes mapping Java objects to the underlying database can be easy, and the default rules can be applied. At other times, these rules do not meet your needs, and you must customise the mapping. Elementary mapping annotations focus on customising the table, the primary key, and the columns, and they let you modify certain naming conventions or typing (not-null column, length etc.).

4.2.1. Tables

Rules for configuration by exception mapping state that the entity and the table name are the same (a `Book` entity is mapped to a `BOOK` table, an `AncientBook` entity is mapped to an `ANCIENTBOOK` table etc.). This might suit you in most cases, but you may want to map your data to a different table, or even map a single entity to several tables.

Mapping a Table

The `@javax.persistence.Table` annotation makes it possible to change the default mapping values related to the table. For example, you can specify the name of the table in which the data will be stored, the catalogue, and the database schema. You can also define unique constraints to the table using the `@UniqueConstraint` annotation in conjunction with `@Table`. If the `@Table` annotation is omitted, the name of the table will be the name of the entity. If you want to change the name to `T_BOOK` instead of `BOOK`, you would do as shown in Listing 21.

Listing 21. The Book Entity Being Mapped to a T_BOOK Table

```
@Entity
@Table(name = "t_book")
public class Book {

  @Id
  private Long id;
  private String title;
  private Float price;
  private String description;
  private String isbn;
  private Integer nbOfPages;
  private Boolean illustrations;

  // Constructors, getters, setters
}
```

In the @Table annotation, I include a lowercase table name (t_book). By default, most databases will map the entity to an uppercase table name except if you configure them to honour case.

Mapping Several Tables

Up to now, I have assumed that an entity gets mapped to a single table, also known as a *primary table*. But sometimes when you have an existing data model, you might need to spread the data across multiple tables, or *secondary tables*. To do this, you need to use the annotation @SecondaryTable to associate a secondary table to an entity. You can distribute the data of an entity across columns in both the primary table and the secondary tables simply by defining the secondary tables with annotations and then specifying for each attribute which table it belongs to (with the @Column annotation, which I'll describe in the "Attributes" section in more detail). Listing 22 shows an Address entity mapping its attributes to one primary table and two secondary tables.

Listing 22. Attributes of the Address Entity Mapped in Three Different Tables

```
@Entity
@SecondaryTable(name = "t_city")
@SecondaryTable(name = "t_country")
public class Address {

  @Id
  private Long id;
  private String street1;
  private String street2;
  @Column(table = "t_city")
  private String city;
  @Column(table = "t_city")
  private String state;
  @Column(table = "t_city")
  private String zipcode;
  @Column(table = "t_country")
  private String country;

  // Constructors, getters, setters
}
```

By default, the attributes of the Address entity are mapped to the primary table (which has the default name of the entity, so the table is called ADDRESS). The two annotations @SecondaryTable inform that there are two secondary tables: T_CITY and T_COUNTRY. You then need to specify which attribute is stored in which secondary table (using the annotation @Column(table="t_city") or @Column(table="t_country")). Figure 12 shows the tables structure to which the Address entity will be mapped. Each table contains different attributes, but they all have the same primary key (to join the tables together).

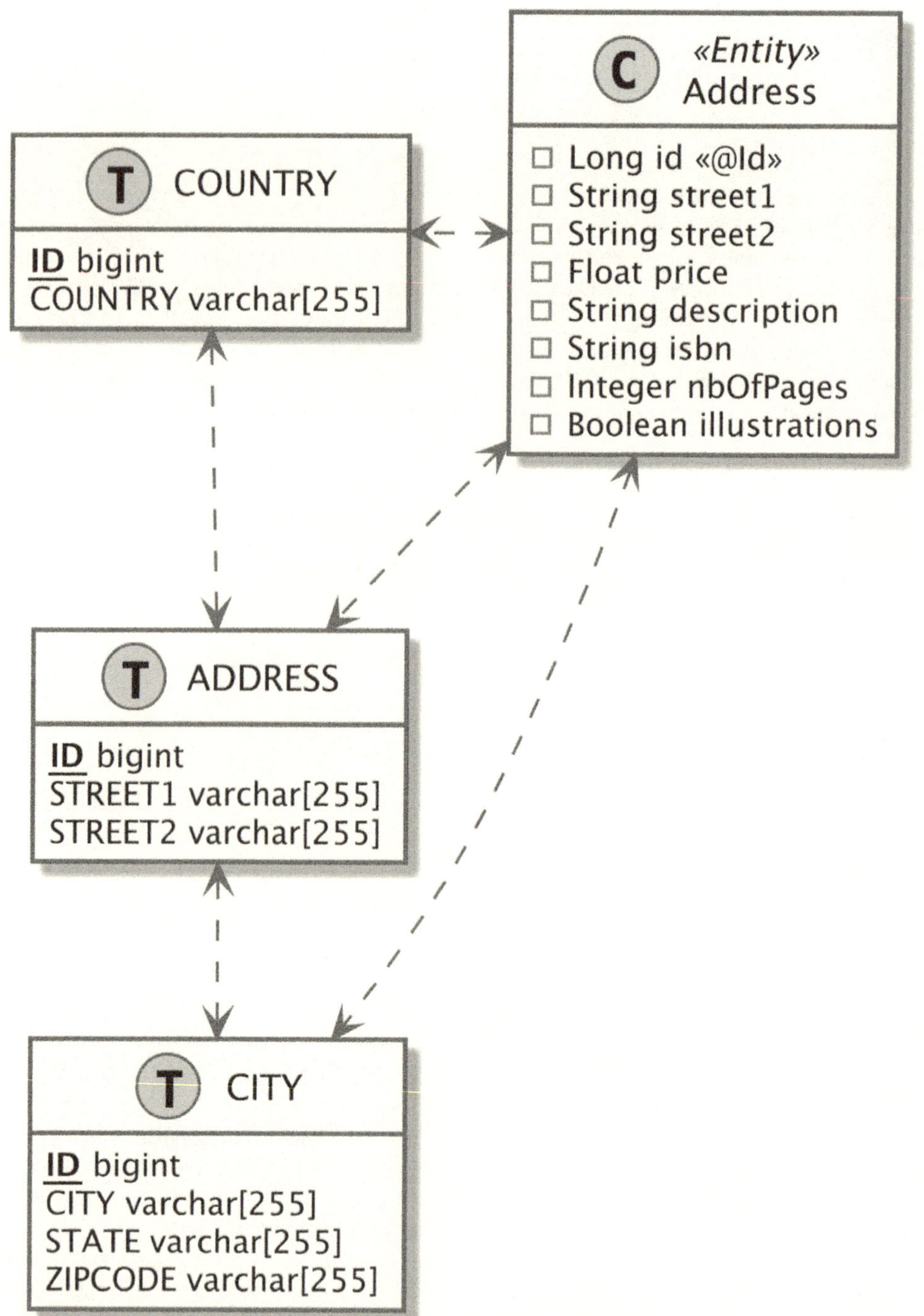

Figure 12. The Address entity is mapped to three tables

As you probably understand by now, you can have several annotations in the same entity. If you want to rename the primary table, you can add the `@Table` annotation as demonstrated in Listing 23.

Listing 23. The Primary Table Is Renamed T_ADDRESS

```
@Entity
@Table(name = "t_address")
@SecondaryTable(name = "t_city")
@SecondaryTable(name = "t_country")
public class Address {

  // Attributes, constructors, getters, setters
}
```

When you use secondary tables, you must consider the issue of performance. Every time you access an entity, the persistence provider accesses several tables and has to join them. On the other hand, secondary tables can be a good thing when you have expensive attributes such as *Binary Large Objects* (BLOBs) that you want to isolate in a different table.

4.2.2. Keys

In relational databases, a primary key uniquely identifies each row in a table. It comprises either a single column or set of columns. Primary keys must be unique, as they identify a single row (a null value is not allowed). Examples of primary keys are a customer identifier, a telephone number, an order reference, or an ISBN. JPA requires entities to have an identifier mapped to a primary key, which will follow the same rule: uniquely identify an entity by either a single attribute or a set of attributes (*composite key*). This entity's primary key value cannot be updated once it has been assigned.

Primary Keys

A simple (i.e. noncomposite) primary key must correspond to a single attribute of the entity class. The `@Id` annotation that you've seen before is used to denote a simple primary key. `@javax.persistence.Id` annotates an attribute as being a unique identifier. It can be one of the following types:

- Primitive Java types: `byte`, `int`, `short`, `long`, `char`
- Wrapper classes of primitive Java types: `Byte`, `Integer`, `Short`, `Long`, `Character`
- Arrays of primitive or wrapper types: `int[]`, `Integer[]` etc.
- Strings, numbers, and dates: `java.lang.String`, `java.math.BigInteger`, `java.util.Date`, `java.sql.Date`, `java.time.LocalDate`, `java.time.LocalTime`, `java.time.LocalDateTime`, `java.time.OffsetTime`, `java.time.OffsetDateTime`

When creating an entity, the value of this identifier can be generated either manually by the application or automatically by the persistence provider using the `@GeneratedValue` annotation. This annotation can have four possible values:

- SEQUENCE and IDENTITY specify use of a database SQL sequence or identity column, respectively.
- TABLE instructs the persistence provider to store the sequence name and its current value in a table, increasing the value each time a new instance of the entity is persisted.
- The generation of a key is done automatically (AUTO) by the underlying persistence provider, which will pick an appropriate strategy for a particular database. AUTO is the default value of the @GeneratedValue annotation.

Note that the attribute id is annotated twice, once with @Id and once with @GeneratedValue. If the @GeneratedValue annotation is not defined, the application has to create its own identifier by applying any algorithm that will return a unique value. The code in Listing 24 shows how to have an automatically generated identifier. GenerationType.AUTO being the default value, I could have omitted the strategy element.

Listing 24. The Book Entity with an Automatically Generated Identifier

```
@Entity
public class Book {

  @Id
  @GeneratedValue(strategy = GenerationType.AUTO)
  private Long id;
  private String title;
  private Float price;
  private String description;
  private String isbn;
  private Integer nbOfPages;
  private Boolean illustrations;

  // Constructors, getters, setters
}
```

Composite Primary Keys

When mapping entities, it is good practice to designate a single dedicated column as the primary key. However, there are cases where a composite primary key is required (such as having to map to a legacy database or when the primary keys have to follow certain business rules, for example a date and a value, or a country code and a time stamp). To do this, a primary key class must be defined to represent the composite key. Then, we have two available annotations for defining this class, depending on how we want to structure the entity: @EmbeddedId and @IdClass. As you'll see, the final result is the same, and you will end up having the same database schema, but the way to query the entity is slightly different.

Let's say that the Vintage Store application needs to post news frequently on the main page where you can see daily news about books, music, or artists. The news has content, a title, and, because it can be written in several languages, a language code (EN for English, PT for Portuguese etc.). The primary key of the news could then be the title and the language code because an article can be translated into multiple languages but keep its original title. So, the primary key class NewsId is composed of two attributes of type String: title and language. Primary key classes must include method definitions for `equals()` and `hashCode()` in order to manage queries and internal collections (equality for these methods must be consistent with the database equality), and their attributes must be in the set of valid types listed previously. They must also be public, implement `Serializable` if they need to cross architectural layers (e.g. they will be managed in the persistent layer and used in the presentation layer), and have a no-arg constructor.

@EmbeddedId

As you will see later in this chapter, JPA uses different sorts of embedded objects. To summarise, an embedded object doesn't have any identity (no primary key of its own), and its attributes will end up as columns in the table of the entity that contains it.

Listing 25 shows the `NewsId` class as an embeddable class. It is just an embedded object (annotated with `@Embeddable`) that happens to be composed of two attributes (`title` and `language`). This class must have no-arg constructor, getter, setter, `equals()`, and `hashCode()` implementations; that is, it needs to use the JavaBean conventions.[51] The class itself doesn't have an identity of its own (no `@Id` annotation). That's a characteristic of an embeddable.

Listing 25. The Primary Key Class Is Annotated with @Embeddable

```
@Embeddable
public class NewsId implements Serializable {

  private String title;
  private String language;

  // Constructors, getters, setters, equals, and hashcode
}
```

The `News` entity, shown in Listing 26, then has to embed the primary key class `NewsId` with the `@EmbeddedId` annotation. With this approach, there is no need to use `@Id`. Every `@EmbeddedId` must refer to an embeddable class marked with `@Embeddable`.

Listing 26. The Entity Embeds the Primary Key Class with @EmbeddedId

```
@Entity
public class News {

  @EmbeddedId
  private NewsId id;
  private String content;

  // Constructors, getters, setters, equals, and hashcode
}
```

In the next chapter, I describe how to find entities using their composite primary key. Just as a first glimpse, here is how it works: the primary key is a class with a constructor. You have to instantiate this class with the values that form your unique key, and pass this object to the entity manager (the `em` attribute) as shown in the code that follows:

```
NewsId pk = new NewsId("Richard Wright has died on September 2008", "EN")
News news = em.find(News.class, pk);
```

@IdClass

The other method of declaring a composite key is through the `@IdClass` annotation. It's a different approach whereby each attribute on the primary key class also needs to be declared on the entity class and annotated with `@Id`.

The composite primary key in the example `NewsId` in Listing 27 is just a POJO that does not require any annotation (in the previous example of Listing 26, the primary key class needs to be annotated with `@EmbeddedId`).

Listing 27. The Primary Key Class Has No Annotation

```
public class NewsId implements Serializable {

  private String title;
  private String language;

  // Constructors, getters, setters, equals, and hashcode
}
```

Then, the entity `News`, shown in Listing 28, has to define the primary key using the `@IdClass` annotation and annotate each key with `@Id`. To persist the `News` entity, you will have to set a value to the `title` and the `language` attributes.

Listing 28. The Entity Defines Its Primary Class with the @IdClass Annotation

```
@Entity
@IdClass(NewsId.class)
public class News {

  @Id
  private String title;
  @Id
  private String language;
  private String content;

  // Constructors, getters, setters, equals, and hashcode
}
```

Both approaches, `@EmbeddedId` and `@IdClass`, will be mapped to the same table structure. This structure is defined in Listing 29 using the *Data Definition Language* (DDL). The attributes of the entity and the primary key will end up in the same table, and the primary key will be formed with the attributes of the composite class (`title` and `language`).

Listing 29. DDL of the NEWS Table with a Composite Primary Key

```
CREATE TABLE NEWS
(
  LANGUAGE VARCHAR NOT NULL,
  TITLE    VARCHAR NOT NULL,
  CONTENT  VARCHAR,
  PRIMARY KEY (LANGUAGE, TITLE)
)
```

The `@IdClass` approach is more prone to error, as you need to define each primary key attribute in both the `@IdClass` and the entity, taking care to use the same name and Java type. The advantage is that you don't need to change the code of the primary key class (no annotation is needed). For example, you could use a legacy class that, for legal reasons, you are not allowed to change but that you can reuse.

One visible difference is in the way you reference the entity in JPQL. In the case of `@IdClass`, you would do something like the following:

```
select n.title from News n
```

With `@EmbeddedId`, you would have something like the following:

```
select n.newsId.title from News n
```

4.2.3. Attributes

An entity must have a primary key (simple or compound) to be able to have an identity in a relational database. It also has all sorts of different attributes, making up its state, that have to be mapped to the table. This state can include almost every Java type that you would want to map:

- Java primitive types (`int`, `double`, `float` etc.) and the wrapper classes (`Integer`, `Double`, `Float` etc.);
- Arrays of bytes and characters (`byte[]`, `Byte[]`, `char[]`, `Character[]`);
- String, large numeric, and temporal types (`java.lang.String`, `java.math.BigInteger`, `java.math.BigDecimal`, `java.util.Date`, `java.util.Calendar`, `java.sql.Date`, `java.sql.Time`, `java.sql.Timestamp`, `java.time.LocalDate`, `java.time.LocalTime`, `java.time.LocalDateTime`, `java.time.OffsetTime`, `java.time.OffsetDateTime`);
- Enumerated types and user-defined types that implement the `Serializable` interface; and
- Collections of basic and embeddable types.

Of course, an entity can also have an entity as an attribute or a collection of entities. But this requires introducing relationships between entities which will be covered in the "Relationship Mapping" section.

With configuration by exception, attributes are mapped using default mapping rules. However, sometimes you need to customise parts of this mapping. That's where JPA annotations (or their XML equivalent) come into play.

Basic

The optional `@javax.persistence.Basic` annotation (see Listing 30) is the simplest type of mapping an attribute to a database column.

Listing 30. @Basic Annotation Elements

```
@Target({METHOD, FIELD})
@Retention(RUNTIME)
public @interface Basic {

  FetchType fetch() default EAGER;
  boolean optional() default true;
}
```

This annotation has two parameters: `optional` and `fetch`. The `optional` element gives a hint as to whether the value of the attribute may be null. It is disregarded for primitive types. The `fetch` element can take two values: `LAZY` or `EAGER`. It gives a hint to the persistence provider runtime that data should be fetched lazily (only when the application asks for the property) or eagerly (when the entity is initially loaded by the provider).

A hint specifies a preference on the part of the application. While a hint defined by JPA should be observed by the provider if possible, a hint may or may not always be observed. A portable application must not depend on the observance of a hint.

For example, take the `Track` entity shown in Listing 31. A CD album is made up of several tracks, and each track has a title, a description, and a WAV file of a certain duration that you can listen to. The WAV file is a BLOB (*Binary Large Object*) that can be a few megabytes long. When you access the `Track` entity, you don't want to eagerly load the WAV file; you can annotate the attribute with `@Basic(fetch = FetchType.LAZY)` so the data will be retrieved from the database lazily (only when you access the `wav` attribute using its getter, for example).

Listing 31. The Track Entity with Lazy Loading on the WAV Attribute

```
@Entity
public class Track {

  @Id
  @GeneratedValue(strategy = GenerationType.AUTO)
  private Long id;
  private String title;
  private Float duration;
  @Basic(fetch = FetchType.LAZY)
  @Lob
  private byte[] wav;
  private String description;

  // Constructors, getters, setters
}
```

Note that the `wav` attribute of type `byte[]` is also annotated with `@Lob` to store the value as a *large object* (LOB). Database columns that can store these types of large objects require special JDBC calls to be accessed from Java. To inform the provider, an additional `@Lob` annotation must be added to the basic mapping.

Columns

The `@javax.persistence.Column` annotation, shown in Listing 32, defines the properties of a column. You can change the column name (which by default is mapped to an attribute of the same name); specify the size; and authorise (or not) the column to have a null value, to be unique, or to allow its value to be updatable or insertable. Listing 32 shows the `@Column` annotation API with the elements and their default values.

Listing 32. @Column Annotation Elements

```
@Target({METHOD, FIELD})
@Retention(RUNTIME)
public @interface Column {

  String  name()        default "";
  boolean unique()      default false;
  boolean nullable()    default true;
  boolean insertable() default true;
  boolean updatable()  default true;
  String  columnDefinition() default "";
  String  table()       default "";
  int     length()      default 255;
  int     precision()  default 0; // decimal precision
  int     scale()       default 0; // decimal scale
}
```

To redefine the default mapping of the original Book entity (Listing 21), you can use the @Column annotation in various ways (see Listing 33). For example, you can change the name of the title and nbOfPages column or the length of the description, and not allow null values. Notice that not all the combinations of attributes on data types are valid (e.g. length only applies to string-valued column, scale and precision only to decimal column).

Listing 33. Customising Mapping for the Book Entity

```
@Entity
public class Book {

  @Id
  @GeneratedValue(strategy = GenerationType.AUTO)
  private Long id;
  @Column(name = "book_title", nullable = false, updatable = false)
  private String title;
  private Float price;
  @Column(length = 2000)
  private String description;
  private String isbn;
  @Column(name = "nb_of_pages", nullable = false)
  private Integer nbOfPages;
  private Boolean illustrations;

  // Constructors, getters, setters
}
```

The Book entity in Listing 33 will get mapped to the table definition in Listing 34.

Listing 34. BOOK Table Definition

```
CREATE TABLE BOOK
(
  ID            BIGINT  NOT NULL,
  BOOK_TITLE    VARCHAR NOT NULL,
  PRICE         DOUBLE,
  DESCRIPTION   VARCHAR(2000),
  ISBN          VARCHAR,
  NB_OF_PAGES   INTEGER NOT NULL,
  ILLUSTRATIONS BOOLEAN,
  PRIMARY KEY (ID)
)
```

Most of the elements of the @Column annotation have an influence on the DDL generated by the provider. If you change the length of the description attribute to 2000 and generate the DDL, the DESTINATION column length will be set at 2000. But if you don't generate the DDL, keep in mind that the @Column(length = 2000) annotation will not serve any purpose. If the attribute description is annotated with @Column(length = 2000), and you do not generate the DDL, and map it to an existing table with DESTINATION column length set to 10, then the database will limit it to 10, not 2000.

On the other hand, `updatable` and `insertable` have an influence during runtime. It means that an attribute can be inserted or not, updated or not, in the database. You can set them to `false` when you want the persistence provider to ensure that it will not insert or update the data to the table in response to changes in the entity. Note that this does not imply that the entity attribute will not change in memory. You can still change the value in memory, but it will not be synchronised with the database. That's because, during the runtime, the generated SQL statement (`INSERT` or `UPDATE`) will not include the columns. In other words, these elements do not affect the relational mapping; they affect the dynamic behaviour of the entity manager when accessing the relational data.

Temporal

In Java, you can use the `java.time` classes to store dates in different formats, such as a date, an hour, or milliseconds. Listing 35 defines a `Customer` entity that has a date of birth (`LocalDate`) and an attribute that stores the exact time it was created in the system (`LocalDateTime`).

Listing 35. The Customer Entity Using LocalDate and LocalDateTime Attributes

```
@Entity
public class Customer {

  @Id
  @GeneratedValue
  private Long id;
  private String firstName;
  private String lastName;
  private String email;
  private String phoneNumber;
  private LocalDate dateOfBirth;
  private LocalDateTime creationDate;

  // Constructors, getters, setters
}
```

The `Customer` entity in Listing 35 will get mapped to the table defined in Listing 36. The `dateOfBirth` attribute is mapped to a column of type `DATE` and the `creationDate` attribute to a column of type `TIMESTAMP`.

Listing 36. CUSTOMER Table Definition

```
CREATE TABLE CUSTOMER
(
  ID           BIGINT NOT NULL,
  FIRSTNAME    VARCHAR,
  LASTNAME     VARCHAR,
  EMAIL        VARCHAR,
  PHONENUMBER  VARCHAR,
  DATEOFBIRTH  DATE,
  CREATIONDATE TIMESTAMP,
  PRIMARY KEY (ID)
)
```

Table 5 shows the mapping between each `java.time` class and its JDBC representation.

Table 5. Java to JDBC Date Type Mappings

Java type	JDBC type
`java.time.Duration`	`BIGINT`
`java.time.Instant`	`TIMESTAMP`
`java.time.LocalDateTime`	`TIMESTAMP`
`java.time.LocalDate`	`DATE`
`java.time.LocalTime`	`TIME`
`java.time.OffsetDateTime`	`TIMESTAMP`
`java.time.OffsetTime`	`TIME`
`java.time.ZonedDateTime`	`TIMESTAMP`

If you have legacy Java code using `java.util.Date` and `java.util.Calendar`, you need to specify which format to map it to using the `@javax.persistence.Temporal` annotation. This annotation has three possible values: `DATE`, `TIME`, or `TIMESTAMP` precision (i.e. the actual date, only the time, or both). Listing 37 shows the `Customer` entity using the legacy Java `Date` and `Calendar` APIs.

Listing 37. The Customer Entity with Two @Temporal Attributes

```
@Entity
public class Customer {

  @Id
  @GeneratedValue
  private Long id;
  private String firstName;
  private String lastName;
  private String email;
  private String phoneNumber;
  @Temporal(TemporalType.DATE)
  private Date dateOfBirth;
  @Temporal(TemporalType.TIMESTAMP)
  private Date creationDate;

  // Constructors, getters, setters
}
```

Transient

With JPA, as soon as a class is annotated with `@Entity`, all its attributes are automatically mapped to a table. If you do not need to map an attribute, you can use the `@javax.persistence.Transient` annotation or the java `transient` keyword. For example, let's take the same `Customer` entity and add an `age` attribute (see Listing 38). Because age can be automatically calculated from the date of birth, the `age` attribute does not need to be mapped and therefore can be transient.

Listing 38. The Customer Entity with a Transient Age

```
@Entity
public class Customer {

  @Id
  @GeneratedValue
  private Long id;
  private String firstName;
  private String lastName;
  private String email;
  private String phoneNumber;
  private LocalDate dateOfBirth;
  @Transient
  private Integer age;
  private LocalDateTime creationDate;

  // Constructors, getters, setters
}
```

As a result, the `age` attribute doesn't need any `AGE` column to be mapped to.

4.2.4. Enumerations

Java SE 5 introduced enumeration types, which are now so frequently used that they are commonly part of the developer's life. The values of an enum are constant and have an implicit ordinal assignment that is determined by the order in which they are declared in the enum. This ordinal cannot be modified at runtime but can be used to store the value of the enumerated type in the database. Listing 39 shows a credit card type enumeration.

Listing 39. CreditCardType Enumeration

```
public enum CreditCardType {

  VISA,
  MASTER_CARD,
  AMERICAN_EXPRESS
}
```

The ordinals assigned to the values of this enumerated type at compile time are `0` for `VISA`, `1` for `MASTER_CARD`, and `2` for `AMERICAN_EXPRESS`. By default, the persistence providers will map this enumerated type to the database assuming that the column is of type `Integer`. Looking at the code in Listing 40, you see a `CreditCard` entity that uses the previous enumeration with the default mapping.

Listing 40. Mapping an Enumerated Type with Ordinals

```
@Entity
@Table(name = "credit_card")
public class CreditCard {

  @Id
  private String number;
  private String expiryDate;
  private Integer controlNumber;
  private CreditCardType creditCardType;

  // Constructors, getters, setters
}
```

Because the defaults are applied, the enumeration will get mapped to an integer column, and it will work fine. But imagine introducing a new constant to the top of the enumeration. Because ordinal assignment is determined by the order in which values are declared, the values already stored in the database will no longer match the enumeration. A better solution would be to store the name of the value as a String instead of storing the ordinal. You can do this by adding an `@Enumerated` annotation to the attribute and specifying a value of `STRING` (`ORDINAL` is the default value), as shown in Listing 41.

Listing 41. Mapping an Enumerated Type with String

```
@Entity
@Table(name = "credit_card")
public class CreditCard {

  @Id
  private String number;
  private String expiryDate;
  private Integer controlNumber;
  @Enumerated(EnumType.STRING)
  private CreditCardType creditCardType;

  // Constructors, getters, setters
}
```

Now the `CreditCardType` database column will be of type `VARCHAR` and a Visa card will be stored with the String `VISA`.

4.2.5. Collection of Basic Types

Collections of things are extremely common in Java. In the upcoming sections, you will learn about relationships between entities (which can be collections of entities). Basically, this means that one entity has a collection of other entities or embeddables. In terms of mapping, each entity is mapped to its own table, and references between primary and foreign keys are created. As you know, an entity is a Java class with an identity and many other attributes. But what if you only need to store a collection of Java types such as Strings or Integers? Since JPA 2.0, you can easily do this without having to go through the trouble of creating a separate class by using the `@ElementCollection` and `@CollectionTable` annotations.

We use the `@ElementCollection` annotation to indicate that an attribute of type `java.util.Collection` contains a collection of instances of basic types (i.e. nonentities) or embeddables (more on that in the "Embeddables" section). In fact, this attribute can be of the following types:

- `java.util.Collection`: Generic root interface in the collection hierarchy.
- `java.util.Set`: Collection that prevents the insertion of duplicate elements.
- `java.util.List`: Collection used when the elements need to be retrieved in some user-defined order.

In addition, the `@CollectionTable` annotation allows you to customise details of the collection table (i.e. the table that will join the entity table with the basic types table) such as its name. If this annotation is missing, the table name will be the concatenation of the name of the containing entity and the name of the collection attribute, separated by an underscore.

Once again, using the example `Book` entity, let's see how to add an attribute to store tags. Today, tags and tag clouds are everywhere; these tend to be very useful for classifying data, so imagine for this example you want to add as many tags as you can to a book to describe it and to find it quickly. A tag is just a String, so the `Book` entity could have a collection of Strings to store this information, as shown in Listing 42.

Listing 42. The Book Entity with a Collection of Strings

```
@Entity
public class Book {

  @Id
  @GeneratedValue(strategy = GenerationType.AUTO)
  private Long id;
  private String title;
  private Float price;
  private String description;
  private String isbn;
  @ElementCollection(fetch = FetchType.LAZY)
  @CollectionTable(name = "Tag")
  @Column(name = "Value")
  private List<String> tags = new ArrayList<>();

  // Constructors, getters, setters
}
```

The `@ElementCollection` annotation in Listing 42 is used to inform the persistence provider that the tags attribute is a list of Strings and should be fetched lazily. If `@CollectionTable` is missing, the table name defaults to `BOOK_TAGS` (a concatenation of the name of the containing entity and the name of the collection attribute, separated by an underscore) instead of `TAG` as specified in the name element (`name = "Tag"`). Notice that I've added a complementary `@Column` annotation to rename the column as `VALUE` in the `TAG` table (if not, the column would be named like the attribute, `TAGS`). Figure 13 shows the result.

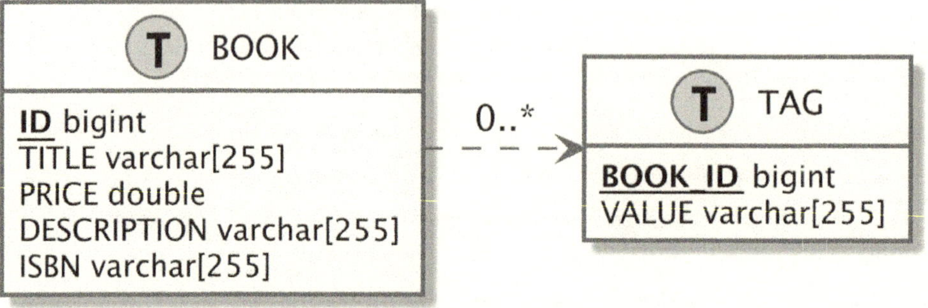

Figure 13. Relationship between the BOOK and the TAG tables

In JPA 1.0, these annotations didn't exist. However, you were still able to store a list of primitive types as a BLOB in the database. Why? Because `java.util.ArrayList` implements `Serializable`, and JPA can map `Serializable` objects to BLOBs automatically. However, if you used `java.util.List` instead, you would have an exception as it doesn't extend `Serializable`. The `@ElementCollection` is a more elegant and useful way of storing lists of basic types. Storing lists in an inaccessible binary format makes it opaque to queries and not portable to other languages (since only Java runtimes can make use of the underlying serialised object - not Ruby, PHP etc.).

4.2.6. Map of Basic Types

Like collections, maps are very useful for storing data. In JPA 1.0, keys could only be a basic data type and values only entities. Now, maps can contain any combination of basic types, embeddable objects, and entities as keys or values, which brings significant flexibility to the mapping. But let's focus on maps of basic types.

When the map key and value are basic data types, the `@ElementCollection` and `@CollectionTable` annotations can be used in the same way you saw previously with collections. A collection table is then used to store the data of the map.

Let's take an example with a CD album that contains tracks (see Listing 43). A track can be seen as a title and a position (the first track of the album, the second track of the album etc.). You could then have a map of tracks with an integer for the position (the key of the map) and a String for the title (the value of the map).

Listing 43. A CD Album with a Map of Tracks

```
@Entity
public class CD {

  @Id
  @GeneratedValue
  private Long id;
  private String title;
  private Float price;
  private String description;
  @Lob
  private byte[] cover;
  @ElementCollection
  @CollectionTable(name = "track")
  @MapKeyColumn(name = "position")
  @Column(name = "title")
  private Map<Integer, String> tracks = new HashMap<>();

  // Constructors, getters, setters
}
```

As discussed previously, the `@ElementCollection` annotation is used to indicate the objects in the map that are stored in a collection table. The `@CollectionTable` annotation changes the default name of the collection table to `TRACK`.

The difference with collections is the introduction of a new annotation: `@MapKeyColumn`. This annotation is used to specify the mapping for the key column of the map. If it is not specified, the column is named with the concatenation of the name of the referencing relationship attribute and `_KEY`. Listing 43 shows the annotation renamed as `POSITION` from the default (`TRACKS_KEY`) in order to be clearer.

The `@Column` annotation indicates that the column containing the map value should be renamed `TITLE`. Figure 14 shows the result.

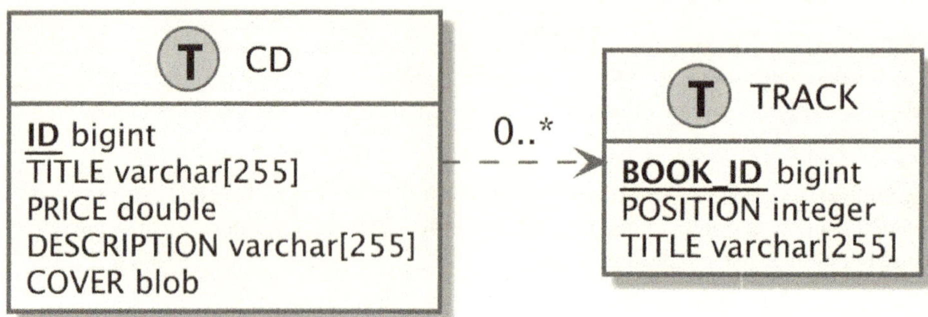

Figure 14. Relationship between the CD and the TRACK tables

4.3. Type Conversion

Thanks to *configuration by exception* we've seen that JPA uses default mapping rules to map a `String` to a `VARCHAR` or a `Long` to a `BIGINT`. But what if we want to manipulate a `Long` in Java and store it as a `VARCHAR`? What if we want to manipulate a `Date` in Java and store it as a `BIGINT`? Thanks to type conversion, you can convert a data type from one format to any other format.

Listing 44 shows the enum `CreditCardType`. As we've seen before, by default, JPA will map the ordinal number of this enum to the database. Another option is to map the String representation of this enum using `Enumerated(EnumType.STRING)`.

Listing 44. CreditCardType Enumeration

```
public enum CreditCardType {

  VISA,
  MASTER_CARD,
  AMERICAN_EXPRESS
}
```

But what if we want to map `VISA` to a `V`, `MASTER_CARD` to an `M` and `AMERICAN_EXPRESS` to an `A`? Well, we need to create a converter that transforms the `CreditCardType` enum to a database column of type `CHAR` and vice-versa. To do so in JPA, we have to annotate a class with `@Converter` and implement the

AttributeConverter interface. We parametrise the interface with the types of the enum and the database column. Listing 45 shows the CreditCardTypeConverter that implements the method convertToDatabaseColumn which takes the enum and converts it to a Character and the method convertToEntityAttribute that does the opposite.

Listing 45. Converts the Enum CreditCardType to a Character and Back

```
@Converter
public class CreditCardTypeConverter implements AttributeConverter<CreditCardType,
Character> {

  @Override
  public Character convertToDatabaseColumn(CreditCardType creditCardType) {
    switch (creditCardType) {
      case VISA:
        return 'V';
      case AMERICAN_EXPRESS:
        return 'A';
      case MASTER_CARD:
        return 'M';
      default:
        throw new IllegalArgumentException("Unknown" + creditCardType);
    }
  }

  @Override
  public CreditCardType convertToEntityAttribute(Character dbData) {
    switch (dbData) {
      case 'V':
        return VISA;
      case 'A':
        return AMERICAN_EXPRESS;
      case 'M':
        return MASTER_CARD;
      default:
        throw new IllegalArgumentException("Unknown" + dbData);
    }
  }
}
```

To use our converter, we just need to add the @Convert annotation to the attribute and specify the converter class we want to use as shown in Listing 46. The persistence provider runtime is responsible for invoking the specified conversion methods for the target attribute type when loading the entity attribute from the database and before storing the entity to the database.

Listing 46. The CreditCard Entity Using the CreditCardTypeConverter

```
@Entity
public class CreditCard {

  @Id
  private String number;
  private String expiryDate;
  private Integer controlNumber;
  @Convert(converter = CreditCardTypeConverter.class)
  private CreditCardType creditCardType;

  // Constructors, getters, setters
}
```

4.4. Mapping with XML

Now that you are more familiar with elementary mapping using annotations, let's take a look at XML mapping. If you have used an object-relational framework such as the early versions of Hibernate, you will be familiar with how to map your entities in a separate XML deployment descriptors file. Since the beginning of this chapter, you haven't seen a single line of XML, just annotations. JPA also offers, as an option, an XML syntax to map entities. I will not go into too much detail about the XML mapping because, nowadays, developers prefer to use annotations over XML mapping. But there are still some valid use cases where you could use a little XML instead of annotations.

Keep in mind that every single annotation you see in this chapter has an XML equivalent, and this section would be huge if I covered them all. I encourage you to check out Chapter 12 (XML Object/Relational Mapping Descriptor) of the JPA 2.2 specification, which covers all the XML tags in more detail.[52]

XML deployment descriptors are an alternative to using annotations. However, although each annotation has an equivalent XML tag and vice versa, there is a difference in that the XML overrides annotations. If you annotate an attribute or an entity with a certain value, and at the same time you deploy an XML descriptor with a different value, the XML will take precedence.

The question is, when should you use annotations over XML and why? First of all, it's a matter of taste, as the behaviour of both is exactly the same. When the metadata are really coupled to the code (e.g. a primary key), it does make sense to use annotations, since the metadata are just another aspect of the program. Other kinds of metadata, such as the column length or other schema details, can be changed depending on the deployment environment (e.g. the database schema is different in the development, test, or production environments). A similar situation arises when a JPA-based product needs to support several different database vendors. Certain `id` generation, column options, and so on, may need to be adjusted depending on the database type in use. This may be better expressed in external XML deployment descriptors (one per environment) so the code doesn't have to be modified.

Let's again turn to the `Book` entity example. This time imagine you have two environments, and you want to map the Book entity to the BOOK table in the development environment and to the BOOK_XML_MAPPING table in the test environment. The class will only be annotated with @Entity (see Listing 47) and not include information about the table it should be mapped to (i.e. it will have no @Table annotation). The @Id annotation defines the primary key as being auto-generated, and a @Column annotation sets the size of the description to 500 characters long.

Listing 47. The Book Entity with Only a Few Annotations

```
@Entity
public class Book {

  @Id
  @GeneratedValue(strategy = GenerationType.AUTO)
  private Long id;
  private String title;
  private Float price;
  @Column(length = 500)
  private String description;
  private String isbn;
  private Integer nbOfPages;
  private Boolean illustrations;

  // Constructors, getters, setters
}
```

In a separate book_mapping.xml file (see Listing 48), following a specified XML schema, you can change the mapping for any data in the entity. The <table> tag allows you to change the name of the table to which the entity will be mapped (BOOK_XML_MAPPING instead of the default BOOK). Inside the <attributes> tag , you can customise the attributes, specifying not only their name and length but also their relationships with other entities. For example, you can change the mapping for the title column and the number of pages (nbOfPages).

Listing 48. Mapping the File META-INF/book_mapping.xml

```
<entity-mappings xmlns:xsi="http://www.w3.org/2001/XMLSchema-instance"
                 xmlns="http://xmlns.jcp.org/xml/ns/persistence/orm"
                 xsi:schemaLocation="http://xmlns.jcp.org/xml/ns/persistence/orm
http://xmlns.jcp.org/xml/ns/persistence/orm_2_2.xsd"
                 version="2.2">

  <entity class="org.agoncal.fascicle.jpa.mapping.Book">
    <table name="book_xml_mapping"/>
    <attributes>
      <basic name="title">
        <column name="book_title" nullable="false" updatable="false"/>
      </basic>
      <basic name="description">
        <column length="2000"/>
      </basic>
      <basic name="nbOfPages">
        <column name="nb_of_pages" nullable="false"/>
      </basic>
    </attributes>
  </entity>
</entity-mappings>
```

An important notion to always have in mind is that the XML takes precedence over annotations. Even if the `description` attribute is annotated by `@Column(length = 500)`, the length of the column used is the one in the `book_mapping.xml` file (Listing 48), which is `2000`. This can be confusing as you look at the code and see `500` and then check the DDL and see `2000`; always remember to check the XML deployment descriptor if it exists.

A result of merging the XML metadata and the annotations metadata is that the `Book` entity will get mapped to the `BOOK_XML_MAPPING` table structure defined in Listing 49. If you want to completely ignore the annotations and define your mapping with XML only, you can add the `<xml-mapping-metadata-complete>` tag to the `book_mapping.xml` file (in this case, all the annotations will be ignored even if the XML does not contain an override).

Listing 49. BOOK_XML_MAPPING Table Structure

```
CREATE TABLE BOOK_XML_MAPPING
(
  ID            BIGINT       NOT NULL,
  BOOK_TITLE    VARCHAR(255) NOT NULL,
  PRICE         FLOAT,
  DESCRIPTION   VARCHAR(2000),
  ISBN          VARCHAR(255),
  NB_OF_PAGES   INTEGER      NOT NULL,
  ILLUSTRATIONS BOOLEAN,
  PRIMARY KEY (ID)
)
```

There is only one piece of information missing to make this work. In your persistence.xml file, you need to reference the book_mapping.xml file, and for this you have to use the <mapping-file> tag. The persistence.xml defines the entity persistence context and the database it should be mapped to. It is the central piece of information that the persistence provider needs to reference external XML mapping. Deploy the Book entity with both XML files in the META-INF directory and you are done (see Listing 50).

Listing 50. A persistence.xml File Referring to an External Mapping File

```
<persistence xmlns:xsi="http://www.w3.org/2001/XMLSchema-instance"
             xmlns="http://xmlns.jcp.org/xml/ns/persistence"
             xsi:schemaLocation="http://xmlns.jcp.org/xml/ns/persistence
http://xmlns.jcp.org/xml/ns/persistence/persistence_2_2.xsd"
             version="2.2">

  <persistence-unit name="cdbookstorePU" transaction-type="RESOURCE_LOCAL">
    <provider>org.eclipse.persistence.jpa.PersistenceProvider</provider>
    <mapping-file>META-INF/book_mapping.xml</mapping-file>
  </persistence-unit>
</persistence>
```

4.5. Embeddables

In the "Composite Primary Keys" section earlier in the chapter, you saw how a class could be embedded and used as a primary key with the @EmbeddedId annotation. Embeddables are objects that don't have a persistent identity on their own; they can only be embedded within an owning entity. The owning entity can have embeddables, either as attributes or collections. They are stored as an intrinsic part of the owning entity and share the same identity. This means each attribute of the embedded object is mapped to the table of the owning entity. It is a strict ownership relationship (a.k.a. composition), so that if the owning entity is removed, the embedded object is also removed.

This composition between two classes uses annotations. The included class uses the @Embeddable annotation, whereas the entity that includes the class uses @Embedded. Let's take the example of a customer that has an identifier, a name, an email address, and an address. All these attributes could be in a Customer entity (see Listing 52), but, for object-modelling reasons, they are split into two classes: Customer and Address. Because Address has no identity of its own but is merely part of the Customer state, it is a good candidate to become an embeddable object instead of an entity (see Listing 51).

Listing 51. The Address Class Is an Embeddable

```
@Embeddable
public class Address {

  private String street1;
  private String street2;
  private String city;
  private String state;
  private String zipcode;
  private String country;

  // Constructors, getters, setters
}
```

As you can see in Listing 51, the Address class is not annotated as being an entity but as an embeddable. It has no @Entity annotation, nor an @Id annotation. The @Embeddable annotation specifies that Address can be embedded in another entity class (or another embeddable). On the other side of the composition, the Customer entity has to use the @Embedded annotation to specify that Address is a persistent attribute that will be stored as an intrinsic part and share its identity (see Listing 52).

Listing 52. The Customer Entity Embedding an Address

```
@Entity
public class Customer {

  @Id
  @GeneratedValue
  private Long id;
  private String firstName;
  private String lastName;
  private String email;
  private String phoneNumber;
  @Embedded
  private Address address;

  // Constructors, getters, setters
}
```

Each attribute of Address is mapped to the table of the owning entity Customer. There will only be one table with the structure defined in Listing 53. As you'll see in Chapter 8 in the section "Overriding Attributes," entities can override the attributes of embeddables (using the @AttributeOverrides annotation).

Listing 53. Structure of the CUSTOMER Table with All the Address Attributes

```
CREATE TABLE CUSTOMER
(
  ID          BIGINT NOT NULL,
  FIRSTNAME   VARCHAR,
  LASTNAME    VARCHAR,
  EMAIL       VARCHAR,
  PHONENUMBER VARCHAR,
  STREET1     VARCHAR,
  STREET2     VARCHAR,
  CITY        VARCHAR,
  STATE       VARCHAR,
  ZIPCODE     VARCHAR,
  COUNTRY     VARCHAR,
  PRIMARY KEY (ID)
)
```

4.5.1. Collections of Embeddables

We've previously seen how to map collections and maps of basic data types. Since JPA 2.1, the same is possible with embeddables. You can map collections of embeddables as well as maps of embeddables (the embeddable can be either the key or the value of the `Map`). As you can see in Listing 54, you need to use the `@ElementCollection` annotation instead of `@Embedded`.

Listing 54. Customer Entity with a List of Embeddable Addresses

```
@Entity
public class Customer {

  @Id
  @GeneratedValue
  private Long id;
  private String firstName;
  private String lastName;
  private String email;
  private String phoneNumber;
  @ElementCollection
  private List<Address> addresses;

  // Constructors, getters, setters
}
```

To map a collection of embeddables, the JPA provider needs a separate table to join each address to a customer. As you can see in Listing 55, the `CUSTOMER` table does not have any attributes related to addresses. Instead, JPA stores all the customer addresses in a separate table named `Customer_ADDRESSES` (remember that you can override the default collection table with the `@CollectionTable` annotation). The join between the two tables is made through the foreign key `Customer_ID`.

Listing 55. Structure of the CUSTOMER and CUSTOMER_ADDRESSES Tables

```
CREATE TABLE CUSTOMER
(
  ID          BIGINT NOT NULL,
  FIRSTNAME   VARCHAR,
  LASTNAME    VARCHAR,
  EMAIL       VARCHAR,
  PHONENUMBER VARCHAR,
  PRIMARY KEY (ID)
);
CREATE TABLE CUSTOMER_ADDRESSES
(
  STREET1     VARCHAR,
  STREET2     VARCHAR,
  CITY        VARCHAR,
  STATE       VARCHAR,
  ZIPCODE     VARCHAR,
  COUNTRY     VARCHAR,
  CUSTOMER_ID BIGINT
);
```

4.6. Mapping Relationships

Having collections of embeddables is an interesting way of mapping a list of data. But remember that embeddables do not have an identity. What if we want to map the fact that a `CD` album has been recorded by a list of musicians and each `Musician` must be identified in the database? `Musician` then needs to be an entity. Relationships between entities is an important feature in JPA.

4.6.1. Relationships in Objects

The world of object-oriented programming abounds with classes and associations between classes. These associations are structural in that they link objects of one kind to objects of another. Several types of associations can exist between classes.

First of all, an association has a direction. It can be *unidirectional* (i.e. one object can navigate towards another) or *bidirectional* (i.e. one object can navigate towards another and vice versa). In Java, you use the dot (`.`) syntax to navigate through objects. For example, when you write `customer.getAddress().getCountry()`, you navigate from the object `Customer` to `Address` and then to `Country`.

In UML (*Unified Modeling Language*), to represent a unidirectional association between two classes, you use an arrow to indicate the orientation. In Figure 15, `Class1` (the source) can navigate to `Class2` (the target), but not the inverse.

Figure 15. A unidirectional association between two classes

To indicate a bidirectional association, no arrows are used. As demonstrated in Figure 16, `Class1` can navigate to `Class2` and vice versa. In Java, this is represented as `Class1` having an attribute of type `Class2` and `Class2` having an attribute of type `Class1`.

Figure 16. A bidirectional association between two classes

An association also has a *multiplicity* (or *cardinality*). Each end of an association can specify how many referring objects are involved in the association. The UML diagram in Figure 17 shows that `Class1` refers to zero or more instances of `Class2`.

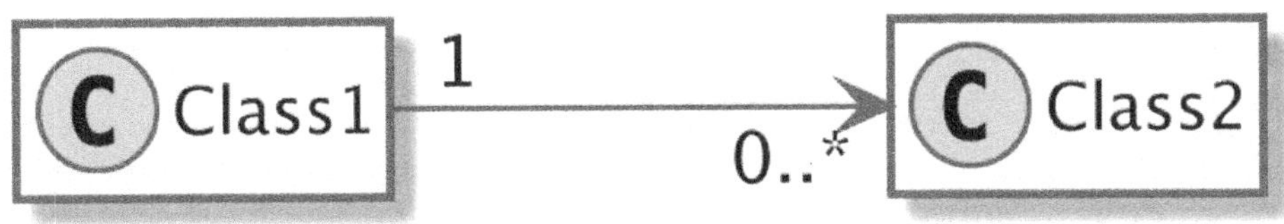

Figure 17. Multiplicity on class associations

In UML, a cardinality is a range between a minimum and a maximum number. So `0..1` means that you will have, at a minimum, zero objects and, at a maximum, one object. `1` means that you have one and only one instance. `1..*` means that you can have one or many instances, and `3..6` means that you have a range of between three and six objects. In Java, an association that represents more than one object uses the data types `java.util.Collection`, `java.util.Set`, `java.util.List`, or even `java.util.Map`.

A relationship has an ownership (i.e. one side of the relationship is the owner of that relationship). In a unidirectional relationship, ownership is implied: in Figure 15, there is no doubt that the owner is `Class1`, but in a bidirectional relationship, as depicted in Figure 16, the owner has to be specified explicitly. For example, `Class1` is the owner, which specifies the database mapping, and `Class2` is called the inverse side (the non-owning side).

Before looking at how to map collections of entities in JPA, let's have a look at the way relational databases store relationships.

4.6.2. Relationships in Relational Databases

In the relational world, things are different because, strictly speaking, a relational database is a collection of *relations* (also called *tables*), which means anything you model is a table. To model an association, you don't have lists, sets, or maps; you have tables. In JPA, when you have an association between two entities, you can model it in the database in two different ways: by using a *foreign key* (a.k.a. *join column*) or by using a *join table*. In database terms, a column that refers to a key of another table is a *foreign key column*.

As an example, consider that a customer has one address. Previously, in Listing 54, we modelled this relation as an embeddable, but let's now turn it into a one-to-one relationship. In Java, you would have a `Customer` class with an `Address` attribute. In the relational world, you could have a `CUSTOMER` table pointing to an `ADDRESS` table through a foreign key column (or join column), as described in Figure 18.

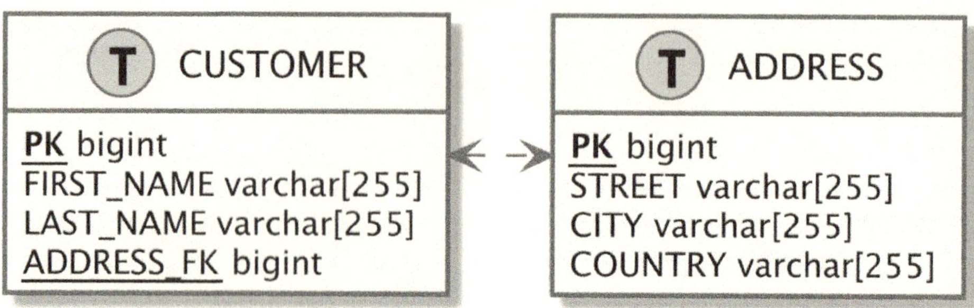

Figure 18. A relationship using a join column

There is a second way of modelling - using a join table. The `CUSTOMER` table in Figure 19 doesn't store the foreign key of the `ADDRESS` anymore. An intermediate table is created to hold the relationship information by storing the foreign keys of both tables.

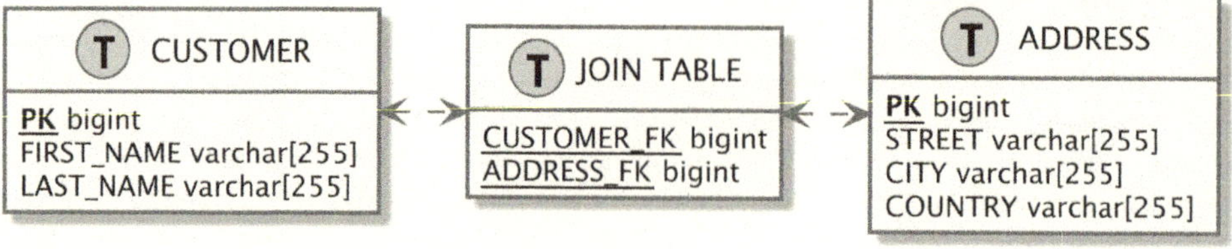

Figure 19. A relationship using a join table

You wouldn't use a join table to represent a one-to-one relationship, as this could have performance issues (you always need to access a third table to get the address of a customer). Join tables are generally used when you have one-to-many or many-to-many cardinalities. As you will see in the next section, JPA uses these two ways to map object associations.

4.6.3. Entity Relationships

Now back to JPA. Most entities need to be able to reference, or have relationships with, other entities. This is what produces the domain model graphs that are common in business applications. JPA makes it possible to map associations so that an entity can be linked to another in a relational model. Like the elementary mapping annotations that you saw previously, JPA uses configuration by exception for associations. It has a default way of defining a relationship but, if this doesn't suit your database model, you have several annotations you can use to customise the mapping.

The cardinality between two entities may be one-to-one, one-to-many, many-to-one, or many-to-many. Each respective mapping is named after the cardinality of the source and target: `@OneToOne`, `@OneToMany`, `@ManyToOne`, or `@ManyToMany`. Each annotation can be used in a unidirectional or bidirectional way.

You will see that unidirectional and bidirectional are repetitive concepts that apply in the same way to all cardinalities. Next, you will see the difference between unidirectional and bidirectional relationships and then implement some of these combinations. I will not go through the complete catalogue of combinations but just focus on a subset. Explaining all the combinations would get repetitive. The important point is that you understand how to map cardinality and direction in relationships.

Unidirectional and Bidirectional

From an object-modelling point of view, direction between classes is natural. In a unidirectional association, object `A` points to object `B` and not the other way round; in a bidirectional association, both objects refer to each other. However, some work is necessary when mapping a bidirectional relationship to a relational database, as illustrated by the following example.

In a unidirectional relationship, a `Customer` entity has an attribute of type `Address` (see Figure 20). The relationship is one-way, navigating from one side to the other. `Customer` is said to be the owner of the relationship. In terms of the database, this means the `CUSTOMER` table will have a foreign key (join column) pointing to `ADDRESS`, and, when you own a relationship, you are able to customise the mapping of this relationship. For example, if you need to change the name of the foreign key, the mapping will be done in the `Customer` entity (i.e. the `owner`).

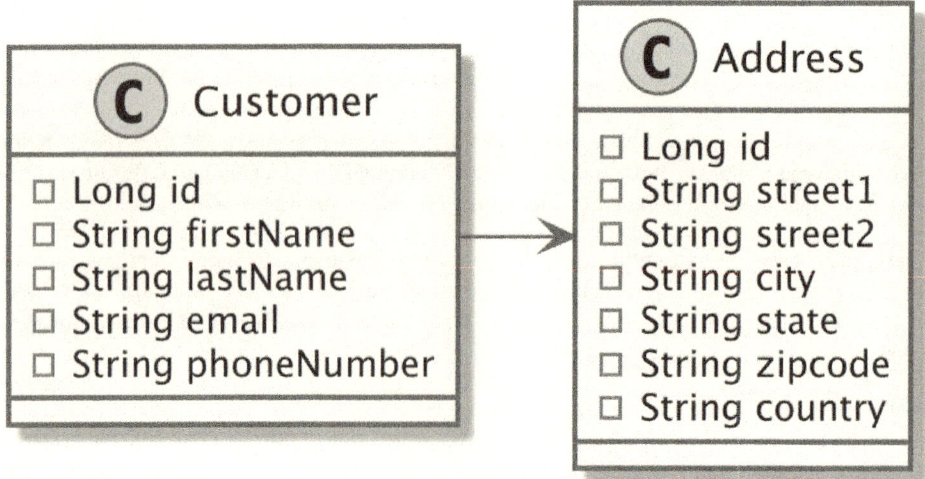

Figure 20. A unidirectional association between Customer and Address

As mentioned previously, relationships can also be bidirectional. To be able to navigate between `Address` and `Customer`, you need to transform a unidirectional relationship into a bidirectional one by adding a `Customer` attribute to the `Address` entity (see Figure 21).

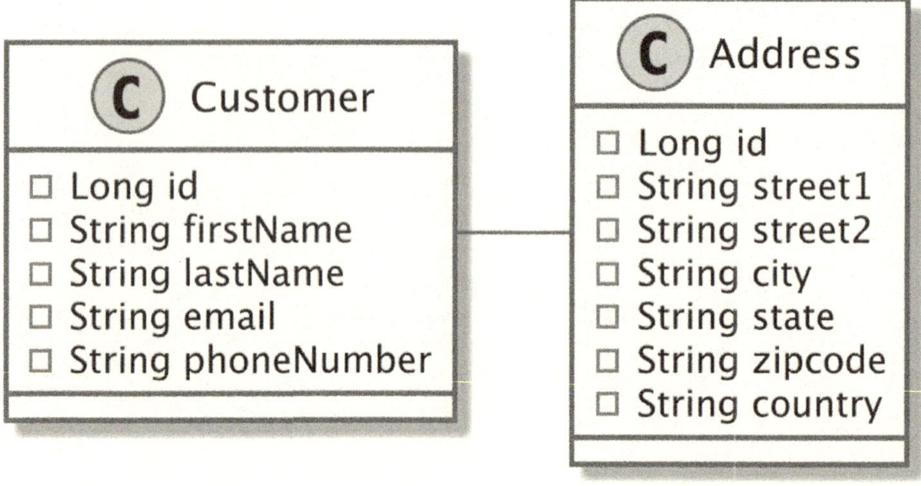

Figure 21. A bidirectional association between Customer and Address

In terms of Java code and annotations, it is similar to having two separate one-to-one mappings, one in each direction. You can think of a bidirectional relationship as a pair of unidirectional relationships, going both ways (see Figure 22).

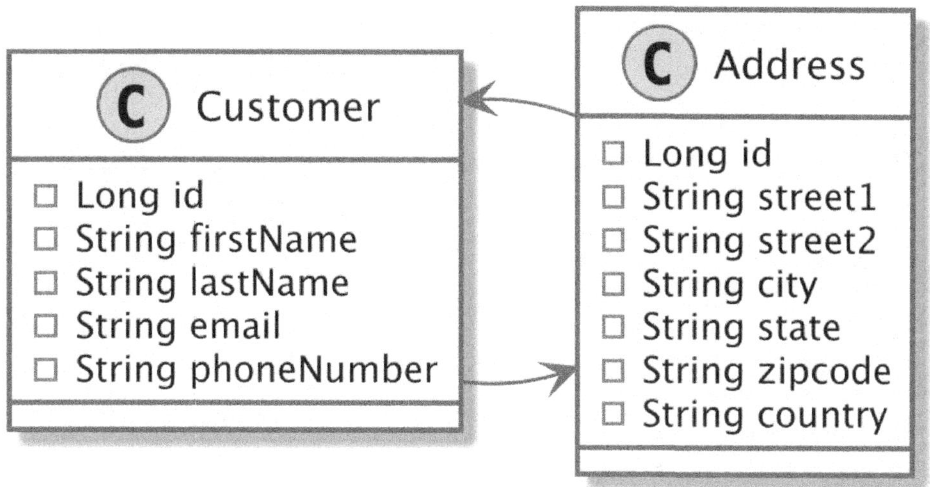

Figure 22. A bidirectional association represented with two arrows

How do you map a pair of unidirectional relationships? Who is the owner of this bidirectional relationship? Who owns the mapping information of the join column or the join table? Unidirectional relationships have an owning side while bidirectional relationships have both an owning and an inverse side, which have to be explicitly specified with the `mappedBy` element of the `@OneToOne`, `@OneToMany`, and `@ManyToMany` annotations. `mappedBy` identifies the attribute that owns the relationship and is required for bidirectional relationships.

By way of explanation, let's compare the Java code (on one side) and the database mapping (on the other). As you can see on the left side of Figure 23, both entities point to each other through attributes: `Customer` has an `address` attribute annotated with `@OneToOne`, and the `Address` entity has a `customer` attribute also with an annotation. On the right side, the database mapping shows a `CUSTOMER` and an `ADDRESS` table. `CUSTOMER` is the owner of the relationship because it contains the `ADDRESS` foreign key.

```
@Entity
public class Customer

    @Id @GeneratedValue
    private Long id;
    private String firstName;
    private String lastName;
    private String email;
    private String phoneNumber;
    @OneToOne
    @JoinColumn(name = "address_fk")
    private Address address;
}

@Entity
public class Address {

    @Id @GeneratedValue
    private Long id;
    private String street1;
    private String street2;
    private String city;
    private String state;
    private String zipcode;
    private String country;
    @OneToOne(mappedBy = "address")
    private Customer customer;
}
```

CUSTOMER		
+ID	bigint	Nullable = false
LASTNAME	varchar(255)	Nullable = true
PHONENUMBER	varchar(255)	Nullable = true
EMAIL	varchar(255)	Nullable = true
FIRSTNAME	varchar(255)	Nullable = true
#ADDRESS_FK	bigint	Nullable = true

ADDRESS		
+ID	bigint	Nullable = false
STREET2	varchar(255)	Nullable = true
STREET1	varchar(255)	Nullable = true
ZIPCODE	varchar(255)	Nullable = true
STATE	varchar(255)	Nullable = true
COUNTRY	varchar(255)	Nullable = true
CITY	varchar(255)	Nullable = true

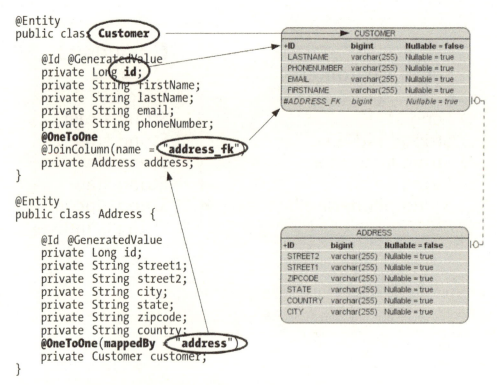

Figure 23. Customer and Address code with database mapping

In Figure 23 the Address entity uses the mappedBy element on its @OneToOne annotation. Address is called the *inverse owner* of the relationship because it has a mappedBy element. The mappedBy element indicates that the join column (address) is specified at the other end of the relationship. In fact, at the other end, the Customer entity defines the join column by using the @JoinColumn annotation and renames the foreign key ADDRESS_FK. Customer is the owning side of the relationship, and, as the owner, is the one to define the join column mapping. Address is the inverse side where the table of the owning entity contains the foreign key (the CUSTOMER table is the one with the ADDRESS_FK column). That is why we said, mappedBy identifies the attribute that owns the relationship and is required for bidirectional relationships.

There is a mappedBy element on the @OneToOne, @OneToMany, and @ManyToMany annotations, but not on the @ManyToOne annotation. You cannot have a mappedBy attribute on both sides of a bidirectional association. It would also be incorrect to not have it on either side as the provider would treat it as two independent unidirectional relationships. This would imply that each side is the owner and can define a join column.

If you are familiar with earlier versions of Hibernate, you might think of the JPA mappedBy as the equivalent of the Hibernate inverse attribute.

One-To-One Unidirectional

A one-to-one unidirectional relationship between entities has a reference of cardinality 1, which can be reached in only one direction. Referring to the example of a customer and their address, assume the customer has only one address (cardinality 1). It is important to navigate from the customer (the source) towards the address (the target) to know where the customer lives. The model shown in Figure 24 is assuming that we don't need to navigate in the opposite direction (e.g. you don't need to know which customer lives at a given address).

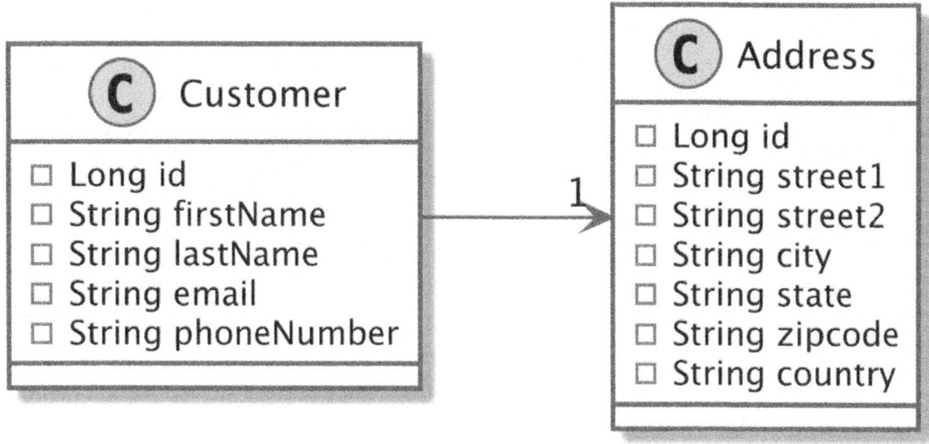

Figure 24. One customer has one address

In Java, a unidirectional relationship means that the `Customer` has an `Address` attribute (Listing 56) but `Address` does not have a `Customer` attribute (Listing 57).

Listing 56. A Customer with One Address

```
@Entity
public class Customer {

  @Id
  @GeneratedValue
  private Long id;
  private String firstName;
  private String lastName;
  private String email;
  private String phoneNumber;
  private Address address;

  // Constructors, getters, setters
}
```

Listing 57. An Address Entity

```
@Entity
public class Address {

  @Id
  @GeneratedValue
  private Long id;
  private String street1;
  private String street2;
  private String city;
  private String state;
  private String zipcode;
  private String country;

  // Constructors, getters, setters
}
```

As you can see in Listing 56 and Listing 57, these two entities have the minimum required annotations: `@Entity` plus `@Id` and `@GeneratedValue` for the primary key, that's all. With configuration by exception, the persistence provider will map these two entities to two tables and a foreign key for the relationship (from the customer pointing to the address). A one-to-one mapping is triggered by the fact that `Customer` is declared an entity and includes the `Address` entity as an attribute. We automatically imply a relationship by using an entity as a property in another entity so we don't need a `@OneToOne` annotation, as it relies on the defaults (see Listing 58 and Listing 59).

Listing 58. The CUSTOMER Table with a Foreign Key to ADDRESS

```
CREATE TABLE CUSTOMER
(
  ID          BIGINT NOT NULL,
  EMAIL       VARCHAR,
  FIRSTNAME   VARCHAR,
  LASTNAME    VARCHAR,
  PHONENUMBER VARCHAR,
  ADDRESS_ID  BIGINT,
  PRIMARY KEY (ID)
)
```

Listing 59. The ADDRESS Table

```
CREATE TABLE ADDRESS
(
  ID      BIGINT NOT NULL,
  CITY    VARCHAR,
  COUNTRY VARCHAR,
  STATE   VARCHAR,
  STREET1 VARCHAR,
  STREET2 VARCHAR,
  ZIPCODE VARCHAR,
  PRIMARY KEY (ID)
)
```

As you now know, with JPA, if you do not annotate an attribute, the default mapping rules are applied. So, by default, the name of the foreign key column is `ADDRESS_ID` (see Listing 58), which is the concatenation of the name of the relationship attribute (here, `address`), the symbol _, and the name of the primary key column of the destination table (here it will be the column `ID` of the `ADDRESS` table). Also notice that, in the DDL, the `ADDRESS_ID` column is nullable by default, meaning that, by default, a one-to-one association is mapped to a zero (null value) or one.

To customise this mapping, you can use two annotations. The first one is `@OneToOne` (that's because the cardinality of the relation is one), and it can modify some attributes of the association itself such as the way the target entity has to be fetched. Listing 60 defines the API of the `@OneToOne` annotation.

Listing 60. @OneToOne Annotation API

```
@Target({METHOD, FIELD})
@Retention(RUNTIME)
public @interface OneToOne {

  Class targetEntity() default void.class;
  CascadeType[] cascade() default {};
  FetchType fetch() default EAGER;
  boolean optional() default true;
  String mappedBy() default "";
  boolean orphanRemoval() default false;
}
```

The other annotation is `@JoinColumn` (its API is very similar to `@Column` shown in Listing 32). It is used to customise the join column, meaning the foreign key, of the owning side. Listing 61 shows how you would use these two annotations.

Listing 61. The Customer Entity with Customised Relationship Mapping

```
@Entity
public class Customer {

  @Id
  @GeneratedValue
  private Long id;
  private String firstName;
  private String lastName;
  private String email;
  private String phoneNumber;
  @OneToOne(fetch = FetchType.LAZY)
  @JoinColumn(name = "add_fk", nullable = false)
  private Address address;

  // Constructors, getters, setters
}
```

In JPA, a foreign key column is called a join column. The `@JoinColumn` annotation allows you to customise the mapping of a foreign key. Listing 61 uses it to rename the foreign key column to `ADD_FK` and to make the relationship obligatory by refusing the null value (`nullable=false`). The `@OneToOne` annotation gives the persistence provider a hint to fetch the relationship lazily (more on that later).

One-To-Many Unidirectional

A one-to-many relationship is when one source object refers to an ensemble of target objects. For example, a purchase order is composed of several order lines (see Figure 25). The order line could refer to the purchase order with a corresponding `@ManyToOne` annotation, but it's not the case as the relationship is unidirectional. `PurchaseOrder` is the "one" side and the source of the relationship, and `OrderLine` is the "many" side and the target.

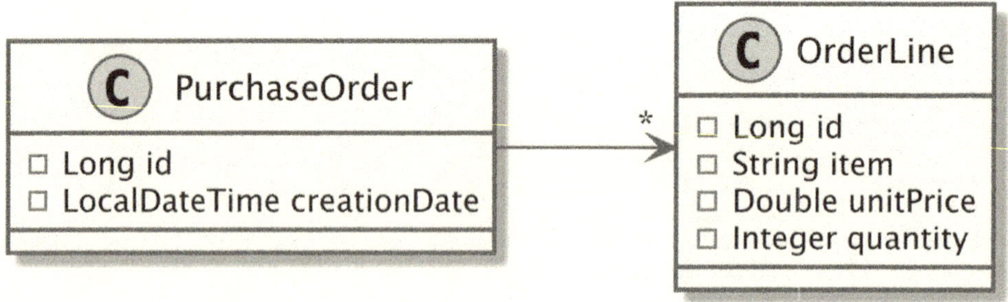

Figure 25. One purchase order has several lines

The cardinality is multiple, and the navigation is done only from `PurchaseOrder` towards `OrderLine`. In Java, this multiplicity is described by the `Collection`, `List`, and `Set` interfaces of the `java.util` package. Listing 62 shows the code of the `PurchaseOrder` entity with a one-way, one-to-many relationship towards `OrderLine` (see Listing 63).

Listing 62. A PurchaseOrder Contains OrderLines

```
@Entity
@Table(name = "purchase_order")
public class PurchaseOrder {

  @Id
  @GeneratedValue
  private Long id;
  private LocalDateTime creationDate;
  private List<OrderLine> orderLines;

  // Constructors, getters, setters
}
```

Listing 63. An OrderLine

```
@Entity
@Table(name = "order_line")
public class OrderLine {

  @Id
  @GeneratedValue
  private Long id;
  private String item;
  private Double unitPrice;
  private Integer quantity;

  // Constructors, getters, setters
}
```

The PurchaseOrder in Listing 62 doesn't have any special annotation and relies on the configuration by exception paradigm. The fact that a collection of an entity type is being used as an attribute on this entity triggers a OneToMany relationship mapping by default. By default, one-to-many unidirectional relationships use a join table to keep the relationship information, with two foreign key columns. One foreign key column refers to the table PURCHASE_ORDER and has the same type as its primary key, and the other refers to ORDER_LINE. The name of this joined table is the name of both entities, separated by the _ symbol. The join table is named PURCHASE_ORDER_ORDER_LINE and will result in the schema structure illustrated in Figure 26.

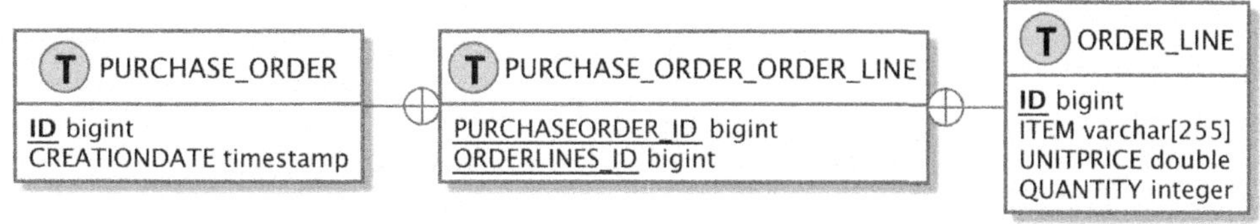

Figure 26. Join table between PURCHASE_ORDER and ORDER_LINE

If you don't like the join table and foreign key names, or if you are mapping to an existing table, you can use JPA annotations to redefine these default values. The default value for a join column is the concatenation of the name of the attribute that maps the association, the symbol _, and the name of the referenced primary key. As the `@JoinColumn` annotation can be used to change the foreign key columns, the `@JoinTable` annotation (see Listing 64) can do the same for the join table mapping. You can also use the `@OneToMany` annotation (see Listing 65) which, like `@OneToOne`, customises the relationship itself (using fetch mode etc.).

Listing 64. @JoinTable Annotation API

```
@Target({METHOD, FIELD})
@Retention(RUNTIME)
public @interface JoinTable {

  String name() default "";
  String catalog() default "";
  String schema() default "";
  JoinColumn[] joinColumns() default {};
  JoinColumn[] inverseJoinColumns() default {};
  ForeignKey foreignKey() default @ForeignKey(PROVIDER_DEFAULT);
  ForeignKey inverseForeignKey() default @ForeignKey(PROVIDER_DEFAULT);
  UniqueConstraint[] uniqueConstraints() default {};
  Index[] indexes() default {};
}
```

Listing 65. The PurchaseOrder Entity with Annotated One-to-many Relationship

```
@Entity
@Table(name = "purchase_order")
public class PurchaseOrder {

  @Id
  @GeneratedValue
  private Long id;
  private LocalDateTime creationDate;
  @OneToMany
  @JoinTable(name = "jnd_ord_line",
    joinColumns = @JoinColumn(name = "order_fk"),
    inverseJoinColumns = @JoinColumn(name = "order_line_fk")
  )
  private List<OrderLine> orderLines;

  // Constructors, getters, setters
}
```

On the API of the `@JoinTable` annotation in Listing 64, you can see two attributes that are of type `@JoinColumn`: `joinColumns` and `inverseJoinColumns`. These two attributes are distinguished by means of the owning side and the inverse side. The `joinColumns` element describes the owning side (the owner of the relationship) and, in our example, refers to the `PURCHASE_ORDER` table. The `inverseJoinColumns` element specifies the inverse side, the target of the relationship, and refers to

ORDER_LINE.

Using the PurchaseOrder entity (see Listing 65), you can add the @OneToMany and @JoinTable annotations on the orderLines attribute by renaming the join table to JND_ORD_LINE (instead of PURCHASE_ORDER_ORDER_LINE), as well as the two foreign key columns.

The PurchaseOrder entity in Listing 65 will be mapped to the join table described in Listing 66.

Listing 66. Structure of the Join Table Between PURCHASE_ORDER and ORDER_LINE

```
CREATE TABLE JND_ORD_LINE
(
  ORDER_FK      BIGINT NOT NULL,
  ORDER_LINE_FK BIGINT NOT NULL,
  PRIMARY KEY (ORDER_FK, ORDER_LINE_FK)
);
ALTER TABLE JND_ORD_LINE
  ADD CONSTRAINT FK_JND_ORD_LINE_ORDER_LINE_FK
    FOREIGN KEY (ORDER_LINE_FK) REFERENCES ORDERLINE (ID);
ALTER TABLE JND_ORD_LINE
  ADD CONSTRAINT FK_JND_ORD_LINE_ORDER_FK
    FOREIGN KEY (ORDER_FK) REFERENCES PURCHASE_ORDER (ID);
```

The default rule for a one-to-many unidirectional relationship is to use a join table, but it is very easy (and useful for legacy databases) to change to using foreign keys. The PurchaseOrder entity has to provide a @JoinColumn annotation instead of a @JoinTable, allowing the code to be changed as shown in Listing 67.

Listing 67. The PurchaseOrder Entity with a Join Column

```
@Entity
@Table(name = "purchase_order")
public class PurchaseOrder {

  @Id
  @GeneratedValue
  private Long id;
  private LocalDateTime creationDate;
  @OneToMany(fetch = FetchType.EAGER)
  @JoinColumn(name = "order_fk")
  private List<OrderLine> orderLines;

  // Constructors, getters, setters
}
```

The code of the OrderLine entity (shown previously in Listing 63) doesn't change. By using @JoinColumn, the foreign key strategy then maps the unidirectional association. The foreign key is renamed to ORDER_FK by the annotation and exists in the target table (ORDER_LINE). The result is the database structure shown in Figure 27. There is no join table, and the reference between both tables is through the foreign key ORDER_FK.

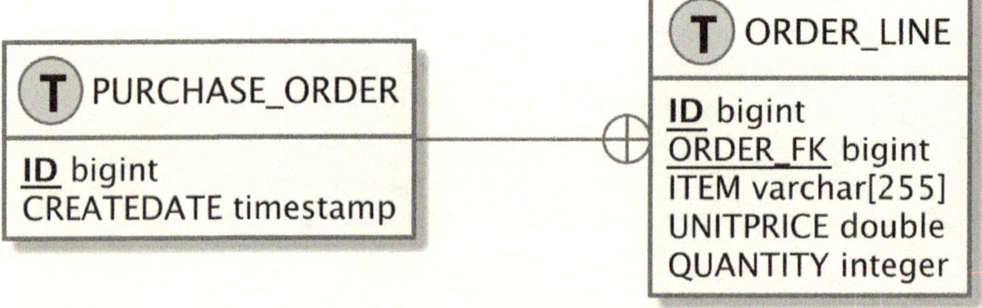

Figure 27. Join column between PURCHASE_ORDER and ORDER_LINE

Many-To-Many Bidirectional

A many-to-many bidirectional relationship exists when one source object refers to many targets, and when a target refers to many sources. For example, a CD album is created by several artists, and an artist appears on several albums. In the Java world, each entity will have a collection of target entities. In the relational world, the only way to map a many-to-many relationship is to use a join table (a join column does not work), and, as you've seen previously, in a bidirectional relationship you need to explicitly define the owner (with the `mappedBy` element).

Assuming the `Artist` entity is the owner of the relationship means that the `CD` is the reverse owner (see Listing 68). Therefore, `CD` needs to use the `mappedBy` element on its `@ManyToMany` annotation. `mappedBy` tells the persistence provider that `appearsOnCDs` is the name of the corresponding attribute of the owning entity.

Listing 68. Several Artists Appear on One CD

```
@Entity
public class CD {

  @Id
  @GeneratedValue
  private Long id;
  private String title;
  private Float price;
  private String description;
  @ManyToMany(mappedBy = "appearsOnCDs")
  private List<Artist> createdByArtists;

  // Constructors, getters, setters
}
```

So, if the `Artist` is the owner of the relationship, as shown in Listing 69, it is the one to customise the mapping of the join table via the `@JoinTable` and `@JoinColumn` annotations.

Listing 69. One Artist Appears on Several CD Albums

```
@Entity
public class Artist {

  @Id
  @GeneratedValue
  private Long id;
  private String firstName;
  private String lastName;
  @ManyToMany
  @JoinTable(name = "jnd_art_cd",
    joinColumns = @JoinColumn(name = "artist_fk"),
    inverseJoinColumns = @JoinColumn(name = "cd_fk")
  )
  private List<CD> appearsOnCDs;

  // Constructors, getters, setters
}
```

As you can see in Listing 69, the join table between `Artist` and `CD` is renamed to `JND_ART_CD` as well as each join column (thanks to the `@JoinTable` annotation). The `joinColumns` element refers to the owning side (the `Artist`) and the `inverseJoinColumns` refers to the inverse owning side (the `CD`). Figure 28 illustrates the database structure.

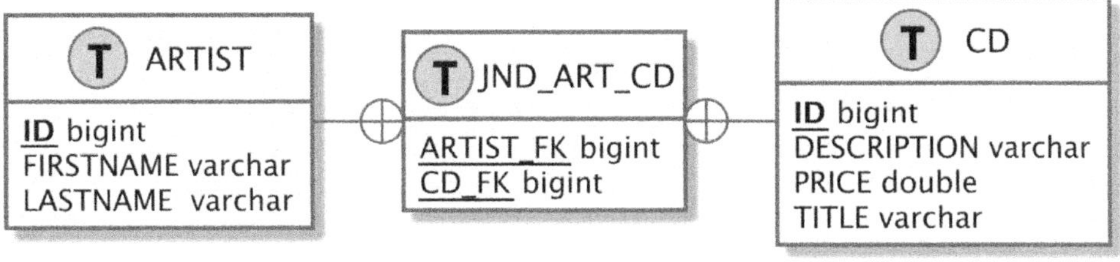

Figure 28. Join table between ARTIST and CD

Note that on a many-to-many and one-to-one bidirectional relationship, either side may be designated as the owning side. No matter which side is designated as the owner, the other side should include the `mappedBy` element. If not, the provider will think that both sides are the owner and will treat it as two separate one-to-many unidirectional relationships. That could result in four tables: `ARTIST` and `CD`, plus two joining tables, `ARTIST_CD` and `CD_ARTIST`. Nor would it be legal to have a `mappedBy` on both sides.

4.6.4. Fetching Relationships

All the annotations that you have seen (`@OneToOne`, `@OneToMany`, `@ManyToOne`, and `@ManyToMany`) define a fetching attribute, specifying the associated objects to be loaded immediately (eagerly) or deferred (lazily), with a resulting impact on performance. Depending on your application, certain relationships are accessed more often than others, while some relationships are not necessarily required to be fetched all the times. In these situations, you can optimise performance by loading data from the database when the entity is initially read (eagerly) or when it is accessed (lazily). As an example, let's look at some extreme cases.

Imagine four entities all linked to each other with different cardinalities (one-to-one, one-to-many). In the first case (see Figure 29), they all have eager relationships. This means that, as soon as you load `Class1` (by a find by Id or a query), all the dependent objects are automatically loaded in memory. This can have an impact on the performance of your system.

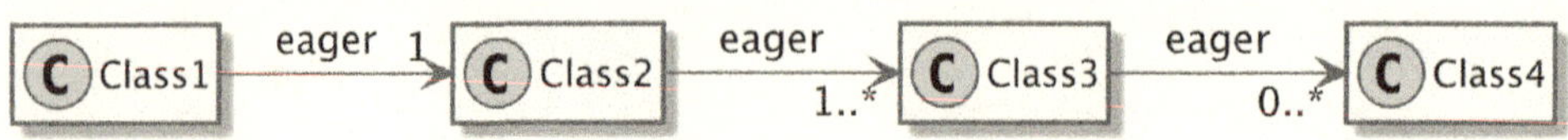

Figure 29. Four entities with eager relationships

Looking at the opposite scenario, all the relationships use a lazy `fetch` mode (see Figure 30). If you load `Class1`, nothing else is loaded (except the direct attributes of `Class1`, of course). You need to explicitly access `Class2` (e.g. by using the getter method) to tell the persistence provider to load the data from the database, and so on. If you want to manipulate the entire object graph, you need to explicitly call each entity.

```
class1.getClass2().getClass3().getClass4()
```

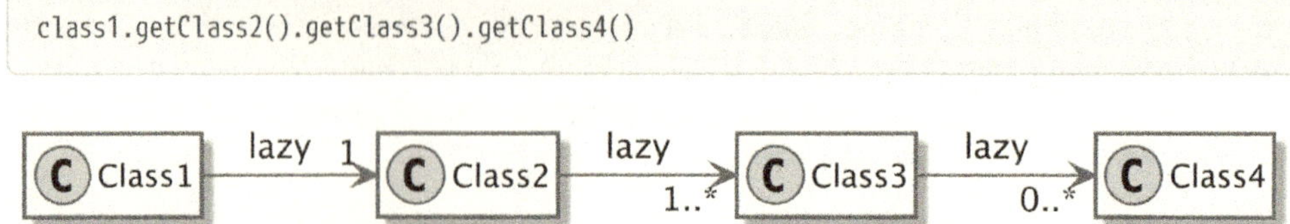

Figure 30. Four entities with lazy relationships

But don't think that `EAGER` is evil and `LAZY` is good. `EAGER` will bring all the data into memory using a small amount of database access (the persistence provider will probably use join queries to join the tables together and extract the data). With `LAZY`, you don't take the risk of filling up your memory because you control which object is loaded. But you have to access the database every time.

The `fetch` parameter is very important because, if it is misused, it can cause performance problems. Each annotation has a default `fetch` value that you have to be aware of and, if not appropriate for your problem, change (see Table 6).

Table 6. Default Fetching Strategies

Annotation	Default Fetching Strategy
`@OneToOne`	`EAGER`
`@ManyToOne`	`EAGER`
`@OneToMany`	`LAZY`
`@ManyToMany`	`LAZY`

In the above example, if we always need to access the order lines of a purchase order when a purchase order is loaded in the application, then it may be efficient to change the default `fetch` mode of the `@OneToMany` annotation to `EAGER` (see Listing 70).

Listing 70. A PurchaseOrder with an Eager Relationship to OrderLine

```
@Entity
public class PurchaseOrder {

  @Id
  @GeneratedValue
  private Long id;
  private LocalDateTime creationDate;
  @OneToMany(fetch = FetchType.EAGER)
  private List<OrderLine> orderLines;

  // Constructors, getters, setters
}
```

4.6.5. Ordering Relationships

With one-to-many or many-to-many relationships, your entities deal with collections of objects. On the Java side, these collections are usually unordered. Neither do relational databases preserve any order in their tables. Therefore, if you want an ordered list, it is necessary to either sort your collection programmatically or use a JPQL query with an `Order By` clause (more on JPQL in Chapter 6). JPA has easier mechanisms, based on annotations that can help in ordering relationships.

Ordered By

Dynamic ordering can be done with the `@OrderBy` annotation. "Dynamic" means that you order the elements of a collection when you retrieve the association.

The example of the Vintage Store application allows a user to write news about music and books. This news is displayed on the website and once published, people are allowed to add comments (see Listing 71). On the website you want to display the comments chronologically, so ordering comes into account.

Listing 71. A Comment Entity with a Posted Date

```
@Entity
public class Comment {

  @Id
  @GeneratedValue
  private Long id;
  private String nickname;
  private String content;
  private Integer note;
  @Column(name = "posted_date")
  private LocalDateTime postedDate;

  // Constructors, getters, setters
}
```

The comments are modelled using the `Comment` entity, shown in Listing 71. It has content, is posted by a user (identified by a nickname) who leaves a note on the news, and has a posted date of type `LocalDateTime`. In the `News` entity, shown in Listing 72, you want to be able to arrange the list of comments ordered by posted date in descending order. To achieve this, you use the `@OrderBy` annotation.

Listing 72. The Comments of a News Entity Are Ordered by Descending Posted Date

```
@Entity
public class News {

  @Id
  @GeneratedValue
  private Long id;
  @Column(nullable = false)
  private String content;
  @OrderBy("postedDate DESC")
  private List<Comment> comments;

  // Constructors, getters, setters
}
```

The `@OrderBy` annotation takes the names of the attributes on which the sorting has to be made (the `postedDate` attribute from the `Comment` entity), as well as the method (ascending or descending). The String `ASC` or `DESC` can be used for sorting in either an ascending or descending manner, respectively. You can have several columns used in the `@OrderBy` annotation. If you need to order by posted date and note, you can use `OrderBy("postedDate DESC, note ASC")`.

The `@OrderBy` annotation doesn't have any impact on the database mapping. The persistence provider is simply informed to use an `Order By` clause when the collection is retrieved at runtime.

Ordered Column

Dynamic ordering using the `@OrderBy` annotation was supported from JPA 1.0 onwards. But this does not include support for maintaining a persistent ordering. Since JPA 2.0, this has been possible by adding the annotation `@OrderColumn` (its API is similar to `@Column` in Listing 32). This annotation informs the persistence provider that it is required to maintain the ordered list using a separate column where the index is stored. The `@OrderColumn` defines this separate column.

Let's use the news and comments example and change it slightly. This time the `Comment` entity, shown in Listing 73, has no `postedDate` attribute, and therefore there is no way to chronologically sort the comments.

Listing 73. A Comment Entity with No Posted Date

```
@Entity
public class Comment {

  @Id
  @GeneratedValue
  private Long id;
  private String nickname;
  private String content;
  private Integer note;

  // Constructors, getters, setters
}
```

To keep an ordering without a posted date, the News entity (shown in Listing 74) can annotate the relationship with @OrderColumn. The persistence provider will then map the News entity to the NEWS table with an additional column called PUBLICATION_INDEX in order to store the ordering.

Listing 74. The Ordering of Comments Is Persisted

```
@Entity
public class News {

  @Id
  @GeneratedValue
  private Long id;
  @Column(nullable = false)
  private String content;
  @JoinColumn
  @OrderColumn(name = "publication_index")
  private List<Comment> comments;

  // Constructors, getters, setters
}
```

In Listing 74, the @OrderColumn renames the additional column to PUBLICATION_INDEX. If the name is not overridden, by default the column name is the concatenation of the name of the entity attribute and the _ORDER string (COMMENTS_ORDER in our example). The type of this column must be a numerical type. This ordering will get mapped to the column PUBLICATION_INDEX as shown in Listing 75.

Listing 75. The Column PUBLICATION_INDEX Persists the Ordering

```
CREATE TABLE COMMENT
(
  ID                BIGINT NOT NULL,
  CONTENT           VARCHAR,
  NICKNAME          VARCHAR,
  NOTE              INTEGER,
  COMMENTS_ID       BIGINT,
  PUBLICATION_INDEX INTEGER,
  PRIMARY KEY (ID)
)
```

There are performance impacts to be aware of; as with the `@OrderColumn` annotation, the persistence provider must also track changes to the index. It is responsible for maintaining the order upon insertion, deletion, or reordering.

Portable applications should not expect a list to be ordered by the database, under the pretext that some database engines automatically optimise their indexes so that the datatable appears as sorted. Instead, it should use either the `@OrderColumn` or `@OrderBy` construct. Note that you can't use both annotations at the same time.

4.7. Mapping Inheritance

Since their creation, object-oriented languages have used the inheritance paradigm. C++ allows multiple inheritance, and Java supports single-class inheritance. In object-oriented languages, developers commonly reuse code by inheriting the attributes and behaviour of root classes.

You have just studied relationships, and relationships between entities have a very straightforward mapping to a relational database. This is not the case with inheritance. Inheritance is a completely unknown concept and not natively implemented in a relational world. The concept of inheritance throws in several tweaks when saving objects into a relational database.

How do you organise a hierarchical model into a flat relational one? Because databases do not support table inheritance, JPA has three different inheritance mapping strategies you can choose from.

- *A single-table-per-class hierarchy strategy*: The sum of the attributes of the entire entity hierarchy is flattened down to a single table (this is the default strategy). For instance, the `ITEM` table will have all the attributes of `Book`, `Item` and `CD` in a single table and an extra discriminator column to differentiate which type each row is.
- *A joined-subclass strategy*: In this approach, each entity in the hierarchy, concrete or abstract, is mapped to its own dedicated table. So `Book`, `Item` and `CD` will have their own tables, each with its own attributes and will be linked together by having the same identifier.
- *A table-per-concrete-class strategy*: This strategy maps each concrete entity class to its own separate table. For instance, the `BOOK` table will contain all the `Book` and `Item` attributes, and the `CD` table will contain all the `CD` and `Item` attributes.

Support for the table-per-concrete-class inheritance mapping strategy is still optional in JPA 2.2. Portable applications should avoid using it until officially mandated.

Leveraging the easy use of annotations, JPA delivers declarative support for defining and mapping inheritance hierarchies, including entities, abstract entities, mapped classes, and transient classes. The `@Inheritance` annotation is used on the root entity to dictate the mapping strategy to itself and to the leaf classes. JPA also transposes the object notion of overriding to the mapping, which allows root class attributes to be overridden by child classes. In Chapter 8 you will also see how the access type can be used with inheritance to mix field access and property access.

4.7.1. Inheritance Strategies

When an entity hierarchy exists, it always has an entity as its root. The root entity class can define the inheritance strategy by using the `strategy` element of `@Inheritance` to one of the options defined in the `javax.persistence.InheritanceType` enumerated type. If it doesn't, the default single-table-per-class hierarchy strategy will be applied. To explore each strategy, I am going to discuss how to map a `CD` and a `Book` entity, both inheriting from the `Item` entity (see Figure 31).

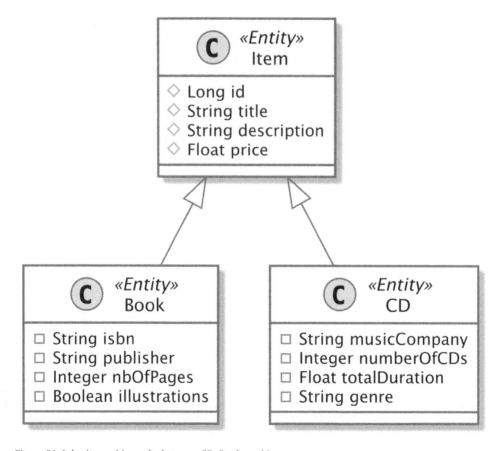

Figure 31. Inheritance hierarchy between CD, Book, and Item

The Item entity is the root entity and has an identifier, a title, a description, and a price. Both the CD and Book entities inherit from Item. Each of these leaf classes adds extra attributes such as an ISBN for the Book entity or a total time duration for the CD entity.

Single-table-per-class Hierarchy Strategy

The default inheritance mapping strategy is the single-table-per-class strategy. In this strategy, all the entities in the hierarchy are mapped to a single table. As it is the default strategy, thanks to configuration by exception, you can even omit the @Inheritance annotation on the root entity (see the Item entity in Listing 76).

Listing 76. The Item Entity Uses the Default Single-table-per-class Strategy

```
@Entity
public class Item {

  @Id
  @GeneratedValue
  protected Long id;
  protected String title;
  protected String description;
  protected Float price;

  // Constructors, getters, setters
}
```

Item (Listing 76) is the root class for the Book entity (see Listing 77) and CD entity (see Listing 78). These entities inherit the attributes from Item as well as the default inheritance strategy and therefore don't have to use the @Inheritance annotation.

Listing 77. Book Extends Item

```
@Entity
public class Book extends Item {

  private String isbn;
  private String publisher;
  private Integer nbOfPages;
  private Boolean illustrations;

  // Constructors, getters, setters
}
```

Listing 78. CD Extends Item

```
@Entity
public class CD extends Item {

  private String musicCompany;
  private Integer numberOfCDs;
  private Float totalDuration;
  private String genre;

  // Constructors, getters, setters
}
```

With what you have seen so far, without inheritance, these three entities would be mapped into their own separate tables, but with inheritance it's different. With the single-table-per-class strategy (the default one), they all end up in the same database table, which defaults to the name of the root class: `ITEM`. Figure 32 shows the `ITEM` table structure.

Figure 32. ITEM table structure

As you can see in Figure 32, the `ITEM` table sums all the attributes of the `Item`, `Book`, and `CD` entities. But there's an additional column that doesn't relate to any of the entities' attributes: it's the discriminator column, `DTYPE`.

The `ITEM` table will be filled with items, books, and CD albums. When accessing the data, the persistence provider needs to know which row belongs to which entity. This way, the provider will instantiate the appropriate object type (`Item`, `Book`, or `CD`) when reading the `ITEM` table. That's why a discriminator column is used to explicitly type each row.

Table 7 shows a fragment of the `ITEM` table with some data. As you can see, the single-table-per-class strategy has some holes; not every column is useful for each entity. The first row is the data stored for an `Item` entity (the `DTYPE` column contains the name of the entity). Items only have a title, a price, and a description (see Listing 76 earlier); they don't have a music company, an ISBN, and so on. So, these columns will always remain empty.

Table 7. Fragment of the ITEM Table Filled with Data

ID	DTYPE	TITLE	PRICE	DESCRIPTION	MUSICCOMPANY	ISBN	...
1	Item	Pen	2.10	Beautiful black pen			...
2	CD	Soul Trane	23.50	Fantastic jazz album	Prestige		...
3	CD	Zoot Allures	18	One of the best from Zappa	Warner		...
4	Book	The Robots of Dawn	22.30	Robots everywhere		0-8764	...
5	Book	H2G2	17.50	Funny IT book ;o)		1-1689	...

The discriminator column is called `DTYPE` by default, is of type `String` (mapped to a `VARCHAR`), and contains the name of the entity. If the defaults don't suit, the `@DiscriminatorColumn` annotation allows you to change the name and the data type. By default, the value of this column is the entity name to which it refers, although an entity may override this value using the `@DiscriminatorValue` annotation.

Listing 79 renames the discriminator column to `DISC` (instead of `DTYPE`) and changes its data type to `Char` instead of `String`; each entity should then change its discriminator value to `I` for `Item`, `B` for `Book` (see Listing 80), and `C` for `CD` (see Listing 81).

Listing 79. Item Redefines the Discriminator Column

```
@Entity
@Inheritance(strategy = InheritanceType.SINGLE_TABLE)
@DiscriminatorColumn(name = "disc", discriminatorType = DiscriminatorType.CHAR)
@DiscriminatorValue("I")
public class Item {

  @Id
  @GeneratedValue
  protected Long id;
  protected String title;
  protected String description;
  protected Float price;

  // Constructors, getters, setters
}
```

Listing 80. Book Redefines the Discriminator Value to B

```
@Entity
@DiscriminatorValue("B")
public class Book extends Item {

  private String isbn;
  private String publisher;
  private Integer nbOfPages;
  private Boolean illustrations;

  // Constructors, getters, setters
}
```

Listing 81. CD Redefines the Discriminator Value to C

```
@Entity
@DiscriminatorValue("C")
public class CD extends Item {

  private String musicCompany;
  private Integer numberOfCDs;
  private Float totalDuration;
  private String genre;

  // Constructors, getters, setters
}
```

The root entity `Item` defines the discriminator column once for the entire hierarchy with `@DiscriminatorColumn`. It then changes its own default value to `I` with the `@DiscriminatorValue` annotation. Child entities have to redefine their own discriminator value only.

Table 8 shows the result. The discriminator column and its values are different from those shown earlier in Table 7.

Table 8. The ITEM Table with a Different Discriminator Name and Values

ID	DISC	TITLE	PRICE	DESCRIPTION	MUSICCOMPANY	ISBN	...
1	I	Pen	2.10	Beautiful black pen			...
2	C	Soul Trane	23.50	Fantastic jazz album	Prestige		...
3	C	Zoot Allures	18	One of the best from Zappa	Warner		...
4	B	The Robots of Dawn	22.30	Robots everywhere		0-8764	...
5	B	H2G2	17.50	Funny IT book ;o)		1-1689	...

The single-table-per-class strategy is the default inheritance strategy, is the easiest to understand,

and works well when the hierarchy is relatively simple and stable. However, it has some drawbacks; adding new entities to the hierarchy, or adding attributes to existing entities, involves adding new columns to the table, migrating data, and changing indexes. This strategy also requires the columns of the child entities to be nullable. If the ISBN of the `Book` entity happens to be non-null, you cannot insert a `CD` anymore, because the `CD` entity doesn't have an ISBN.

Joined-subclass Strategy

In the joined-subclass strategy, each entity in the hierarchy is mapped to its own table. The root entity maps to a table that defines the primary key to be used by all tables in the hierarchy, as well as the discriminator column. Each subclass is represented by a separate table that contains its own attributes (not inherited from the root class) and a primary key that refers to the root table's primary key. The non-root tables do not hold a discriminator column.

You can implement a joined-subclass strategy by annotating the root entity with the `@Inheritance` annotation as shown in Listing 82 (the code of `CD` and `Book` is unchanged, the same as before).

Listing 82. The Item Entity with a Joined-subclass Strategy

```
@Entity
@Inheritance(strategy = InheritanceType.JOINED)
public class Item {

  @Id
  @GeneratedValue
  protected Long id;
  protected String title;
  protected String description;
  protected Float price;

  // Constructors, getters, setters
}
```

From a developer's point of view, the joined-subclass strategy is natural, as each entity, abstract or concrete, will have its state mapped to a different table. Figure 33 shows how the `Item`, `Book`, and `CD` entities will be mapped.

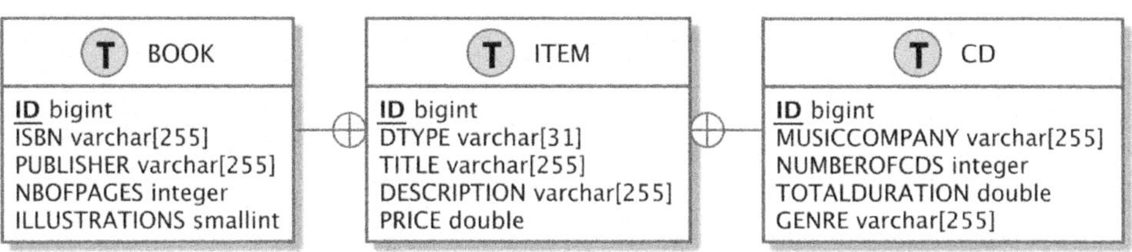

Figure 33. Mapping inheritance with a joined-subclass strategy

You can still use `@DiscriminatorColumn` and `@DiscriminatorValue` annotations in the root entity to customise the discriminator column and values (the `DTYPE` column is in the `ITEM` table).

The joined-subclass strategy is intuitive and is close to what you know from the object inheritance mechanism. But querying can have a performance impact. This strategy is called *joined* because, to reassemble an instance of a subclass, the subclass table has to be joined with the root class table. The deeper the hierarchy, the more joins needed to assemble a leaf entity. This strategy provides good support for polymorphic relationships but requires one or more join operations to be performed when instantiating entity subclasses. This may result in poor performance for extensive class hierarchies. Similarly, queries that cover the entire class hierarchy require join operations between the subclass tables, resulting in decreased performance.

Table-per-concrete-class Strategy

In the table-per-class (or table-per-concrete-class) strategy, each entity is mapped to its own dedicated table like the joined-subclass strategy. The difference is that all attributes of the root entity will also be mapped to columns of the child entity table. From a database point of view, this strategy de-normalises the model and causes all root entity attributes to be redefined in the tables of all leaf entities that inherit from it. With the table-per-concrete-class strategy, there is no shared table, no shared columns, and no discriminator column.

Mapping our example to this strategy is a matter of specifying a `TABLE_PER_CLASS` on the `@Inheritance` annotation (see Listing 83) of the root entity (`Item`).

Listing 83. The Item Entity with a Table-per-concrete-class Strategy

```
@Entity
@Inheritance(strategy = InheritanceType.TABLE_PER_CLASS)
public class Item {

  @Id
  @GeneratedValue
  protected Long id;
  protected String title;
  protected String description;
  protected Float price;

  // Constructors, getters, setters
}
```

Figure 34 shows the `ITEM`, `BOOK`, and `CD` tables. You can see that `BOOK` and `CD` duplicate the `ID`, `TITLE`, `PRICE`, and `DESCRIPTION` columns of the `ITEM` table. Note that the tables are not linked.

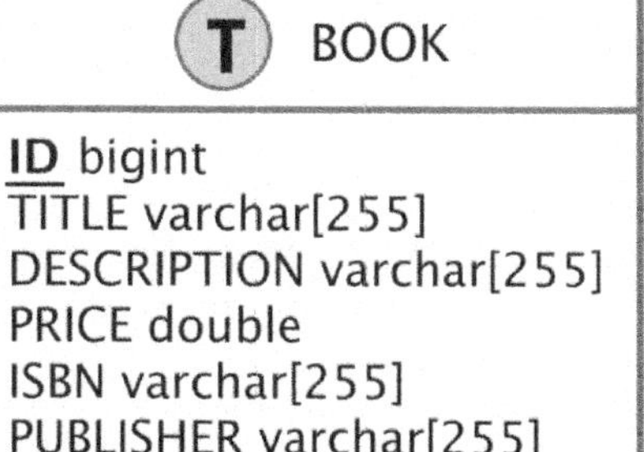

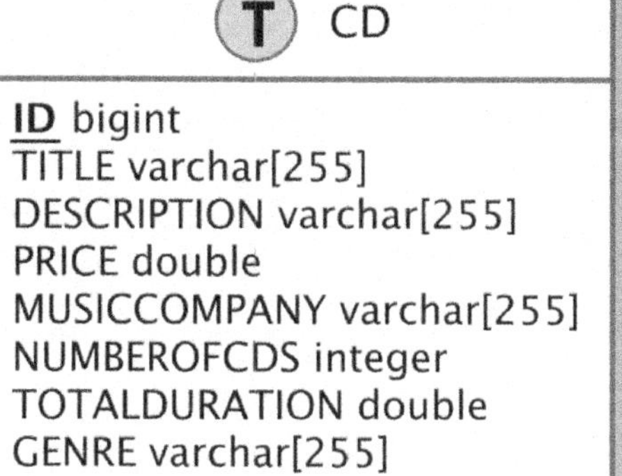

Figure 34. BOOK and CD tables duplicating ITEM columns

Of course, remember that each table can be redefined by annotating each entity with the `@Table` annotation.

The table-per-concrete-class strategy performs well when querying instances of one entity, as it is similar to using the single-table-per-class strategy: the query is confined to a single table. The downside is that it makes polymorphic queries across a class hierarchy (e.g. finding all the items, including CDs and books) more expensive than the other strategies; it must query all subclass tables using a `UNION` operation, which is expensive when a large amount of data is involved. Support for table-per-concrete-class strategy is still optional in JPA 2.2.

4.7.2. Type of Classes in the Inheritance Hierarchy

The previous examples used to explain the mapping strategies only use entities. `Item` is an entity as well as `Book` and `CD`. But entities don't always have to inherit from entities. A hierarchy of classes can mix all sorts of different classes: entities and also nonentities (or transient classes), abstract entities, and mapped superclasses. Inheriting from these different types of classes will have an impact on the mapping.

Abstract Entity

In the previous examples, the `Item` entity was a concrete class. It was annotated with `@Entity` and didn't have an `abstract` keyword, but an abstract class can also be specified as an entity. An abstract entity differs from a concrete entity only in that it cannot be directly instantiated with the `new` keyword. It provides a common data structure for its leaf entities (`Book` and `CD`) and follows the mapping strategies. Abstract entities can be queried just like concrete entities. In fact, for the persistence provider, abstract entities are like concrete entities but cannot be instantiated.

Nonentity

Nonentities are also called *transient classes*, meaning they are POJOs. An entity may subclass a nonentity or may be extended by a nonentity. Why would you have nonentities in a hierarchy? Object modelling and inheritance are the means through which state and behaviour are shared. Nonentities can be used to provide a common data structure to leaf entities. The state of a nonentity superclass is not persistent because it is not managed by the persistence provider (remember that the condition for a class to be managed by the persistence provider is the presence of an `@Entity` annotation).

For example, `Book` is an entity (Listing 85) and extends from an `Item` nonentity (`Item` doesn't have any annotation) as shown in Listing 84.

Listing 84. Item Is a Simple POJO with No @Entity

```
public class Item {

  protected String title;
  protected String description;
  protected Float price;

  // Constructors, getters, setters
}
```

The `Book` entity (Listing 85) inherits from `Item`, so the Java code can access the `title`, `price`, and `description` attributes, plus any other method that is defined, in a normal, object-oriented way. `Item` can be concrete or abstract and does not have any impact on the final mapping.

Listing 85. The Book Entity Extends from a POJO

```
@Entity
public class Book extends Item {

  @Id
  @GeneratedValue
  protected Long id;
  private String isbn;
  private String publisher;
  private Integer nbOfPages;
  private Boolean illustrations;

  // Constructors, getters, setters
}
```

Book is an entity and extends Item. But only the attributes of Book would be mapped to a table. No attributes from Item appear in the table structure defined in Listing 86. To persist a Book, you need to create an instance of Book, set values to any attributes you want (title, price, isbn, publisher etc.), but only the Book's attributes (id, isbn etc.) will get persisted.

Listing 86. The BOOK Table Has No Attributes from Item

```
CREATE TABLE BOOK
(
  ID            BIGINT NOT NULL,
  ILLUSTRATIONS BOOLEAN,
  ISBN          VARCHAR,
  NBOFPAGES     INTEGER,
  PUBLISHER     VARCHAR,
  PRIMARY KEY (ID)
)
```

Mapped Superclass

JPA defines a special kind of class, called a *mapped superclass*, to share state and behaviour, as well as mapping information that entities inherit from. However, mapped superclasses are not entities. They are not managed by the persistence provider, do not have any table to be mapped to, and cannot be queried or be part of a relationship, but they may provide persistent properties to any entities that extend from them. They are similar to embeddable classes except they can be used with inheritance. A class is indicated as being a mapped superclass by annotating it with the @MappedSuperclass annotation. Mapped superclasses can be abstract or concrete.

Using the root class, Item is annotated with @MappedSuperclass, not @Entity, as Listing 87 illustrates. It defines an inheritance strategy (JOINED) and annotates some of its attributes with @Column. Because mapped superclasses are not mapped to tables, the @Table annotation is not permitted.

Listing 87. Item Is a Mapped Superclass

```
@MappedSuperclass
@Inheritance(strategy = JOINED)
public abstract class Item {

  @Id
  @GeneratedValue
  protected Long id;
  @Column(length = 50, nullable = false)
  protected String title;
  @Column(length = 2000)
  protected String description;
  protected Float price;

  // Constructors, getters, setters
}
```

As you can see in Listing 87, the `title` and `description` attributes are annotated with `@Column`. Listing 88 shows the `Book` entity extending `Item`.

Listing 88. Book Extends from a Mapped Superclass

```
@Entity
public class Book extends Item {

  private String isbn;
  private String publisher;
  private Integer nbOfPages;
  private Boolean illustrations;

  // Constructors, getters, setters
}
```

This hierarchy will be mapped into only one table. `Item` is not an entity and does not have any table. Attributes of `Item` and `Book` would be mapped to columns of the `BOOK` table, but mapped superclasses also share their mapping information. The `@Column` annotations of `Item` will be inherited.

As mapped superclasses are not managed entities, you would not be able to persist or query them. Listing 89 shows the `BOOK` table structure with customised `TITLE` and `DESCRIPTION` columns.

Listing 89. The BOOK Table Has All the Attributes from Item

```
CREATE TABLE BOOK
(
  ID            BIGINT       NOT NULL,
  DESCRIPTION   VARCHAR(2000),
  ILLUSTRATIONS BOOLEAN,
  ISBN          VARCHAR,
  NBOFPAGES     INTEGER,
  PRICE         DOUBLE,
  PUBLISHER     VARCHAR,
  TITLE         VARCHAR(50) NOT NULL,
  PRIMARY KEY (ID)
)
```

[51] **JavaBean** https://docs.oracle.com/javase/8/docs/api/java/beans/package-summary.html

[52] **JPA Specification** https://jcp.org/en/jsr/detail?id=338

Chapter 5. Managing Entities

Java Persistence API has two sides. The first is the ability to map objects to a relational database. Configuration by exception allows persistence providers to do most of the work without much code, but the richness of JPA also allows customised mapping from objects to tables using either annotation or XML descriptors. From simple mapping (changing the name of a column) to more complex mapping (inheritance), JPA offers a wide spectrum of customisations. As a result, you can map almost any object model to a legacy database.

The other aspect of JPA is the ability to query these mapped objects. In JPA, the centralised service for manipulating instances of entities is the entity manager. It provides an API to create, find, remove, and synchronise objects with the database. It also allows the execution of different sorts of JPQL queries, such as dynamic, static, or native queries, against entities. Locking mechanisms are also possible with the entity manager.

The code in this chapter can be found at https://github.com/agoncal/agoncal-fascicle-jpa/tree/2.2/managing

5.1. Entity Management APIs

Before we look at how to manage entities, let's first have a brief overview of APIs used to manage entities. Figure 35 shows the main interfaces which are located in three different packages. Under the root package `javax.persistence` we find everything related to obtaining an `EntityManager`, transactions and queries. The subpackage `javax.persistence.criteria` hosts the interfaces related to criteria queries, while the sub-package `javax.persistence.metamodel` is related to the entity metamodel.

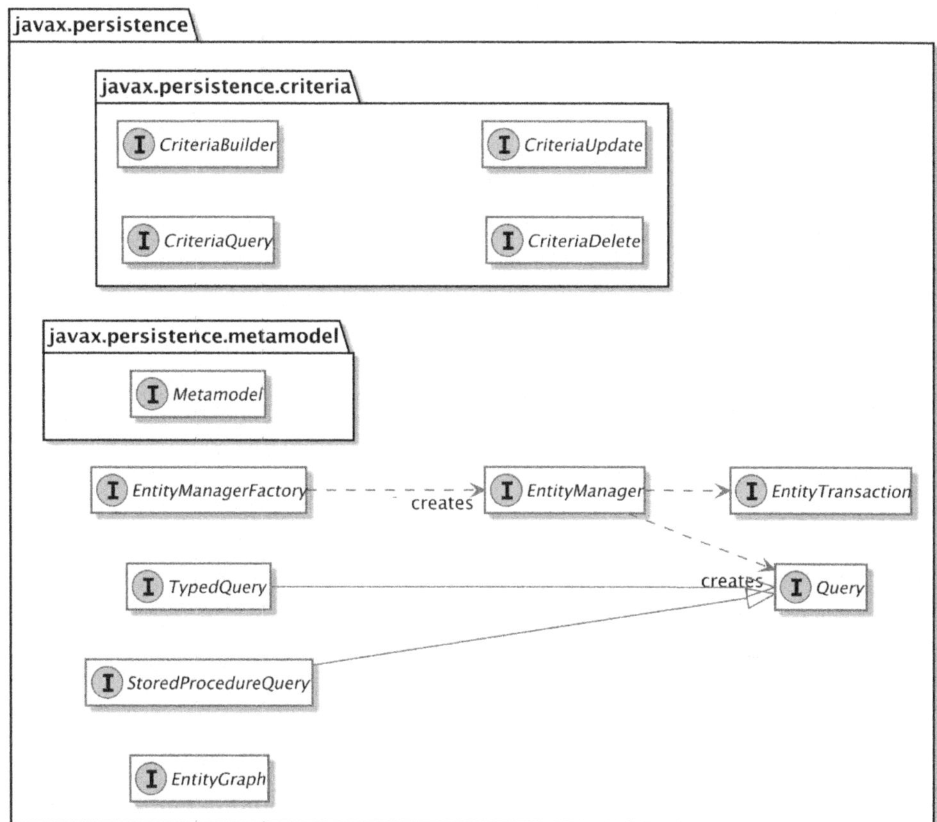

Figure 35. Entity management APIs

Let's dig into these APIs.

5.1.1. Entity Manager API

The entity manager manages the state and life cycle of entities as well as querying entities within a persistence context. The entity manager is responsible for creating and removing persistent entity instances and finding entities by their primary key. It can lock entities in order to protect against concurrent access by using optimistic or pessimistic locking and can use JPQL queries to retrieve entities following certain criteria (more on concurrency and locks in Chapter 8).

When an entity manager obtains a reference to an entity, the entity is said to be "managed." Up to that point, the entity is seen as a regular POJO (i.e. detached). The strength of JPA is that entities can be used as regular objects by different layers of an application and become managed by the entity manager when you need to load or insert data into the database. When an entity is managed, you can carry out persistence operations, and the entity manager will automatically synchronise the state of the entity with the database. When the entity is detached (i.e. not managed), it returns to a simple POJO and can then be used by other layers (e.g. the presentation layer) without synchronising its state with the database.

With regard to persistence, the real work begins with the entity manager. `EntityManager` is an interface implemented by a persistence provider that will generate and execute SQL statements. The `javax.persistence.EntityManager` interface provides the API to manipulate entities (subset shown in Listing 90).

Listing 90. Subset of the EntityManager API

```
public interface EntityManager {

  // Factory to create an entity manager, close it and check if it's open
  public void close();
  public boolean isOpen();
  public EntityManagerFactory getEntityManagerFactory();

  // Return the underlying provider object for the EntityManager
  public <T> T unwrap(Class<T> cls);
  public Object getDelegate();

  // Sets and gets an entity manager property or hint
  public void setProperty(String propertyName, Object value);
  public Map<String, Object> getProperties();
```

The entity manager can be seen as a first-level cache for entities. Therefore, it has a few methods to check if an entity is in the first-level cache (a.k.a. managed), flush the cache to the database or refresh the cache from the database. The methods `clear` and `detach` remove an entity from the entity manager.

```
// Synchronises the persistence context to the underlying database
public void flush();
public void setFlushMode(FlushModeType flushMode);
public FlushModeType getFlushMode();

// Refreshes the state of the entity from the database, overwriting any changes made
public void refresh(Object entity);
public void refresh(Object entity, LockModeType lockMode);

// Clears the persistence context and checks if it contains an entity
public void clear();
public void detach(Object entity);
public boolean contains(Object entity);
```

For basic CRUD operations, the entity manager has a few methods that allow you to persist, merge, remove and find entities by their primary key.

```
// Persists, merges, removes and finds an entity to/from the database
public void persist(Object entity);
public <T> T merge(T entity);
public void remove(Object entity);
public <T> T find(Class<T> entityClass, Object primaryKey);
public <T> T getReference(Class<T> entityClass, Object primaryKey);
```

When CRUD is not enough, JPA allows you to create a certain number of queries using JPQL, native SQL, criteria queries or stored procedures.

```
  // Creates an instance of Query or TypedQuery for executing a JPQL statement
  public Query createQuery(String qlString);
  public <T> TypedQuery<T> createQuery(String qlString, Class<T> resultClass);

  // Creates an instance of Query or TypedQuery for executing a named query
  public Query createNamedQuery(String name);
  public <T> TypedQuery<T> createNamedQuery(String name, Class<T> resultClass);

  // Creates an instance of Query for executing a native SQL query
  public Query createNativeQuery(String sqlString);
  public Query createNativeQuery(String sqlString, Class resultClass);
  public Query createNativeQuery(String sqlString, String resultSetMapping);

  // Creates a StoredProcedureQuery for executing a stored procedure in the database
  public StoredProcedureQuery createNamedStoredProcedureQuery(String name);
  public StoredProcedureQuery createStoredProcedureQuery(String procedureName);
  public StoredProcedureQuery createStoredProcedureQuery(
    String procedureName, Class... resultClasses);
  public StoredProcedureQuery createStoredProcedureQuery(
    String procedureName, String... resultSetMappings);

  // Metamodel and criteria builder for criteria queries (select, update and delete)
  public CriteriaBuilder getCriteriaBuilder();
  public Metamodel getMetamodel();
  public <T> TypedQuery<T> createQuery(CriteriaQuery<T> criteriaQuery);
  public Query createQuery(CriteriaUpdate updateQuery);
  public Query createQuery(CriteriaDelete deleteQuery);

  // Creates and returns an entity graph
  public <T> EntityGraph<T> createEntityGraph(Class<T> rootType);
  public EntityGraph<?> createEntityGraph(String graphName);
  public  EntityGraph<?> getEntityGraph(String graphName);
  public <T> List<EntityGraph<? super T>> getEntityGraphs(Class<T> entityClass);
}
```

The entity manager has a few methods that let you obtain a transaction or join an existing one. It also lets you lock an entity with either optimistic or pessimistic locks.

```java
// Returns an entity transaction
public EntityTransaction getTransaction();

// Indicates if a JTA transaction is active and joins the persistence context to it
public void joinTransaction();
public boolean isJoinedToTransaction();

// Locks an entity with the specified lock mode type (optimistic, pessimistic...)
public void lock(Object entity, LockModeType lockMode);
public LockModeType getLockMode(Object entity);
```

Don't get scared by the API in Listing 90, as this chapter covers most of the methods.

5.1.2. Obtaining an Entity Manager

The entity manager is the central interface used to interact with entities, but it first has to be obtained by the application. Depending on whether it is a container-managed environment (e.g. see Spring or CDI in Chapter 9) or an application-managed environment, the code can be quite different. For example, in a container-managed environment, the transactions are managed by the container. That means you don't need to explicitly write the commit or rollback, which you have to do in an application-managed environment.

The term *application managed* means the application is responsible for explicitly obtaining an instance of `EntityManager` and managing its life cycle (creating and then closing the entity manager programmatically). The code in Listing 91 demonstrates how a class running in a Java SE environment gets an instance of an entity manager. It uses the `Persistence` class to bootstrap an `EntityManagerFactory` associated with a persistence unit (`vintageStorePU`), which is then used to create an entity manager. Notice that, in an application-managed environment, the developer is responsible for creating and closing the entity manager (i.e. managing its life cycle). It will throw a `javax.persistence.PersistenceException` if it cannot create or close the entity manager.

Listing 91. Obtaining an EntityManager within an Application-managed Component

```
public class BookService {

  public void createBook() {

    // Obtains an entity manager
    EntityManagerFactory emf = Persistence.createEntityManagerFactory("cdbookstorePU"
);
    EntityManager em = emf.createEntityManager();

    // Obtains a transaction
    EntityTransaction tx = em.getTransaction();

    // Creates an instance of book
    Book book = new Book().title("H2G2").price(12.5F).isbn("1-84023-742-2").nbOfPages
(354);

    // Persists the book to the database
    tx.begin();
    em.persist(book);
    tx.commit();

    // Closes the entity manager and the factory
    em.close();
    emf.close();
  }
}
```

In a container-managed environment, the way to acquire an entity manager is through injection. Depending on the container, injection can happen with the `@PersistenceContext` annotation or `@Inject` (more on injection in Chapter 9). Also, we don't need to programmatically create or close the entity manager, as its life cycle is managed by the container. Listing 92 shows the code of a transactional service (see the `@Transactional` annotation) into which the container injects a reference of the `vintageStorePU` persistence unit.

Listing 92. Obtaining an EntityManager within a Container-managed Component

```
@Transactional
public class BookService {

  // Obtains an entity manager
  @PersistenceContext(unitName = "cdbookstorePU")
  private EntityManager em;

  public void createBook() {

    // Creates an instance of book
    Book book = new Book().title("H2G2").price(12.5F).isbn("1-84023-742-2").nbOfPages
(354);

    // Persists the book to the database
    em.persist(book);
  }
}
```

Compared with Listing 91, the code in Listing 92 is much simpler. First, there is no `Persistence` or `EntityManagerFactory` as the container injects the entity manager instance. The application is not responsible for managing the life cycle of the `EntityManager` (creating and closing the `EntityManager`). Second, because transactional beans manage the transactions, there is no explicit commit or rollback. Chapter 9 shows how to integrate Java Persistence API with container-managed technologies such as CDI and Spring.

5.1.3. Persistence Context

Before exploring the `EntityManager` API in detail, you need to understand a crucial concept: the *persistence context*. A persistence context is a set of managed entity instances at a given time for a given user's transaction: only one entity instance with the same persistent identity can exist in a persistence context. For example, if a `Book` instance with an Id of 12 exists in the persistence context, no other book with this ID can exist within that same persistence context. Only entities that are contained in the persistence context are managed by the entity manager, meaning that changes will be reflected in the database.

The entity manager updates or consults the persistence context whenever a method of the `javax.persistence.EntityManager` interface is called. For example, when a `persist()` method is called, the entity passed as an argument will be added to the persistence context if it doesn't already exist. Similarly, when an entity is found by its primary key, the entity manager first checks whether the requested entity is already present in the persistence context. The persistence context can be seen as a first-level cache. It's a short-lived space where the entity manager stores entities before flushing the content to the database. By default, objects just live in the persistent context for the duration of the transaction.

To summarise, let's look at Figure 36 where two users need to access entities whose data is stored in the database. Each user has his their persistence context that lasts for the duration of their own transaction. User 1 gets the `Book` entities with IDs equal to 12 and 56 from the database, so both books get stored in their persistence context. User 2 gets the entities 12 and 34. As you can see, both entities with ID = 12 are stored in each user's persistence context. While the transaction runs, the persistence context acts like a first-level cache, storing the entities that can be managed by the `EntityManager`. Once the transaction ends, the persistence context ends and the entities are cleared.

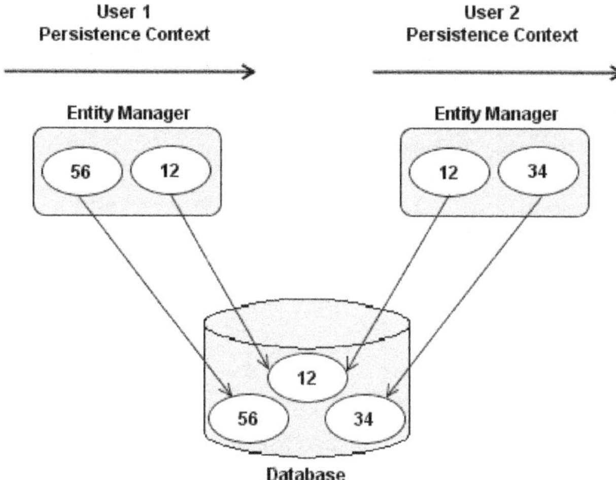

Figure 36. Entities living in different users' persistence context

The configuration for an entity manager is bound to the factory that created it. Whether application or container managed, the factory needs a persistence unit from which to create an entity manager. A persistence unit dictates the settings to connect to the database and the list of entities that can be managed in a persistence context. The `persistence.xml` file (see Listing 93) located in the `META-INF` directory defines a persistence unit. The persistence unit has a name (`vintageStorePU`) and a set of attributes.

Listing 93. A Persistence Unit with a Set of Manageable Entities

```
<persistence xmlns:xsi="http://www.w3.org/2001/XMLSchema-instance"
             xmlns="http://xmlns.jcp.org/xml/ns/persistence"
             xsi:schemaLocation="http://xmlns.jcp.org/xml/ns/persistence
http://xmlns.jcp.org/xml/ns/persistence/persistence_2_2.xsd"
             version="2.2">

  <persistence-unit name="cdbookstorePU" transaction-type="RESOURCE_LOCAL">
    <provider>org.eclipse.persistence.jpa.PersistenceProvider</provider>
    <class>org.agoncal.fascicle.jpa.managing.Book</class>
    <properties>
      <property name="javax.persistence.schema-generation.database.action" value=
"drop-and-create"/>
      <property name="javax.persistence.schema-generation.scripts.action" value="drop-
and-create"/>
      <property name="javax.persistence.schema-generation.scripts.create-target"
value="cdbookstoreCreate.ddl"/>
      <property name="javax.persistence.schema-generation.scripts.drop-target" value=
"cdbookstoreDrop.ddl"/>
      <property name="javax.persistence.jdbc.driver" value="org.h2.Driver"/>
      <property name="javax.persistence.jdbc.url" value="jdbc:h2:mem:cdbookstoreDB"/>
    </properties>
  </persistence-unit>
</persistence>
```

The persistence unit is the bridge between the persistence context and the database. On the one hand, the `<class>` tag lists all the entities that could be managed in the persistence context and, on the other, it defines all the information to physically connect to the database (using properties). The persistence unit also defines the transaction mode. In an application-managed environment, the transaction mode is local (`transaction-type="RESOURCE_LOCAL"`). Chapter 9 will cover container-managed environments (e.g. Spring and Java EE). In container-managed environments, the `persistence.xml` would define a datasource instead of the database connection properties and set the transaction type to JTA (`transaction-type="JTA"`) or *Java Transaction API*.

From JPA 2.1 onwards, some properties of the `persistence.xml` file have been standardised (see Table 9). They all start with `javax.persistence` such as `javax.persistence.jdbc.url`. JPA providers are required to support these standard properties, but they may provide custom properties of their own (e.g. the EclipseLink property `eclipselink.logging.level` to setup the log level).

Table 9. Standard persistence.xml Properties

Property	Description
`javax.persistence.jdbc.driver`	Fully qualified name of the driver class
`javax.persistence.jdbc.url`	Driver-specific URL
`javax.persistence.jdbc.user`	Username used by database connection
`javax.persistence.jdbc.password`	Password used by database connection
`javax.persistence.database-product-name`	Name of the targeted database (e.g. H2)

Property	Description
`javax.persistence.database-major-version`	Version number of the targeted database
`javax.persistence.database-minor-version`	Minor version number of the targeted database
`javax.persistence.ddl-create-script-source`	Name of the script creating the database
`javax.persistence.ddl-drop-script-source`	Name of the script dropping the database
`javax.persistence.sql-load-script-source`	Name of the script loading data into the database
`javax.persistence.schema-generation.database.action`	Specifies the action to be taken with regard to the database (`none`, `create`, `drop-and-create`, `drop`)
`javax.persistence.schema-generation.scripts.action`	Specifies the action to be taken with regard to DDL scripts (`none`, `create`, `drop-and-create`, `drop`)
`javax.persistence.schema-generation.scripts.create-target`	If scripts are to be generated, name of the create script
`javax.persistence.schema-generation.scripts.drop-target`	If scripts are to be generated, name of the drop script
`javax.persistence.lock.timeout`	Value in milliseconds for pessimistic lock timeout
`javax.persistence.query.timeout`	Value in milliseconds for query timeout
`javax.persistence.validation.group.pre-persist`	Groups targeted for validation upon pre-persist
`javax.persistence.validation.group.pre-update`	Groups targeted for validation upon pre-update
`javax.persistence.validation.group.pre-remove`	Groups targeted for validation upon pre-remove

5.2. Manipulating Entities

Being the central piece of JPA, we use the entity manager for both simple entity manipulation and complex JPQL query execution. When manipulating single entities, the `EntityManager` interface can be seen as a generic *Data Access Object* (DAO), which allows CRUD operations on any entity.[53]

To help you gain a better understanding of these methods, I use a simple example of a one-way, one-to-one relationship between a `Customer` and an `Address`. Both entities have automatically generated identifiers (thanks to the `@GeneratedValue` annotation), and `Customer` (see Listing 94) has a link to `Address` (see Listing 95).

Listing 94. The Customer Entity with a One-way, One-to-one Address

```
@Entity
public class Customer {

  @Id
  @GeneratedValue
  private Long id;
  private String firstName;
  private String lastName;
  private String email;
  @OneToOne(fetch = LAZY)
  @JoinColumn(name = "address_fk")
  private Address address;

  // Constructors, getters, setters
}
```

Listing 95. The Address Entity

```
@Entity
public class Address {

  @Id
  @GeneratedValue
  private Long id;
  private String street1;
  private String city;
  private String zipcode;
  private String country;

  // Constructors, getters, setters
}
```

These two entities will get mapped into the database structure shown in Figure 37. Note the `ADDRESS_FK` column is the foreign key to `ADDRESS`.

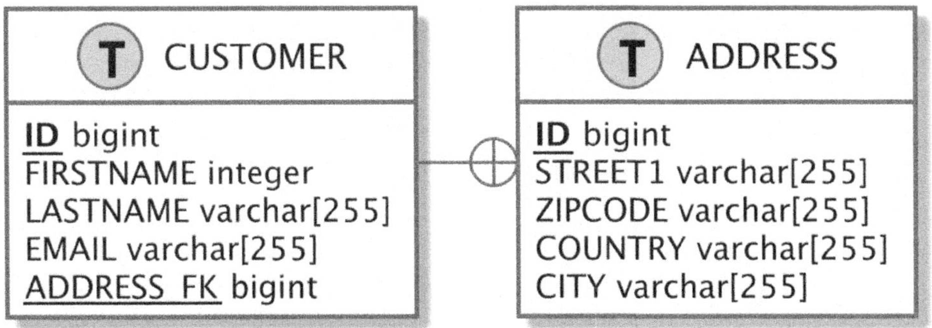

Figure 37. CUSTOMER and ADDRESS tables

For better readability, the fragments of code used in the upcoming sections assume that the `em` attribute is of type `EntityManager`. As for the variable `tx`, it is of type `EntityTransaction`.

5.2.1. Persisting an Entity

Persisting an entity means inserting data into the database when the data doesn't already exist. To do so, it's necessary to create a new entity instance using the `new` operator, set the values of the attributes, bind one entity to another when there are associations (`customer.setAddress(address)`), and finally call the `EntityManager.persist()` method as shown in the JUnit test case in Listing 96.

Listing 96. Persisting a Customer with an Address

```
Customer customer = new Customer("Anthony", "Balla", "aballa@mail.com");
Address address = new Address("Ritherdon Rd", "London", "8QE", "UK");
customer.setAddress(address);

// Persists the object
tx.begin();
em.persist(customer);
em.persist(address);
tx.commit();

assertNotNull(customer.getId());
assertNotNull(address.getId());
```

In Listing 96, `customer` and `address` are just two objects that reside in the JVM memory. Both become managed entities when the entity manager (variable `em`) takes them into account by persisting them (`em.persist()`). At this time, both objects become eligible for insertion in the database. When the transaction is committed, the data is flushed to the database, an address row is inserted into the `ADDRESS` table, and a customer row is inserted into the `CUSTOMER` table. As the `Customer` is the owner of the relationship, its table holds the foreign key to `ADDRESS`. The `assertNotNull` expressions check that both entities have received a generated identifier (thanks to the persistence provider and the `@Id` and `@GeneratedValue` annotations).

Note the ordering of the `persist()` methods: a customer is persisted and then an address. If it were the other way round, the result would be the same. Earlier, the entity manager was described as a first-level cache. Until the transaction is committed, the data stays in memory and there is no access to the database. The entity manager caches data and, when the transaction is committed, flushes the data in the order that the underlying database is expecting (respecting integrity constraints). Because of the foreign key in the `CUSTOMER` table, the `insert` statement for `ADDRESS` will be executed first, followed by that for `CUSTOMER`.

Most of the entities in this chapter do not implement the `Serializable` interface. That's because entities don't have to be in order to get persisted in the database. They are passed by reference from one method to the other, and, when they have to be persisted, the `EntityManager.persist()` method is invoked. But, if you need to pass entities by value (remote invocation, external container etc.), they must implement the `java.io.Serializable` marker (no method) interface. It indicates to the compiler that it must enforce all fields on the entity class to be serialisable, so that any instance can be serialised to a byte stream and passed using *Remote Method Invocation* (RMI).

5.2.2. Finding by Id

To find an entity by its identifier, you can use two different methods. The first is the `EntityManager.find()` method, which has two parameters: the entity class and the unique identifier (see Listing 97). If the entity is found, it is returned; if it is not found, a null value is returned.

Listing 97. Finding a Customer by Id

```
Customer customer = em.find(Customer.class, id);
if (customer != null) {
  // Process the object
}
```

The second method is `getReference()` (see Listing 98). It is very similar to the `find` operation, as it has the same parameters, but it retrieves a reference to an entity (via its primary key) but does not retrieve its data. Think of it as a proxy to an entity, not the entity itself. It is intended for situations where a managed entity instance is needed, but no data, other than potentially the entity's primary key, being accessed. With `getReference()`, the state data is fetched lazily, which means that if you don't access state before the entity is detached, the data might not be there. If the entity is not found, an `EntityNotFoundException` is thrown.

Listing 98. Finding a Customer by Reference

```
try {
  Customer customer = em.getReference(Customer.class, id);
  // Process the object
  assertNotNull(customer);
} catch (
  EntityNotFoundException ex) {
  // Entity not found
}
```

5.2.3. Removing an Entity

An entity can be removed with the `EntityManager.remove()` method. Once removed, the entity is deleted from the database, is detached from the entity manager, and cannot be synchronised with the database anymore. In terms of Java objects, the entity is still accessible until it goes out of scope and the garbage collector cleans it up. The code in Listing 99 shows how to remove an object after it has been created.

Listing 99. Creating and Removing Customer and Address Entities

```
Customer customer = new Customer("Anthony", "Balla", "aballa@mail.com");
Address address = new Address("Ritherdon Rd", "London", "8QE", "UK");
customer.setAddress(address);

// Persists the object
tx.begin();
em.persist(customer);
em.persist(address);
tx.commit();

assertNotNull(customer.getId());
assertNotNull(address.getId());

// Removes the object from the database
tx.begin();
em.remove(customer);
tx.commit();

// The objects are still available until GC
assertEquals(customer.getFirstName(), "Anthony");
assertEquals(address.getCity(), "London");

// The entities are not in the database
customer = em.find(Customer.class, customer.getId());
assertNull(customer);
address = em.find(Address.class, address.getId());
assertNotNull(address);
```

The code in Listing 99 creates an instance of `Customer` and `Address`, links them together (`customer.setAddress(address)`), and persists them. In the database, the customer row is linked to the address through a foreign key; later on, in the code, only the `Customer` is deleted. Depending on how the cascading is configured (discussed later in this chapter), the `Address` could be left with no other entity referencing it and the address row becomes an orphan.

5.2.4. Orphan Removal

For data consistency, orphans are not desirable, as they result in having rows that are not referenced by any other table in the database, without means of access. With JPA, you can inform the persistence provider to automatically remove orphans or cascade a remove operation as you'll see later. If a target entity (`Address`) is privately owned by a source (`Customer`), meaning a target must never be owned by more than one source, and that source is deleted by the application, the provider should also delete the target.

Associations that are specified as one-to-one, or one-to-many, support the use of the orphan-removal option. To include this option in the example, we just add the `orphanRemoval=true` element to the `@OneToOne` annotation (see Listing 100).

Listing 100. The Customer Entity Dealing with Orphan Address Removal

```
@Entity
public class Customer {

  @Id
  @GeneratedValue
  private Long id;
  private String firstName;
  private String lastName;
  private String email;
  @OneToOne(orphanRemoval = true)
  @JoinColumn(name = "address_fk")
  private Address address;

  // Constructors, getters, setters
}
```

With this mapping, the code in Listing 101 will automatically remove the `Address` entity when the customer is removed, or when the relationship is broken (by setting the `address` attribute to null, or by removing the child entity from the collection in a one-to-many case). The remove operation is applied at the time of the flush operation (transaction committed).

Listing 101. Removing Only the Customer Entity

```
Customer customer = new Customer("Anthony", "Balla", "tballa@mail.com");
Address address = new Address("Ritherdon Rd", "London", "8QE", "UK");
customer.setAddress(address);

// Persists the object
tx.begin();
em.persist(customer);
em.persist(address);
tx.commit();

assertNotNull(customer.getId());
assertNotNull(address.getId());

// Removes only the customer entity from the database
tx.begin();
em.remove(customer);
tx.commit();

// Customer is not in the database, nor address
customer = em.find(Customer.class, customer.getId());
assertNull(customer);
address = em.find(Address.class, address.getId());
assertNull(address);
```

5.2.5. Synchronising with the Database

Up to now, the synchronisation with the database has been done at commit time. The entity manager is a first-level cache, waiting for the transaction to be committed in order to flush the data to the database, but what happens when a customer and an address need to be inserted?

```
tx.begin();
em.persist(customer);
em.persist(address);
tx.commit();
```

All pending changes require an SQL statement; here, two `insert` statements are produced and made permanent only when the database transaction commits. For most applications, this automatic data synchronisation is sufficient. The database is synchronised with the entities in the persistence context, but data can be explicitly flushed (`flush`) to the database, or entities refreshed with data from the database (`refresh`).

If the data is flushed to the database at one point, and if, later in the code, the application calls the `rollback()` method, the flushed data will be taken out of the database.

5.2.6. Flushing an Entity

With the `EntityManager.flush()` method, the persistence provider can be explicitly forced to flush the data to the database but it won't commit the transaction. This allows a developer to manually trigger the same process used by the entity manager internally to flush the persistence context.

Listing 102. Flushing the Customer Entity to the Database

```
Customer customer = new Customer("Anthony", "Balla", "aballa@mail.com");
Address address = new Address("Ritherdon Rd", "London", "8QE", "UK");
customer.setAddress(address);

assertThrows(IllegalStateException.class, () -> {
  tx.begin();
  em.persist(customer);
  em.flush();
  em.persist(address);
  tx.commit();
});
```

Two interesting things happen in Listing 102. The first is that `em.flush()` will not wait for the transaction to commit and will force the provider to flush the persistence context. An insert statement will be generated and executed at the flush. The second is that this code will not work because of the integrity constraint. Without an explicit flush, the entity manager caches all changes and orders and executes them in a coherent way for the database. With an explicit flush, the insert statement to `CUSTOMER` will be executed, but the state of the `Address` entity is not consistent. That's because the `Address` entity is not persisted yet, therefore, it doesn't have an id (the id is set to null) but all the other attributes are set (street, city etc.). That's why we get an `IllegalStateException`: the `Customer` entity has an `Address` with set values except for the identifier. That will lead the transaction to roll back. Data that has been flushed will also get rolled back. Explicit flushes should be carefully used and only when needed.

5.2.7. Refreshing an Entity

The `refresh()` method is used for data synchronisation in the opposite direction of the flush, meaning it overwrites the current state of a managed entity with the data present in the database. A typical case is when you use the `EntityManager.refresh()` method to undo changes that have been made to the entity in memory only. The test case snippet in Listing 103 finds a `Customer` by Id, changes its first name, and undoes this change using the `refresh()` method.

Listing 103. Refreshing the Customer Entity from the Database

```
Customer customer = em.find(Customer.class, id);
assertEquals("Anthony", customer.getFirstName());

customer.setFirstName("William");
assertEquals("William", customer.getFirstName());

// Refreshes the customer entity
em.refresh(customer);
assertEquals("Anthony", customer.getFirstName());
```

5.2.8. Content of the Persistence Context

The persistence context holds the managed entities. With the `EntityManager` interface, you can check whether an entity is being managed, detach it, or clear all entities from the persistence context.

Contains

Entities are either managed or not by the entity manager. The `EntityManager.contains()` method returns a `Boolean` and allows you to check whether or not a particular entity instance is currently managed by the entity manager within the current persistence context. In the test case in Listing 104, a `Customer` is persisted, and you can immediately check whether the entity is managed (`em.contains(customer)`). The answer is true. Afterwards, the `remove()` method is called, and the entity is removed from the database and from the persistence context (`em.contains(customer)` returns `false`).

Listing 104. Test Case for Whether the Customer Entity Is in the Persistence Context

```
Customer customer = new Customer("Anthony", "Balla", "aballa@mail.com");

assertFalse(em.contains(customer));

// Persists the object
tx.begin();
em.persist(customer);
tx.commit();

assertTrue(em.contains(customer));

// Removes the object
tx.begin();
em.remove(customer);
tx.commit();

assertFalse(em.contains(customer));
```

Clear and Detach

The `clear()` method is straightforward: it empties the persistence context, causing all managed entities to become detached (check the "Entity Life Cycle" introduced in Chapter 3, more on that in Chapter 7). The `detach(Object entity)` method removes the given entity from the persistence context. Changes made to the entity will not be synchronised to the database after such an eviction has taken place. Listing 105 creates an entity, checks that it is managed, detaches it from the persistence context, and checks that it is detached.

Listing 105. Checking Whether the Customer Entity Is in the Persistence Context

```
Customer customer = new Customer("Anthony", "Balla", "aballa@mail.com");

// Persists the object
tx.begin();
em.persist(customer);
tx.commit();

assertTrue(em.contains(customer));

// Detaches the entity
em.detach(customer);

assertFalse(em.contains(customer));
```

5.2.9. Merging an Entity

A detached entity is no longer associated with a persistence context. If you want to manage it, you need to reattach it (i.e. merge it). Let’s take the example of an entity that needs to be displayed on a web page. The entity is first loaded from the database into the persistent layer (it is managed), it is returned from an invocation of a transactional bean (it is detached because the transaction context ends), the presentation layer displays it (it is still detached), and then it returns to be updated to the database. However, at that moment, the entity is detached and needs to be attached again, in order to synchronise its state with the database. This reattachment happens through the `em.merge()` method.

Listing 106 simulates this case by clearing the persistence context (`em.clear()`), which detaches the entity.

Listing 106. Clearing the Persistence Context and Merging an Entity

```
Customer customer = new Customer("Anthony", "Balla", "aballa@mail.com");

// Persists the object
tx.begin();
em.persist(customer);
tx.commit();
assertTrue(em.contains(customer));

// Clears the Persistence Context
em.clear();
assertFalse(em.contains(customer));

// Re-attaches the entity and updates name
customer.setFirstName("William");
tx.begin();
customer = em.merge(customer);
tx.commit();
assertTrue(em.contains(customer));

// Clears the Persistence Context
em.clear();
assertFalse(em.contains(customer));

// Checks the name has been updated
customer = em.find(Customer.class, customer.getId());
assertEquals(customer.getFirstName(), "William");
assertTrue(em.contains(customer));
```

The code in Listing 106 creates and persists a customer. The call to `em.clear()` forces the detachment of the customer entity, but detached entities continue to live outside the persistence context in which they were located, and their state is no longer guaranteed to be synchronised with the database state. That's what happens with `customer.setFirstName("William")`. This is executed on a detached entity, and the data is not updated in the database. To synchronise this change with the database, you need to reattach the entity (i.e. merge it) with `em.merge(customer)` inside a transaction.

5.2.10. Updating an Entity

Updating an entity is simple, yet at the same time it can be confusing to understand. As you've just seen, you can use `EntityManager.merge()` to attach an entity and synchronise its state with the database. But, if an entity is currently managed, changes to it will be reflected in the database automatically (after the transaction is committed). If not, you will need to explicitly call `merge()`.

Listing 107 demonstrates persisting a customer with a first name set to `Anthony`. When you call the `em.persist()` method, the entity is managed, so any changes made to the entity will be synchronised with the database. When you call the `setFirstName()` method , the entity changes its state. The entity manager caches any entity action starting at `tx.begin()` and synchronises it when committed.

Listing 107. Updating the Customer's First Name

```
Customer customer = new Customer("Anthony", "Balla", "aballa@mail.com");

// Persists the object
tx.begin();
em.persist(customer);

assertEquals(customer.getFirstName(), "Anthony");

// Updates name while managed
customer.setFirstName("William");
assertEquals(customer.getFirstName(), "William");

tx.commit();

customer = em.find(Customer.class, customer.getId());
assertEquals(customer.getFirstName(), "William");
```

5.2.11. Cascading Events

By default, every entity manager operation applies only to the entity supplied as an argument to the operation. But sometimes, when an operation is carried out on an entity, you want to propagate the operation on the entity's associations. This is known as *cascading an event*. The examples so far have relied on default cascade behaviour and not customised behaviour. In Listing 108, to create a customer, you instantiate a `Customer` and an `Address` entity, link them together (`customer.setAddress(address)`), and then persist the two.

Listing 108. Persisting without Cascading a Persist Event to Address

```
Customer customer = new Customer("Anthony", "Balla", "aballa@mail.com");
Address address = new Address("Ritherdon Rd", "London", "8QE", "UK");
customer.setAddress(address);

// Persists the object
tx.begin();
em.persist(customer);
em.persist(address);
tx.commit();

assertNotNull(customer.getId());
assertNotNull(address.getId());
```

Because there's a relationship between `Customer` and `Address`, you could cascade the `persist` action from the customer to the address. That would mean that a call to `em.persist(customer)` would cascade the `persist` event to the `Address` entity if it allows this type of event to be propagated. You could then shrink the code and do away with the `em.persist(address)` as shown in Listing 109.

Listing 109. Cascading a Persist Event to Address

```
Customer customer = new Customer("Anthony", "Balla", "aballa@mail.com");
Address address = new Address("Ritherdon Rd", "London", "8QE", "UK");
customer.setAddress(address);

// Persists the object
tx.begin();
em.persist(customer);
tx.commit();

assertNotNull(customer.getId());
assertNotNull(address.getId());
```

Without cascading, the customer would get persisted but not the address. Cascading an event is possible if the mapping of the relationship is modified. The annotations `@OneToOne`, `@OneToMany`, `@ManyToOne`, and `@ManyToMany` have a `cascade` attribute that takes an array of events to be cascaded. To allow the cascading of the `persist`, you must modify the mapping of the `Customer` entity (see Listing 110) and add a `cascade` attribute with a `PERSIST` event (as well as a `REMOVE` event which is commonly used to perform delete cascades).

Listing 110. Customer Entity Cascading Persist and Remove Events

```
@Entity
public class Customer {

  @Id
  @GeneratedValue
  private Long id;
  private String firstName;
  private String lastName;
  private String email;
  @OneToOne(fetch = LAZY, cascade = {PERSIST, REMOVE})
  @JoinColumn(name = "address_fk")
  private Address address;

  // Constructors, getters, setters
}
```

You can choose from several events to cascade to a target association (Table 10 lists these events) and you can even cascade them all using the `CascadeType.ALL` type.

Table 10. Possible Events to Be Cascaded

Property	Description
`PERSIST`	Cascades persist operations to the target of the association
`REMOVE`	Cascades remove operations to the target of the association
`MERGE`	Cascades merge operations to the target of the association

Property	Description
`REFRESH`	Cascades refresh operations to the target of the association
`DETACH`	Cascades detach operations to the target of the association
`ALL`	Declares that all the previous operations should be cascaded

But remember that, by default, no event is cascaded from the parent to the child entities.

[53] DAO https://en.wikipedia.org/wiki/Data_access_object

Chapter 6. Querying Entities

The relational database world relies on *Structured Query Language*, or SQL. This programming language is designed for managing relational data (retrieval, insertion, updating and deletion), and its syntax is table oriented. You can select columns from tables made of rows, join tables together, combine the results of two SQL queries through unions, and so on. There are no objects here, only rows, columns, and tables. In the Java world, where we manipulate objects, a language made for tables (SQL) has to be tweaked to suit a language made of objects (Java). This is where Java Persistence Query Language comes into play.

JPQL (*Java Persistence Query Language*) is the language defined in JPA to query entities stored in a relational database. JPQL syntax resembles SQL but operates against entity objects rather than directly working with database tables. JPQL does not see the underlying database structure or deal with tables or columns but rather objects and attributes. And, for that, it uses the dot (`.`) notation that Java developers are familiar with.

The code in this chapter can be found at https://github.com/agoncal/agoncal-fascicle-jpa/tree/2.2/querying

6.1. Java Persistence Query Language

You just saw how to manipulate entities individually with the `EntityManager` API. You know how to find an entity by Id, persist it, remove it, and so on. But finding an entity by Id is quite limiting, as you only retrieve a single entity using its unique identifier. In practice, you may need to retrieve an entity by criteria other than the Id (by name, ISBN etc.) or retrieve a set of entities based on different criteria (e.g. all customers living in the United States). This possibility is inherent to relational databases, and JPA has a language that allows this interaction: *Java Persistence Query Language* (JPQL).

JPQL is used to define searches for persistent entities independent of the underlying database. JPQL is a query language that takes its roots in the syntax of SQL, which is the standard language for database interrogation. But the main difference is that, in SQL, the results obtained are in the form of rows and columns (tables), whereas JPQL results will yield an entity or a collection of entities. JPQL syntax is object oriented and therefore more easily understood by developers who are familiar with object-oriented languages. Developers manage their entity domain model, not a table structure, by using the dot notation (e.g. `myClass.myAttribute`).

Under the hood, JPQL uses the mapping mechanism in order to transform a JPQL query into language comprehensible by an SQL database. The query is executed on the underlying database with SQL and JDBC calls, and then entity instances have their attributes set and are returned to the application - all in a very simple and powerful manner, using a rich query syntax.

The simplest JPQL query selects all the instances of a single entity.

```
SELECT b
FROM Book b
```

If you know SQL, this should look familiar to you. Instead of selecting from a table, JPQL selects entities, here Book. The FROM clause is also used to give an alias to the entity: b is an alias for Book. The SELECT clause of the query indicates that the result type of the query is the b entity (the Book). Executing this statement will result in a list of zero or more b (Book instances).

To restrict the result you just add a search criteria using the WHERE clause as follows:

```
SELECT b
FROM Book b
WHERE b.title = 'H2G2'
```

The alias is used to navigate across entity attributes through the dot operator. Since the Book entity has a persistent attribute named title of type String, b.title refers to the title attribute of the Book entity. Executing this statement will result in a list of zero or more Book instances that have a title equal to 'H2G2'.

The simplest select query consists of two mandatory parts: the SELECT and the FROM clause. SELECT defines the format of the query results. The FROM clause defines the entity or entities from which the results will be obtained, and the optional WHERE, ORDER BY, GROUP BY, and HAVING clauses can be used to restrict or order the result of a query. Listing 111 defines a simplified syntax of a JPQL statement.

Listing 111. Simplified JPQL Statement Syntax

```
SELECT <select clause>
FROM <from clause>
[WHERE <where clause>]
[ORDER BY <order by clause>]
[GROUP BY <group by clause>]
[HAVING <having clause>]
```

Listing 111 defines a SELECT statement but DELETE and UPDATE statements can also be used to perform delete and update operations across multiple instances of a specific entity class.

6.1.1. Select

The SELECT clause follows the path expressions syntax and results in one of the following forms: an entity, an entity attribute, a constructor expression, an aggregate function, or some sequence of these path expressions. These are the building blocks of queries and are used to navigate on entity attributes or across entity relationships (or a collection of entities) via the dot (.) navigation, using the following syntax:

```
SELECT [DISTINCT] <expression> [[AS] <identification variable>]
expression ::= { NEW | TREAT | AVG | MAX | MIN | SUM | COUNT }
```

A simple SELECT returns an entity. For example, if a Customer entity has an alias called c, SELECT c will return an entity or a list of entities.

```
SELECT c
FROM Customer AS c
```

The keyword AS being optional, the same query can be simplified as follows:

```
SELECT c
FROM Customer c
```

But a SELECT clause can also return attributes. If the Customer entity has a first name, SELECT c.firstName will return a String or a collection of Strings with the first names.

```
SELECT c.firstName
FROM Customer c
```

To retrieve the first name and the last name of a customer, you create a list containing the following two attributes:

```
SELECT c.firstName, c.lastName
FROM Customer c
```

From JPA 2.0 onwards, an attribute can be retrieved depending on a condition (using a CASE WHEN… THEN…ELSE…END expression). For example, instead of retrieving the price of a book, a statement can return a computation of the price (e.g. 50% discount) depending on the publisher (e.g. 50% discount on Apress books, 20% discount for all other books).

```
SELECT CASE b.editor WHEN 'Apress'
                     THEN b.price * 0.5
                     ELSE b.price * 0.8
       END
FROM Book b
```

If a Customer entity has a one-to-one relationship with Address, c.address refers to the address of the customer, and the result of the following query will return not a list of customers but a list of addresses:

```
SELECT c.address
FROM Customer c
```

Navigation expressions can be chained together to traverse complex entity graphs. Using this technique, path expressions such as c.address.country.code can be constructed, referring to the country code of the customer's address.

```
SELECT c.address.country.code
FROM Customer c
```

A constructor may be used in the `SELECT` expression to return an instance of a Java class initialised with the result of the query. The class doesn't have to be an entity, but the constructor must be fully qualified and match the attributes.

```
SELECT NEW org.agoncal.fascicle.jpa.querying.CustomerDTO(c.firstName, c.lastName, c
.address.country.code)
FROM Customer c
```

The result of this query is a list of `CustomerDTO` objects that have been instantiated with the `new` operator and initialised with the first name, last name, and country code of the customers.

Executing these queries will return either a single value or a collection of zero or more entities (or attributes) including duplicates. To remove the duplicates, the `DISTINCT` operator must be used. So, the query below returns all the customer first names without any duplicate.

```
SELECT DISTINCT c.firstName
FROM Customer c
```

The result of a query may be the result of an aggregate function applied to a path expression. The following aggregate functions can be used in the `SELECT` clause: `AVG`, `COUNT`, `MAX`, `MIN`, `SUM`. The results may be grouped in the `GROUP BY` clause and filtered using the `HAVING` clause.

```
SELECT COUNT(c)
FROM Customer c
```

Scalar expressions also can be used in the `SELECT` clause of a query as well as in the `WHERE` and `HAVING` clauses. These expressions can be used on numeric (`ABS`, `SQRT`, `MOD`, `SIZE`, `INDEX`), String (`CONCAT`, `SUBSTRING`, `TRIM`, `LOWER`, `UPPER`, `LENGTH`, `LOCATE`), and date-time (`CURRENT_DATE`, `CURRENT_TIME`, `CURRENT_TIMESTAMP`) values.

6.1.2. From

The `FROM` clause of a query defines entities by declaring identification variables. An *identification variable*, or *alias*, is an identifier that can be used in the other clauses (`SELECT`, `WHERE` etc.) to identify a specific entity. The syntax of the `FROM` clause consists of an entity and an alias. In the following example, `Customer` is the entity and `c` the identification variable:

```
SELECT c
FROM Customer c
```

6.1.3. Where

The `WHERE` clause of a query consists of a conditional expression used to restrict the result of a `SELECT`, `UPDATE`, or `DELETE` statement. The `WHERE` clause can be a simple expression, or a set of conditional expressions used to filter the query.

The simplest way to restrict the result of a query is to use the attribute of an entity. For example, the following query selects all customers named `'Vincent'`:

```
SELECT c
FROM Customer c
WHERE c.firstName = 'Vincent'
```

You can further restrict queries by using the logical operators `AND` and `OR`. The following example uses `AND` to select all customers named `'Vincent'`, living in `'France'`:

```
SELECT c
FROM Customer c
WHERE c.firstName = 'Vincent' AND c.address.country.code = 'AU'
```

The `WHERE` clause also uses comparison operators: `=`, `>`, `>=`, `<`, `<=`, `<>`, `[NOT] BETWEEN`, `[NOT] LIKE`, `[NOT] IN`, `IS [NOT] NULL`, `IS [NOT] EMPTY`, `[NOT] MEMBER [OF]`. The following shows an example using two of these operators:

```
SELECT c
FROM Customer c
WHERE c.age > 18

SELECT c
FROM Customer c
WHERE c.age NOT BETWEEN 40 AND 50

SELECT c
FROM Customer c
WHERE c.address.country.code IN ('UK', 'FR')
```

The `LIKE` expression consists of a `String` and optional escape characters that define the match conditions: the underscore (`_`) for single-character wildcards and the percent sign (`%`) for multi-character wildcards.

```
SELECT c
FROM Customer c
WHERE c.email LIKE '%mail.com'
```

Binding Parameters

Up to now, the WHERE clauses shown here have only used fixed values. In an application, queries frequently depend on parameters. JPQL supports two types of parameter-binding syntax, allowing dynamic changes to the restriction clause of a query: positional and named parameters.

Positional parameters are designated by a question mark (?) followed by an integer (e.g. ?1). When the query is executed, the parameter numbers that should be replaced need to be specified.

```
SELECT c
FROM Customer c
WHERE c.firstName = ?1 AND c.address.country = ?2
```

Named parameters can also be used and are designated by a String identifier that is prefixed by the colon (:) symbol. When the query is executed, the parameter names that should be replaced need to be specified.

```
SELECT c
FROM Customer c
WHERE c.firstName = :fname AND c.address.country = :country
```

In the "Queries" section later in this chapter, you will see how an application binds parameters.

Subqueries

A subquery is a SELECT query that is embedded within a conditional expression of a WHERE or HAVING clause. The results of the subquery are evaluated and interpreted in the conditional expression of the main query. To retrieve the youngest customers from the database, a subquery with a MIN(age) is first executed and its result is evaluated in the main query.

```
SELECT c
FROM Customer c
WHERE c.age = (
  SELECT MIN(cust.age) FROM Customer cust
)
```

6.1.4. Order By

The ORDER BY clause allows the entities or values that are returned by a SELECT query to be ordered. The ordering applies to the entity attribute specified in this clause followed by the ASC or DESC keyword. The keyword ASC specifies that ascending ordering should be used; DESC, the inverse, specifies that descending ordering should be used. Ascending is the default and can be omitted.

```
SELECT c
FROM Customer c
WHERE c.age > 18
ORDER BY c.age DESC
```

Multiple expressions may also be used to refine the sort order.

```
SELECT c
FROM Customer c
WHERE c.age > 18
ORDER BY c.age DESC, c.address.country.code ASC
```

6.1.5. Group By and Having

The `GROUP BY` construct enables the aggregation of result values according to a set of properties. The entities are divided into groups based on the values of the entity field specified in the `GROUP BY` clause. To group customers by country code and count them, use the following query:

```
SELECT c.address.country.code, COUNT(c)
FROM Customer c
GROUP BY c.address.country.code
```

`GROUP BY` defines the grouping expressions (`c.address.country.code`) over which the results will be aggregated and counted (`count(c)`). Note that expressions that appear in the `GROUP BY` clause must also appear in the `SELECT` clause.

The `HAVING` clause defines an applicable filter after the query results have been grouped, similar to a secondary `WHERE` clause, filtering the result of the `GROUP BY`. So, if we take the previous query and add a `HAVING` clause, we get the total amount of customers in each country other than the UK.

```
SELECT c.address.country.code, COUNT(c)
FROM Customer c
GROUP BY c.address.country.code
HAVING c.address.country.code <> 'UK'
```

`GROUP BY` and `HAVING` can only be used within a `SELECT` clause (not a `DELETE` or an `UPDATE`).

6.1.6. Bulk Delete

You know how to remove an entity with the `EntityManager.remove()` method and query a database to retrieve a list of entities that correspond to certain criteria. To remove a list of entities, you can execute a query, iterate through it, and remove each entity individually. Although this is a valid algorithm, it has an impact in terms of performance (too many database calls). There is a better way to do it: bulk deletes.

JPQL performs bulk delete operations across multiple instances of a specific entity class. These are used to delete a large number of entities in a single operation. Note that entities in the first level cache are not affected by the DELETE statement. They will stay in the cache while their database record is deleted.

The DELETE statement looks like the SELECT statement, as it can have a restricting WHERE clause and use parameters. As a result, the number of entity instances affected by the operation is returned. The syntax of the DELETE statement is:

```
DELETE FROM <entity name> [[AS] <identification variable>]
[WHERE <where clause>]
```

As an example, to delete all customers younger than 18, you can use a bulk removal via a DELETE statement.

```
DELETE FROM Customer c
WHERE c.age < 18
```

6.1.7. Bulk Update

Bulk updates of entities are accomplished with the UPDATE statement, setting one or more attributes of the entity subject to conditions in the WHERE clause. Like the DELETE statement we just saw, entities in the first level cache are not affected by a bulk update. They will stay in the cache while their database record is updated.

The UPDATE statement syntax is:

```
UPDATE <entity name> [[AS] <identification variable>]
SET <update statement> {, <update statement>}*
[WHERE <where clause>]
```

Rather than deleting all the young customers, their first name can be changed to "too young" with the following statement:

```
UPDATE Customer c
SET c.firstName = 'TOO YOUNG'
WHERE c.age < 18
```

6.2. Queries

You've just seen the JPQL syntax and how to describe statements using different clauses (SELECT, FROM, WHERE etc.). But how do you integrate a JPQL statement in your application? And what about SQL? Can you still use SQL statements? The answer to these questions is that you can use queries. In fact, JPA has five different types of queries that can be used in code, each for a different purpose.

- *Dynamic queries*: This is the simplest form of query, consisting of nothing more than a JPQL query string, dynamically specified at runtime.
- *Named queries*: Named queries are static and unchangeable JPQL queries.
- *Criteria API*: JPA 2.0 introduced the concept of object-oriented query API to write type safe JPQL queries.
- *Native queries*: This type of query is useful for executing a native SQL statement instead of a JPQL statement.
- *Stored procedure queries*: JPA 2.1 brought a new API to call stored procedures.

6.2.1. Query APIs

The central point for choosing from these five types of queries is the `EntityManager` interface (see Figure 38), which has several factory methods returning either a `Query`, a `TypedQuery`, or a `StoredProcedureQuery` interface (as shown in Figure 38, both `TypedQuery` and `StoredProcedureQuery` extend `Query`). The `Query` interface is used in cases when the result type is `Object`, and `TypedQuery` is used when a typed result is preferred. `StoredProcedureQuery` is used to control stored procedure query execution.

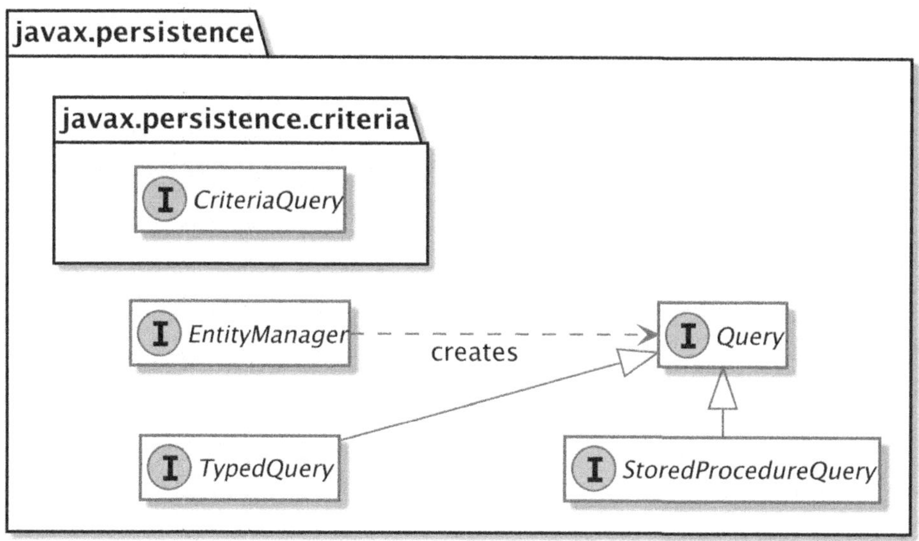

Figure 38. Different query interfaces

Query API

When you obtain an implementation of the `Query`, `TypedQuery`, or `StoredProcedureQuery` interface through one of the factory methods in the `EntityManager` interface, a rich API controls it. The `Query` API, shown in Listing 112, is used for dynamic queries and named queries using JPQL, and native queries in SQL. The `Query` API also supports parameter binding and pagination control.

The methods that are mostly used in this API are ones that execute the query itself. To execute a `SELECT` query, you have to choose between two methods, depending on the required result.

- The `getResultList()` method executes the query and returns a list of results (entities, attributes, expressions etc.).
- The `getResultStream()` method executes the query and returns the query results as a `java.util.stream.Stream`.
- The `getSingleResult()` method executes the query and returns a single result (throws a `NonUniqueResultException` if more than one result is found).

To execute an `UPDATE` or a `DELETE` you need to use the `executeUpdate()` method. This method executes a bulk update or delete query and returns the number of entities affected by the execution of this query.

Listing 112. Query API

```
public interface Query {

  // Executes a query and returns a result
  default Stream getResultStream() {
    return getResultList().stream();
  }
  List getResultList();
  Object getSingleResult();
  int executeUpdate();
```

As you saw in the "JPQL" section earlier, a query can use parameters that are either named (e.g. `:myParam`) or positional (e.g. `?1`). The `Query` API defines several `setParameter` methods for seting parameters before executing a query.

```
// Sets parameters for the query
<T> Query setParameter(Parameter<T> param, T value);
Query setParameter(Parameter<Calendar> param, Calendar value,
                   TemporalType temporalType);
Query setParameter(Parameter<Date> param, Date value,
                   TemporalType temporalType);
Query setParameter(String name, Object value);
Query setParameter(String name, Calendar value,
                   TemporalType temporalType);
Query setParameter(String name, Date value,
                   TemporalType temporalType);
Query setParameter(int position, Object value);
Query setParameter(int position, Calendar value,
                   TemporalType temporalType);
Query setParameter(int position, Date value,
                   TemporalType temporalType);


// Gets parameters from the query
Set<Parameter<?>> getParameters();
Parameter<?> getParameter(String name);
<T> Parameter<T> getParameter(String name, Class<T> type);
Parameter<?> getParameter(int position);
<T> Parameter<T> getParameter(int position, Class<T> type);
boolean isBound(Parameter<?> param);
<T> T getParameterValue(Parameter<T> param);
Object getParameterValue(String name);
Object getParameterValue(int position);
```

When you execute a query, it can return a large number of results. Depending on the application, these can be processed together or in chunks (e.g. a web application only displays ten rows at one time). To control the pagination, the `Query` interface defines `setFirstResult()` and `setMaxResults()` methods to specify the first result to be received (numbered from zero) and the maximum number of results to be returned, relative to that point (examples below).

```
// Constrains the number of results returned by a query
Query setMaxResults(int maxResult);
int getMaxResults();
Query setFirstResult(int startPosition);
int getFirstResult();
```

The flush mode indicates how the persistence provider should handle pending changes and queries. There are two possible flush mode settings: `AUTO` and `COMMIT`. `AUTO` (the default) means that the persistence provider is responsible for ensuring that pending changes are visible to the processing of the query. `COMMIT` is when the effect of updates made to entities does not overlap with changed data in the persistence context (more on locking in Chapter 8).

Queries can be locked using the `setLockMode(LockModeType)` method. Locks are intended to provide a facility that enables the effect of repeatable reads, whether optimistically or pessimistically (more on locking in Chapter 8).

```
// Sets and gets query hints
Query setHint(String hintName, Object value);
Map<String, Object> getHints();


// Sets the flush mode type to be used for the query execution
Query setFlushMode(FlushModeType flushMode);
FlushModeType getFlushMode();


// Sets the lock mode type to be used for the query execution
Query setLockMode(LockModeType lockMode);
LockModeType getLockMode();


// Allows access to the provider-specific API
<T> T unwrap(Class<T> cls);
```

Query and TypedQuery

The `Query` API appeared in the very first version of JPA (1.0). `TypedQuery` arrived later with Java Persistence 2.0. It extends the `Query` API but adds type to it. Listing 113 shows a subset of the `TypedQuery` API. As you can see, it basically redefines all the methods of the `Query` API but adds type. So `List getResultList()` turns into `List<X> getResultList()` and so on.

Listing 113. TypedQuery API

```
public interface TypedQuery<X> extends Query {

  default Stream<X> getResultStream() {
    return getResultList().stream();
  }
  List<X> getResultList();
  X getSingleResult();

  // ...
}
```

In the following code, the JPQL query selects all the customers from the database. The result of this query is a `List` with no type. So when you invoke the `getResultList()` method, it returns a list of `Object` (that we need to cast to `Customer`).

```
Query query = em.createQuery("SELECT c FROM Customer c");
List customers = query.getResultList();

for (Object customer : customers) {
  System.out.println(((Customer) customer).getFirstName());
}
```

When you know that your query only returns a single entity, use the `getSingleResult()` method instead. It returns an `Object` (instead of a list of objects) and avoids the work of retrieving the data as a list.

```
Query query = em.createQuery("SELECT c FROM Customer c WHERE c.firstName = 'Mike'");
Customer customer = (Customer) query.getSingleResult();
```

Both queries above return a `Query` object. When you invoke the `query.getResultList()` or `query.getSingleResult()` methods, it returns untyped objects. If you want the same query to return a list of type `Customer` or one instance of type `Customer`, then you need to use the `TypedQuery` as follows:

```
TypedQuery<Customer> typedQuery = em.createQuery(
  "SELECT c FROM Customer c", Customer.class);
List<Customer> customers = typedQuery.getResultList();

for (Customer customer : customers) {
  System.out.println(customer.getFirstName());
}
```

The same happens when you want to retrieve a single customer. Thanks to the `TypedQuery`, the `getSingleResult()` returns a `Customer`, not an `Object`, therefore you don't need to cast the result.

```
TypedQuery<Customer> typedQuery = em.createQuery(
  "SELECT c FROM Customer c WHERE c.firstName = 'Mike'", Customer.class);
Customer customer = typedQuery.getSingleResult();
```

JPA 2.2 brought support for `java.util.stream`. And, in fact, the method `getResultStream()` is a shortcut for `getResultList().stream()`. So now, you can use Streams with JPA just as you would in Java code:

```
TypedQuery<Customer> typedQuery = em.createQuery(
  "SELECT c FROM Customer c", Customer.class);
Stream<Customer> customers = typedQuery.getResultStream();

customers.forEach(c -> System.out.println(c.getFirstName()));
```

6.2.2. Dynamic Queries

Dynamic queries are defined on the fly as needed by the application. To create a dynamic query, we use the `EntityManager.createQuery()` method, which takes a `String` as a parameter that represents a JPQL query. It's called *dynamic* because the query string can be dynamically created by the application, which can then specify a complex query at runtime not known ahead-of-time. String concatenation can be used to construct the query dynamically, depending on the criteria. The following query retrieves customers named `'Mike'` depending on certain criteria. That's why the query cannot be predicted: if the boolean is true, the query will have a `WHERE` clause, if it's false, it won't.

```
String jpqlQuery = "SELECT c FROM Customer c";
if (someCriteria)
  jpqlQuery += " WHERE c.firstName = 'Mike'";

TypedQuery<Customer> typedQuery = em.createQuery(jpqlQuery, Customer.class);
List<Customer> customers = typedQuery.getResultList();
```

When concatenating strings, you can end-up passing an unchecked value to the database. This can raise security concerns because it can be easily hacked by SQL injection. You have to avoid the above code and use parameter binding instead. For that, there are two possible choices for passing a parameter: using names or positions. In the following example, I use a named parameter called `:fname` (note the : symbol) in the query and bind it with the `setParameter()` method:

```
TypedQuery<Customer> typedQuery = em.createQuery(
  "SELECT c FROM Customer c WHERE c.firstName = :fname", Customer.class);
typedQuery.setParameter("fname", "Mike");
List<Customer> customers = typedQuery.getResultList();
```

Note that the parameter name `fname` does not include the colon used in the query. You can also use positional parameters. It is *1-based* meaning that the first parameter is number *1*, the second parameter number *2*, and so on. The equivalent code would look like the following:

```
TypedQuery<Customer> typedQuery = em.createQuery(
  "SELECT c FROM Customer c WHERE c.firstName = ?1", Customer.class);
typedQuery.setParameter(1, "Mike");
List<Customer> customers = typedQuery.getResultList();
```

If you need to use pagination to display the list of customers in chunks of five, you can use the `setMaxResults()` method as follows:

```
TypedQuery<Customer> typedQuery = em.createQuery(
  "SELECT c FROM Customer c ORDER BY c.age", Customer.class);
typedQuery.setMaxResults(5);
List<Customer> customers = typedQuery.getResultList();
```

And if you need to set the position of the first result to retrieve, then you can use the setFirstResult() method:

```
TypedQuery<Customer> typedQuery = em.createQuery(
  "SELECT c FROM Customer c ORDER BY c.age", Customer.class);
typedQuery.setFirstResult(3);
typedQuery.setMaxResults(10);
List<Customer> customers = typedQuery.getResultList();
```

An issue to consider with dynamic queries is the cost of translating the JPQL string into an SQL statement at runtime. Because the query is dynamically created and cannot be predicted, the persistence provider has to parse the JPQL string, get the ORM metadata, and generate the equivalent SQL. The performance cost of processing each of these dynamic queries can be an issue. If you have static queries that are unchangeable and want to avoid this overhead, then you can use named queries instead.

6.2.3. Named Queries

Named queries are different from dynamic queries in that they are static and unchangeable. In addition to their static nature, which does not allow the flexibility of a dynamic query, named queries can be more efficient to execute because the persistence provider can translate the JPQL string to SQL once the application starts, rather than every time the query is executed.

Named queries are static queries expressed in metadata inside either a @NamedQuery annotation or the XML equivalent. To define these reusable queries, annotate an entity with the @NamedQuery annotation, which takes two elements: the name of the query and its content. So, let's change the Customer entity and statically define three queries using annotations (see Listing 114).

Listing 114. The Customer Entity Defining Named Queries

```
@Entity
@NamedQuery(name = "findAll", query = "SELECT c FROM Customer c")
@NamedQuery(name = "findVincent", query = "SELECT c FROM Customer c WHERE c.firstName
= 'Vincent'")
@NamedQuery(name = "findWithParam", query = "SELECT c FROM Customer c WHERE
c.firstName = :fname")
public class Customer {

  @Id
  @GeneratedValue
  private Long id;
  private String firstName;
  private String lastName;
  private String email;
  private Integer age;
  @OneToOne(cascade = {PERSIST})
  private Address address;

  // Constructors, getters, setters
}
```

The first query, called `findAll`, selects all customers from the database with no restriction (no `WHERE` clause). The `findVincent` named query selects all customers whose first name is `Vincent`. The `findWithParam` query uses the parameter `:fname` to restrict customers by their first name.

The way to execute these named queries resembles the way dynamic queries are used. The `EntityManager.createNamedQuery()` method is invoked and passed to the query name defined by the annotations. This method returns a `Query` or a `TypedQuery` that can be used to set parameters, the max results, fetch modes, and so on. To execute the `findAll` query, write the following code:

```
Query query = em.createNamedQuery("findAll");
List customers = query.getResultList();
```

Again, if you need to type the query to return a list of `Customer` objects, you'll need to use the `TypedQuery` as follows:

```
TypedQuery<Customer> typedQuery = em.createNamedQuery("findAll", Customer.class);
List<Customer> customers = typedQuery.getResultList();
```

The following is a fragment of code calling the `findWithParam` named query, passing the parameter `:fname`, and setting the maximum result to 2:

```
TypedQuery<Customer> typedQuery = em.createNamedQuery("findWithParam", Customer.class
);
typedQuery.setParameter("fname", "Vincent");
typedQuery.setMaxResults(2);
```

Because most of the methods of the Query API return a Query object, you can use the following elegant shortcut to write queries. You call methods one after the other (`setParameter().setMaxResults()` etc.).

```
TypedQuery<Customer> typedQuery = em
  .createNamedQuery("findWithParam", Customer.class)
  .setParameter("fname", "Vincent")
  .setMaxResults(2);
```

Named queries are useful for organising query definitions and powerful for improving application performance. The organisation comes from the fact that the named queries are defined statically on entities and are typically placed on the entity class that directly corresponds to the query result (here the `findAll` query returns customers, so it should be defined in the `Customer` entity).

There is a restriction in that the name of the query is scoped to the persistence unit and must be unique within that scope, meaning that only one `findAll` method can exist. A `findAll` query for customers and a `findAll` query for addresses should be named differently. A common practice is to prefix the query name with the entity name. For example, the `findAll` query for the `Customer` entity would be named `Customer.findAll`.

Another problem is that the name of the query, which is a String, is manipulated, and, if you make a typo or refactor your code, you may get some exceptions indicating that the query doesn't exist. To limit the risks, you can replace the name of a query with a constant. Listing 115 shows how to refactor the `Customer` entity.

Listing 115. The Customer Entity Defining a Named Query with a Constant

```
@Entity
@NamedQuery(name = Customer.FIND_ALL, query="SELECT c FROM Customer c"),
public class Customer {

  public static final String FIND_ALL = "Customer.findAll";

  // Attributes, constructors, getters, setters
}
```

The `FIND_ALL` constant identifies the `findAll` query unambiguously by prefixing the name of the query with the name of the entity. The same constant is then used in the `@NamedQuery` annotation, and you can use this constant to execute the query as follows:

```
TypedQuery<Customer> typedQuery = em.createNamedQuery(Customer.FIND_ALL, Customer
.class);
```

6.2.4. Criteria API (or Object-oriented Queries)

Up to now, I've been using Strings to write JPQL (dynamic or named queries) statements. This has the advantage of writing a database query concisely but the inconvenience of being error prone and difficult for an external framework to manipulate: it is a String, you end up concatenating Strings and so many typos can be made. For example, you could have typos on JPQL keywords (`SLECT` instead of `SELECT`), class names (`Custmer` instead of `Customer`), or attributes (`firstname` instead of `firstName`). You can also write a syntactically incorrect statement (`SELECT c WHERE c.firstName = 'John' FROM Customer`). Any of these mistakes will be discovered at runtime, and it may sometimes be difficult to find where the bug comes from.

From JPA 2.0 on, there has been a new API, called *Criteria API* and it is defined in the package `javax.persistence.criteria`. It allows you to write any query in an object-oriented and syntactically correct way. Most of the mistakes that a developer could make writing a statement are found at compile time, not at runtime. The idea is that, all the JPQL keywords (`SELECT`, `UPDATE`, `DELETE`, `WHERE`, `LIKE`, `GROUP BY` etc.) are defined in this API. In other words, the Criteria API supports everything JPQL can do but with an object-based syntax. Let's have a first look at a simple JPQL query that retrieves all the customers:

```
SELECT c FROM Customer c
```

This JPQL statement is rewritten in Listing 116 in an object-oriented way using the Criteria API.

Listing 116. A Criteria Query Selecting All the Customers

```
CriteriaBuilder builder = em.getCriteriaBuilder();
CriteriaQuery<Customer> criteriaQuery = builder.createQuery(Customer.class);
Root<Customer> customer = criteriaQuery.from(Customer.class);
criteriaQuery.select(customer);

TypedQuery<Customer> query = em.createQuery(criteriaQuery);
List<Customer> customers = query.getResultList();
```

If we want a query that retrieves all the customers named `'Vincent'`, we add a `WHERE` clause on the first name:

```
SELECT c FROM Customer c WHERE c.firstName = 'Vincent'
```

The JPQL statement with a `WHERE` clause rewritten in an object-oriented way using the Criteria API would look like Listing 117.

Listing 117. A Criteria Query Selecting All the Customers with First Name

```
CriteriaBuilder builder = em.getCriteriaBuilder();
CriteriaQuery<Customer> criteriaQuery = builder.createQuery(Customer.class);
Root<Customer> c = criteriaQuery.from(Customer.class);
criteriaQuery.select(c).where(builder.equal(c.get("firstName"), "Vincent"));

TypedQuery<Customer> query = em.createQuery(criteriaQuery);
List<Customer> customers = query.getResultList();
String param = "Vincent";

CriteriaBuilder builder = em.getCriteriaBuilder();
CriteriaQuery<Customer> criteriaQuery = builder.createQuery(Customer.class);
Root<Customer> c = criteriaQuery.from(Customer.class);
criteriaQuery.select(c).where(builder.equal(c.get("firstName"), param));

TypedQuery<Customer> query = em.createQuery(criteriaQuery);
List<Customer> customers = query.getResultList();
```

Without going into too much detail, you can see that the `SELECT`, `FROM`, and `WHERE` keywords have an API representation through the methods `select()`, `from()`, and `where()`. And this rule applies for every JPQL keyword. Criteria queries are constructed through the `CriteriaBuilder` interface that is obtained by the `EntityManager` (the `em` attribute in Listing 117 and Listing 118). It contains methods to construct the query definition (this interface defines keywords such as `desc()`, `asc()`, `avg()`, `sum()`, `max()`, `min()`, `count()`, `and()`, `or()`, `greaterThan()`, `lowerThan()` etc.). The other role of the `CriteriaBuilder` is to serve as the main factory of criteria queries (`CriteriaQuery`) and criteria query elements. This interface defines methods such as `select()`, `from()`, `where()`, `orderBy()`, `groupBy()`, and `having()`, which have the equivalent meaning in JPQL.

In Listing 117, the way you get the alias `c` (as in `SELECT c FROM Customer`) is through the `Root` interface (`Root<Customer> c`). Then you just have to use the `builder`, the `query`, and the `root` to write any JPQL statement you want: from the simplest (select all the entities from the database) to the most complex (joins, subqueries, case expressions, functions etc.).

Let's take another example. Listing 118 shows a query that retrieves all the customers older than 40. The `c.get("age")` gets the attribute `age` from the `Customer` entity and checks if it's greater than 40.

Listing 118. A Criteria Query Selecting All the Customers Older Than 40

```
CriteriaBuilder builder = em.getCriteriaBuilder();
CriteriaQuery<Customer> criteriaQuery = builder.createQuery(Customer.class);
Root<Customer> c = criteriaQuery.from(Customer.class);
criteriaQuery.select(c).where(builder.greaterThan(c.get("age").as(Integer.class), 40)
);

TypedQuery<Customer> query = em.createQuery(criteriaQuery);
List<Customer> customers = query.getResultList();
```

I started this section saying that the Criteria API allows you to write error-free statements. But it's not completely true yet. When you look at Listing 117 and Listing 118, you can still see some strings ("firstName" and "age") that represent the attributes of the Customer entity. So, typos can still be made. In Listing 118, we even need to cast the age into an Integer(c.get("age").as(Integer.class)) because there is no other way to discover that the age attribute is of type Integer. To solve these problems, the Criteria API comes with a static metamodel class for each entity, bringing type safety to the API.

Type Safe Criteria API

Listing 117 and Listing 118 are almost typesafe: each JPQL keyword can be represented by a method of the CriteriaBuilder and CriteriaQuery interface. The only missing part is the attributes of the entity that are string based: the way to refer to the customer's firstName attribute is by calling c.get("firstName"). The get method takes a String as a parameter. Type safe Criteria API solves this by overriding this method with a path expression from the metamodel API classes, bringing type safety.

Listing 119 shows the Customer entity with several attributes of different types (Long, String, Integer, Address).

Listing 119. A Customer Entity with Several Attributes' Types

```
@Entity
public class Customer {

  @Id
  @GeneratedValue
  private Long id;
  private String firstName;
  private String lastName;
  private String email;
  private Integer age;
  @OneToOne(cascade = {PERSIST})
  private Address address;

  // Constructors, getters, setters
}
```

To bring type safety, JPA can generate a static metamodel class for each entity. The convention is that each entity X will have a metadata class called X_ (with an underscore). So, the Customer entity will have its metamodel representation described in the Customer_ class shown in Listing 120.

Listing 120. The Customer_ Class Describing the Metamodel of Customer

```
@StaticMetamodel(Customer.class)
public class Customer_ {

  public static volatile SingularAttribute<Customer, Long> id;
  public static volatile SingularAttribute<Customer, String> firstName;
  public static volatile SingularAttribute<Customer, String> lastName;
  public static volatile SingularAttribute<Customer, String> email;
  public static volatile SingularAttribute<Customer, Integer> age;
  public static volatile SingularAttribute<Customer, Address> address;

}
```

In the static metamodel class, each attribute of the `Customer` entity is defined by a subclass of `javax.persistence.metamodel.Attribute` (`CollectionAttribute`, `ListAttribute`, `MapAttribute`, `SetAttribute`, or `SingularAttribute`). Each of these attributes uses generics and is strongly-typed (e.g. `SingularAttribute<Customer, Integer>, age`). Listing 121 shows the exact same code as Listing 118 but revisited, with the static metamodel class (the `c.get("age")` being turned into `c.get(Customer_.age)`). Another advantage of type safety is that the metamodel defines the `age` attribute as being an `Integer`, so there is no need to cast the attribute into an `Integer` using `as(Integer.class)`.

Listing 121. A Type Safe Criteria Query Selecting All the Customers Older Than 40

```
CriteriaBuilder builder = em.getCriteriaBuilder();
CriteriaQuery<Customer> criteriaQuery = builder.createQuery(Customer.class);
Root<Customer> c = criteriaQuery.from(Customer.class);
criteriaQuery.select(c).where(builder.greaterThan(c.get(Customer_.age), 40));

TypedQuery<Customer> query = em.createQuery(criteriaQuery);
List<Customer> customers = query.getResultList();
```

Again, these are just examples of what you can do with the Criteria API. It is a very rich API that is completely defined in Chapter 5 (*Metamodel API*) and Chapter 6 (*Criteria API*) of the JPA specification.[54]

The classes used in the static metamodel, such as `Attribute` or `SingularAttribute`, are standard and defined in the package `javax.persistence.metamodel`. But the generation of the static metamodel classes is implementation specific. EclipseLink uses an internal class called `CanonicalModelProcessor`. This processor can be invoked by your *Integrated Development Environment* (IDE) while you develop a Java command, an Ant task, or a Maven plugin.

6.2.5. Native Queries

JPQL has a very rich syntax that allows you to handle entities in any form and ensures portability across databases. JPA enables you to use specific features of a database by using native queries.

Native queries take a native SQL statement (SELECT, UPDATE, or DELETE) as the parameter and return a Query instance for executing that SQL statement. However, native queries are not expected to be portable across databases.

If the code is not portable, why not use JDBC calls? The main reason for using JPA native queries rather than JDBC calls is because the result of the query can be automatically converted back to entities. If you want to retrieve all the customer entities from the database using SQL, you need to use the EntityManager.createNativeQuery() method that has the SQL query and the entity class (that the result should be mapped to) as parameters.

```
Query query = em.createNativeQuery("SELECT * FROM T_CUSTOMER", Customer.class);
List<Customer> customers = query.getResultList();
```

The previous native query result is mapped to a Customer entity. But if you just need to query one column (e.g. FIRSTNAME), you can avoid the mapping. Therefore, the result will return a list of Strings.

```
Query query = em.createNativeQuery("SELECT FIRSTNAME FROM T_CUSTOMER");
List<String> firstNames = query.getResultList();
```

As you can see in the preceding code fragments, the SQL query is a String that can be dynamically created at runtime (just like JPQL dynamic queries). Like named queries, you can use annotations to define native queries (a.k.a. static SQL queries). Named native queries are defined using the @NamedNativeQuery annotation, which must be placed on any entity (see code below). Like JPQL named queries, the name of the query must be unique within the persistence unit.

```
@Entity
@Table(name = "t_customer")
@NamedNativeQuery(name = "findAll", query = "SELECT * FROM t_customer", resultClass =
Customer.class)
public class Customer {

  // ...
```

To execute this named native query, we just use the method we've seen previously: em.createNamedQuery() and the name of the native query (here findAll).

```
Query query = em.createNamedQuery("findAll", Customer.class);
List<Customer> customers = query.getResultList();
```

6.2.6. Stored Procedure Queries

So far, all of the different queries (JPQL or SQL) had the same purpose: send a query from your application to the database that will execute it and send back a result. Stored procedures are different in the sense that they are actually stored in the database itself and executed within this database.

A stored procedure is a subroutine available to applications that access a relational database. Typical usage could be extensive or complex processing that requires execution of several SQL statements or a data-intensive repetitive task. Stored procedures are usually written in a proprietary language close to SQL and are therefore not easily portable across database vendors. But storing the code inside the database, even in a nonportable way, provides many advantages, like:

- Better performance due to pre-compilation of the stored procedure as well as reutilising its execution plan,
- Keeping statistics on the code to keep it optimised,
- Reducing the amount of data passed over a network by keeping the code on the server,
- Altering the code in a central location without replicating it in several different programs,
- Stored procedures, which can be used by multiple programs written in different languages (not just Java),
- Hiding the raw data by allowing only stored procedures to gain access to the data, and
- Enhancing security controls by granting users permission to execute a stored procedure independently of underlying table permissions.

Let's take a look at a practical example: archiving old books and CDs. After a certain date, books and CDs have to be archived in a certain warehouse, meaning they have to be physically transferred from a warehouse to a reseller. Archiving books and CDs can be a time-consuming process as several tables have to be updated (Inventory, Warehouse, Book, CD, Transportation tables etc.). So, we can write a stored procedure to regroup several SQL statements and improve performance. The stored procedure `sp_archive_books` defined in Listing 122 takes an archive date and a warehouse code as parameters and updates the `T_INVENTORY` and the `T_TRANSPORT` tables.

Listing 122. Abstract of a Stored Procedure Archiving Books

```
CREATE PROCEDURE sp_archive_books @archiveDate DATE, @warehouseCode VARCHAR AS
  UPDATE T_INVENTORY
  SET Number_Of_Books_Left - 1
  WHERE Archive_Date < @archiveDate AND Warehouse_Code = @warehouseCode;

  UPDATE T_TRANSPORT
  SET Warehouse_To_Take_Books_From = @warehouseCode;
END
```

The stored procedure in Listing 122 is compiled into the database and can then be invoked through its name (`sp_archive_books`). As you can see, a stored procedure accepts data in the form of input or output parameters. Input parameters (`@archiveDate` and `@warehouseCode` in our example) are utilised in the execution of the stored procedure which, in turn, can produce an output result. This result is returned to the application through the use of a result set.

In JPA, the `StoredProcedureQuery` interface (which extends `Query`) supports stored procedures. Unlike dynamic, named, or native queries, the API only allows you to invoke a stored procedure that already exists in the database, not define it. You can invoke a stored procedure with annotations (with @NamedStoredProcedureQuery) or dynamically.

Listing 123 shows the Book entity that declares the sp_archive_books stored procedure using named query annotations. The NamedStoredProcedureQuery annotation specifies the name of the stored procedure to invoke, the types of all of the parameters (Date.class and String.class), their corresponding parameter modes (IN, OUT, INOUT, REF_CURSOR), and how result sets, if any, are to be mapped. A StoredProcedureParameter annotation needs to be provided for each parameter.

Listing 123. Entity Declaring a Named Stored Procedure

```
@Entity
@NamedStoredProcedureQuery(name = "archiveOldBooks", procedureName = "
sp_archive_books",
  parameters = {
    @StoredProcedureParameter(name = "archiveDate", mode = ParameterMode.IN, type =
LocalDate.class),
    @StoredProcedureParameter(name = "warehouse", mode = ParameterMode.IN, type =
String.class)
  })
public class Book {

  @Id
  @GeneratedValue
  private Long id;
  private String title;
  private Float price;
  private String description;
  private String isbn;

  // Constructors, getters, setters
}
```

To invoke the sp_archive_books stored procedure, you need to use the entity manager and create a named stored procedure query by passing its name (archiveOldBooks). This returns a StoredProcedureQuery on which you can set the parameters and execute it as shown in Listing 124.

Listing 124. Calling a StoredProcedureQuery

```
StoredProcedureQuery query = em.createNamedStoredProcedureQuery("archiveOldBooks");
query.setParameter("archiveDate", LocalDate.now());
query.setParameter("maxBookArchived", 1000);
query.execute();
```

If the stored procedure is not defined using metadata (@NamedStoredProcedureQuery), you can use the API to dynamically specify a stored procedure query. This means that parameters and result set information must be provided programmatically. This can be done using the registerStoredProcedureParameter method of the StoredProcedureQuery interface, as shown in Listing 125.

Listing 125. Registering and Calling a StoredProcedureQuery

```
StoredProcedureQuery query = em.createStoredProcedureQuery("sp_archive_old_books");
query.registerStoredProcedureParameter("archiveDate", LocalDate.class, ParameterMode
.IN);
query.registerStoredProcedureParameter("maxBookArchived", Integer.class,
ParameterMode.IN);

query.setParameter("archiveDate", LocalDate.now());
query.setParameter("maxBookArchived", 1000);
query.execute();
```

[54] JSR 338 https://jcp.org/en/jsr/detail?id=338

Chapter 7. Callbacks and Listeners

By now, you know most of the ins and outs of entities, so let's look at their life cycle. When an entity is instantiated (with the `new` operator), it is just seen as a regular POJO by the JVM (i.e. detached) and can be used as a regular object by the application. Then, when the entity is persisted or loaded by the entity manager, it is said to be managed. When an entity is managed, the entity manager will automatically synchronise the value of its attributes with the underlying database (e.g. if you change the value of an attribute by using a `set` method while the entity is managed, this new value will be automatically synchronized with the database). Let's discuss the entity life cycle in more detail.

The code in this chapter can be found at https://github.com/agoncal/agoncal-fascicle-jpa/tree/2.2/callbacks-listeners

7.1. Entity Life Cycle

To have a better understanding of this process, take a look at Figure 39, a UML state diagram showing the transitions between each state of an entity.

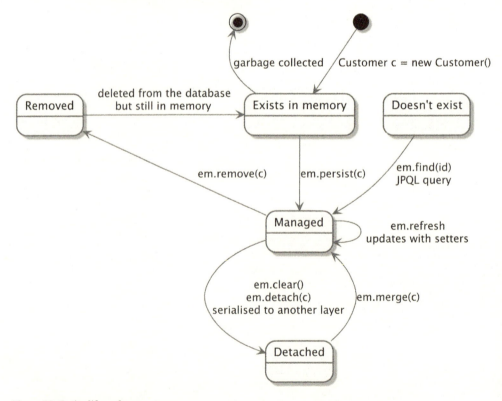

Figure 39. Entity life cycle

To illustrate the state diagram in Figure 39, let's describe the `Customer` entity life cycle. First, to create an instance of the `Customer` object, we use the `new` operator. This object exists in memory, although JPA knows nothing about it. If we do nothing with this object, it will go out of scope and will end up being garbage collected, and that will be the end of its life cycle. What we can do next is persist an instance of `Customer` with the `EntityManager.persist()` method. At that moment, the entity becomes managed, and its state will be synchronised with the database (usually when the transaction commits). During this managed state, we can update attributes using the setter methods (e.g. `customer.setFirstName()`) or refresh the content with an `EntityManager.refresh()` method. All these changes will be synchronised between the entity and the database. During this state, if we call the `EntityManager.contains(customer)` method, it will return `true` because `customer` is contained in the persistence context (i.e. managed).

Another way for an entity to be managed is when it is loaded from the database. When we use the `EntityManager.find()` method, or create a JPQL query to retrieve a list of entities, all are automatically managed, and we can start updating or removing their attributes.

In the managed state, we can call the `EntityManager.remove()` method, and the entity is deleted from the database and not managed anymore. But the Java object continues living in memory, and we can still use it until the garbage collector gets rid of it.

Now let's look at the detached state. You've seen in Chapter 5 how explicitly calling the `EntityManager.clear()` or `EntityManager.detach(customer)` methods will clear the entity from the persistence context; it becomes detached. But there is also another, more subtle, way to detach an entity: when it's serialised. In many examples in this fascicle, entities don't implement anything but, if they need to cross a network to be invoked remotely or cross layers to be displayed in a presentation tier, they need to implement the `java.io.Serializable` interface. This is not a JPA restriction but a Java restriction. When a managed entity is serialised, crosses the network, and gets deserialised, it is seen as a detached object. To reattach an entity, you need to call the `EntityManager.merge()` method.

Callback methods and listeners allow you to add your own business logic when certain life cycle events occur on an entity, or broadly whenever a life cycle event occurs on any entity.

7.2. Callbacks

The life cycle of an entity falls into four categories: persisting, updating, removing, and loading, which correspond to the database operations of inserting, updating, deleting, and selecting, respectively. Each life cycle has a "pre" and "post" event (except for loading, which only has a "post" event) that can be intercepted by the entity manager to invoke a business method. These business methods have to be annotated by one of the annotations described in Table 11. These annotations may be applied to methods of an entity class, a mapped superclass, or a callback listener class.

Table 11. Life Cycle Callback Annotations

Annotation	Description
`@PrePersist`	Marks a method to be invoked before `EntityManager.persist()` is executed.
`@PostPersist`	Marks a method to be invoked after the entity has been persisted. If the entity auto-generates its primary key (with `@GeneratedValue`), the value is available in the method.

Annotation	Description
`@PreUpdate`	Marks a method to be invoked before the entity state is updated.
`@PostUpdate`	Marks a method to be invoked after a database update operation is performed.
`@PreRemove`	Marks a method to be invoked before `EntityManager.remove()` is executed.
`@PostRemove`	Marks a method to be invoked after the entity has been removed.
`@PostLoad`	Marks a method to be invoked after an entity is loaded (with a JPQL query or an `EntityManager.find()`) or refreshed from the underlying database. There is no `@PreLoad` annotation, as it doesn't make sense to preload data on an entity that is not built yet.

Adding the callback annotations to the UML state diagram shown previously in Figure 39 results in the diagram you see in Figure 40.

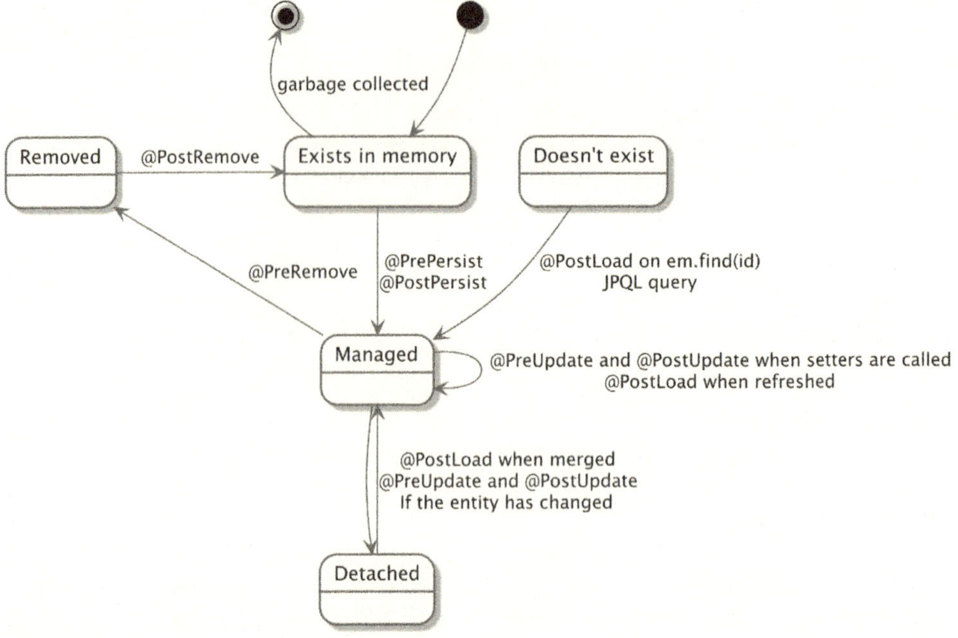

Figure 40. Entity life cycle with callback annotations

Before inserting an entity into the database, the entity manager calls the method annotated with `@PrePersist`. If the insert does not throw an exception, the entity is persisted, its identity is initialised, and the method annotated with `@PostPersist` is then invoked. This is the same behaviour for updates (`@PreUpdate`, `@PostUpdate`) and deletes (`@PreRemove`, `@PostRemove`). A method annotated with `@PostLoad` is called when an entity is loaded from the database (via an `EntityManager.find()` or a JPQL query). When the entity is detached and needs to be merged, the entity manager first has to check whether there are any differences with the database (`@PostLoad`) and, if so, update the data (`@PreUpdate`, `@PostUpdate`).

How does it look in the code? Entities can have not only attributes, constructors, getters, and setters but also business logic used to validate their state or compute some of their attributes. These can consist of normal Java methods that are invoked by other classes or callback annotations (also referred to as callback methods), as shown in Listing 126. The entity manager invokes them automatically depending on the event triggered.

Listing 126. The Customer Entity with Callback Annotations

```
@Entity
public class Customer {

  @Id
  @GeneratedValue
  private Long id;
  private String firstName;
  private String lastName;
  private String email;
  private String phoneNumber;
  private LocalDate dateOfBirth;
  @Transient
  private Integer age;
  private LocalDateTime creationDate;

  @PrePersist
  @PreUpdate
  private void validate() {
    if (firstName == null || firstName.isEmpty())
      throw new IllegalArgumentException("Invalid first name");
    if (lastName == null || lastName.isEmpty())
      throw new IllegalArgumentException("Invalid last name");
  }

  @PostLoad
  @PostPersist
  @PostUpdate
  public void calculateAge() {
    if (dateOfBirth == null) {
      age = null;
      return;
    }

    age =  Period.between(dateOfBirth, LocalDate.now()).getYears();
  }

  // Constructors, getters, setters
}
```

In Listing 126, the `Customer` entity has a method to validate its data (checks the `firstName` and `lastName` attributes). This method is annotated with `@PrePersist` and `@PreUpdate` and will be called before inserting data into or updating data in the database. If the data is not valid, a runtime exception is thrown, and the insert or update will roll back to ensure that the data inserted or updated in the database is valid.

The method `calculateAge()` calculates the age of the customer. The `age` attribute is transient and doesn't get mapped into the database. After the entity gets loaded, persisted, or updated, the `calculateAge()` method takes the date of birth of the customer, calculates the age, and sets the `age` attribute.

The following rules apply to life cycle callback methods:

- Life cycle callback methods can have public, private, protected, or package-level access but must not be static or final. Notice in Listing 126 that the `validate()` method is private.
- A life cycle callback method may be annotated with multiple life cycle event annotations (the `validateData()` method is annotated with `@PrePersist` and `@PreUpdate`). However, only one life cycle annotation of a given type may be present in an entity class (e.g. you can't have two `@PrePersist` annotations in the same entity).
- A life cycle callback method can throw unchecked (runtime) exceptions but not checked exceptions. Throwing a runtime exception will roll back the transaction if one exists.
- A life cycle callback method cannot invoke any `EntityManager` or `Query` operations.
- With inheritance, if a method is specified on the superclass, it will get invoked before the method on the child class. For example, if in Listing 126 `Customer` was inheriting from a `Person` entity, the `Person` `@PrePersist` method would be invoked before the `Customer` `@PrePersist` method.
- If event cascading is used in the relationships, the callback method will also be called in a cascaded way. For example, let's say a `Customer` has a collection of addresses, and a cascade remove is set on the relation. When you delete the customer, the `Address` `@PreRemove` method would be invoked as well as the `Customer` `@PreRemove` method.

7.3. Listeners

Callback methods in an entity work well when you have business logic that is only related to that entity. Entity listeners are used to extract the business logic to a separate class and share it between other entities. An entity listener is just a POJO on which you can define one or more life cycle callback methods. To register a listener, the entity needs to use the `@EntityListeners` annotation.

Using the customer example, let's extract the `calculateAge()` method on the `AgeCalculationListener` (see Listing 127) and the `validate()` method on `DataValidationListener` (see Listing 128).

Listing 127. A Listener Calculating the Customer's Age

```
public class AgeCalculationListener {

  @PostLoad
  @PostPersist
  @PostUpdate
  public void calculateAge(Customer customer) {
    if (customer.getDateOfBirth() == null) {
      customer.setAge(null);
      return;
    }

    customer.setAge(Period.between(customer.getDateOfBirth(), LocalDate.now())
.getYears());
  }
}
```

Listing 128. A Listener Validating the Customer's Attributes

```
public class DataValidationListener {

  @PrePersist
  @PreUpdate
  private void validate(Customer customer) {
    if (customer.getFirstName() == null || customer.getFirstName().isEmpty())
      throw new IllegalArgumentException("Invalid first name");
    if (customer.getLastName() == null || customer.getLastName().isEmpty())
      throw new IllegalArgumentException("Invalid last name");
  }
}
```

Simple rules apply to a listener class. The first is that the class must have a public no-arg constructor. Second, the signatures of the callback methods are slightly different from the ones in Listing 126. When you invoke the callback method on a listener, the method needs to have access to the entity state (e.g. the customer's first name and last name which need to be validated). The methods must have a parameter of a type that is compatible with the entity type (here `Customer`).

A callback method defined on an entity has the following signature with no parameter:

```
void <METHOD>();
```

Callback methods defined on an entity listener can have two different types of signature. If the method has to be used on several entities, it must have an `Object` argument.

```
void <METHOD>(Object anyEntity)
```

If it is only for one entity or its subclasses (when there's inheritance), the parameter can be of the entity type.

```
void <METHOD>(Customer customerOrSubclasses)
```

To designate that these two listeners are notified by the `Customer` entity life cycle, you need to use the `@EntityListeners` annotation (see Listing 129) on the entity class. This annotation can take one entity listener as a parameter, or an array of listeners. When several listeners are defined and the life cycle event occurs, the persistence provider iterates through each listener in the order in which they are listed and invokes the callback method, passing a reference of the entity to which the event applies. It will then invoke the callback methods on the entity itself (if there are any).

Listing 129. The Customer Entity Defining Two Listeners

```
@EntityListeners({DataValidationListener.class, AgeCalculationListener.class})
@Entity
public class Customer {

  @Id
  @GeneratedValue
  private Long id;
  private String firstName;
  private String lastName;
  private String email;
  private String phoneNumber;
  private LocalDate dateOfBirth;
  @Transient
  private Integer age;
  private LocalDateTime creationDate;

  // Constructors, getters, setters
}
```

The result of this code is exactly the same as that of the previous example (shown earlier in Listing 126). The `Customer` entity validates its data before an insert or an update using the `DataValidationListener.validate()` method and calculates its age with the listener's `AgeCalculationListener.calculateAge()` method.

The rules that an entity listener's methods have to follow are similar to the entity callback methods except for a few details.

- Only unchecked exceptions can be thrown. This causes the remaining listeners and callback methods to not be invoked and the transaction to be roll backed if one exists.
- In an inheritance hierarchy, if multiple entities define listeners, the listeners defined on the superclass are invoked before the listeners defined on the subclasses. If an entity doesn't want to inherit the superclass listeners, it can explicitly exclude them by using the `@ExcludeSuperclassListeners` annotation (or its XML equivalent).

Listing 129 shows a Customer entity defining two listeners, but a listener can also be defined by more than one entity. This can be useful in cases where the listener provides more general logic that many entities can benefit from. For example, you could create a debug listener that displays the name of some triggered events, as shown in Listing 130.

Listing 130. A Debug Listener Usable by Any Entity

```
public class DebugListener {

  @PrePersist
  void prePersist(Object object) {
    System.out.println("prePersist");
  }

  @PreUpdate
  void preUpdate(Object object) {
    System.out.println("preUpdate");
  }

  @PreRemove
  void preRemove(Object object) {
    System.out.println("preRemove");
  }
}
```

Notice that each method takes an Object as a parameter, meaning that any type of entity could use this listener by adding the DebugListener class to its @EntityListeners annotation. To have every single entity of your application use this listener, you would have to go through each one and add it manually to the annotation. For this case, JPA has a notion of *default listeners* that can cover all entities in a persistence unit. As there is no annotation targeted for the entire scope of the persistence unit, the default listeners can only be declared in an XML mapping file.

In Chapter 4, you saw how to use XML mapping files instead of annotations. The same steps have to be followed to define the DebugListener as a default listener. A mapping file, with the XML defined in Listing 131, needs to be created and deployed with the application.

Listing 131. A Debug Listener Defined as the Default Listener

```
<entity-mappings xmlns:xsi="http://www.w3.org/2001/XMLSchema-instance"
                 xmlns="http://xmlns.jcp.org/xml/ns/persistence/orm"
                 xsi:schemaLocation="http://xmlns.jcp.org/xml/ns/persistence/orm
http://xmlns.jcp.org/xml/ns/persistence/orm_2_2.xsd"
                 version="2.2">

  <persistence-unit-metadata>
    <persistence-unit-defaults>
      <entity-listeners>
        <entity-listener class=
"org.agoncal.fascicle.jpa.callbackslisteners.DebugListener"/>
      </entity-listeners>
    </persistence-unit-defaults>
  </persistence-unit-metadata>

</entity-mappings>
```

In this file, the `<persistence-unit-metadata>` tag defines all the metadata that don't have any equivalent annotation. The `<persistence-unit-defaults>` tag defines all the defaults of the persistence unit, and the `<entity-listener>` tag defines the default listener. This file needs to be referred in the `persistence.xml` and deployed with the application. The `DebugListener` will then be automatically invoked for every single entity.

When you declare a list of default entity listeners, each listener gets called in the order in which it is listed in the XML mapping file. Default entity listeners are always invoked before any of the entity listeners listed in the `@EntityListeners` annotation. If an entity doesn't want to have the default entity listeners applied to it, it can use the `@ExcludeDefaultListeners` annotation, as shown in Listing 132.

Listing 132. The Customer Entity Excluding Default Listeners

```
@ExcludeDefaultListeners()
@Entity
public class Customer extends Person {

  private String email;
  private String phoneNumber;
  @Transient
  private Integer age;

  // Constructors, getters, setters
}
```

When an event is raised, the listeners are executed in the following order:

1. Default listeners,
2. `@EntityListeners` for the superclasses (highest first) in the array order,

3. `@EntityListeners` for the entity in the array order,
4. Callbacks of the superclasses (highest first), and
5. Callbacks of the entity.

Callbacks and entity listeners are a great way to add business logic to entities depending on the life cycle of the entity.

Chapter 8. Advanced Topics

Up to now, you've seen the core purpose of JPA: map entities to the database and query them, and all that using a defined life cycle. But sometimes you might want to go further and dig into less common use cases. This chapter explains a few corner cases that you might use from time to time.

The code in this chapter can be found at https://github.com/agoncal/agoncal-fascicle-jpa/tree/2.2/advanced

8.1. Mapping Annotations on Fields and Properties

Up to now, I have shown you annotated classes (`@Entity` or `@Table`) and attributes (`@Basic`, `@Column`, `@Temporal` etc.), but the annotations applied on an attribute (or field) can also be set on the corresponding getter method (or property). For example, the annotation `@Id` can be set on the `id` attribute or on the `getId()` method. As this is largely a matter of personal preference, I tend to use property access (annotate the getters), as I find the code more readable. This allows me to quickly read the attributes of an entity without drowning in annotations. In this fascicle, for easy readability, I've decided to annotate the attributes. But in some cases (e.g. with inheritance), it is not simply a matter of personal taste, as it can have an impact upon your mapping.

Java defines a field as an attribute. A property is any field with accessor (getter and setter) methods that follow the Java Bean pattern (starts with `getXXX`, `setXXX`, or `isXXX` for a `Boolean`).

Listing 133 shows how an entity is mapped by annotating the fields.

Listing 133. The Customer Entity with Annotated Fields

```
@Entity
public class Customer {

  @Id
  @GeneratedValue
  private Long id;
  @Column(name = "first_name", nullable = false, length = 50)
  private String firstName;
  @Column(name = "last_name", nullable = false, length = 50)
  private String lastName;
  private String email;
  @Column(name = "phone_number", length = 15)
  private String phoneNumber;

  // Constructors, getters, setters
}
```

Listing 134 shows how an entity is mapped by annotating the property methods.

Listing 134. The Customer Entity with Annotated Properties

```
@Entity
public class Customer {

  private Long id;
  private String firstName;
  private String lastName;
  private String email;
  private String phoneNumber;

  // Constructors and setters

  @Id
  @GeneratedValue
  public Long getId() {
    return id;
  }

  @Column(name = "first_name", nullable = false, length = 50)
  public String getFirstName() {
    return firstName;
  }

  @Column(name = "last_name", nullable = false, length = 50)
  public String getLastName() {
    return lastName;
  }

  public String getEmail() {
    return email;
  }

  @Column(name = "phone_number", length = 15)
  public String getPhoneNumber() {
    return phoneNumber;
  }
}
```

In terms of mapping, the two entities in Listing 133 and Listing 134 are completely identical because the attribute names happen to be the same as the getter names. But if in Listing 134 you add a mapping annotation on a single attribute, then JPA will fall back to the default behaviour: it will use attribute mapping. In this specific case, you will need to explicitly specify the mapping type by means of the `@javax.persistence.Access` annotation.

This annotation takes two possible values, `FIELD` or `PROPERTY`, and can be used on the entity itself and/or on each attribute or getter. For example, when an `@Access(AccessType.FIELD)` is applied to the entity, only mapping annotations placed on the attributes will be taken into account by the persistence provider. It is then possible to selectively designate individual getters for property access with `@Access(AccessType.PROPERTY)`.

Explicit access types can be very useful (e.g. with embeddables and inheritance) but mixing them often results in errors. Listing 135 shows an example of what might happen when you mix access types.

Listing 135. The Customer Entity That Explicitly Mixes Access Types

```
@Entity
@Access(AccessType.FIELD)
public class Customer {

  @Id
  @GeneratedValue
  private Long id;
  @Column(name = "first_name", nullable = false, length = 50)
  private String firstName;
  @Column(name = "last_name", nullable = false, length = 50)
  private String lastName;
  private String email;
  @Column(name = "phone_number", length = 15)
  private String phoneNumber;

  // Constructors, getters, setters

  @Access(AccessType.PROPERTY)
  @Column(name = "phone_number", length = 555)
  public String getPhoneNumber() {
    return phoneNumber;
  }
}
```

The example in Listing 135 explicitly defines the access type as being `FIELD` at the entity level. This indicates to the persistence manager that it should only process annotations on attributes. The `phoneNumber` attribute is annotated with `@Column`, which restricts its length to `15`. Reading this code, you expect to end up with a `VARCHAR(15)` in the database, but this is not what happens. The getter method shows that the access type for the `getPhoneNumber()` method has been explicitly changed, and so has the length of the phone number (to `555`). In this case, the entity `AccessType.FIELD` is overwritten by `AccessType.PROPERTY`. You will then get a `VARCHAR(555)` in the database. You should be careful when mixing mapping access types in entities.

When choosing between field access (attributes) or property access (getters), you are specifying the *access type*. By default, a single access type applies to an entity: it is either field access or property access, but not both (i.e. the persistence provider accesses the persistent state either via attributes or via the getter methods). The JPA specification states that the behaviour of an application that mixes the placement of annotations on fields and properties, without explicitly specifying the access type, is undefined.

8.1.1. Access Type of an Embeddable Class

The access type of an embeddable class is determined by the access type of the entity class in which it exists. If the entity explicitly uses a property access type, an embeddable object will implicitly use property access as well. A different access type for an embeddable class can be specified by means of the `@Access` annotation.

The `Customer` entity (see Listing 136) and `Address` entity (see Listing 137) use different access types.

Listing 136. The Customer Entity with Field Access Type

```
@Entity
@Access(AccessType.FIELD)
public class Customer {

  @Id
  @GeneratedValue
  private Long id;
  @Column(name = "first_name", nullable = false, length = 50)
  private String firstName;
  @Column(name = "last_name", nullable = false, length = 50)
  private String lastName;
  private String email;
  @Column(name = "phone_number", length = 15)
  private String phoneNumber;
  @Embedded
  private Address address;

  // Constructors, getters, setters
}
```

Listing 137. The Embeddable Object with Property Access Type

```
@Embeddable
@Access(AccessType.PROPERTY)
public class Address {

  private String street1;
  private String street2;
  private String city;
  private String state;
  private String zipcode;
  private String country;

  // Constructors and setters

  @Column(nullable = false)
  public String getStreet1() {
    return street1;
  }

  public String getStreet2() {
    return street2;
  }

  @Column(nullable = false, length = 50)
  public String getCity() {
    return city;
  }

  @Column(length = 3)
  public String getState() {
    return state;
  }

  @Column(name = "zip_code", length = 10)
  public String getZipcode() {
    return zipcode;
  }

  public String getCountry() {
    return country;
  }
}
```

Explicitly setting the access type on embeddables is strongly recommended in order to avoid mapping errors when an embeddable is embedded by multiple entities. For example, let's extend our model by adding an `Order` entity as shown in Figure 41. `Address` is now embedded by `Customer` (the home address of the customer) and `Order` (the delivery address).

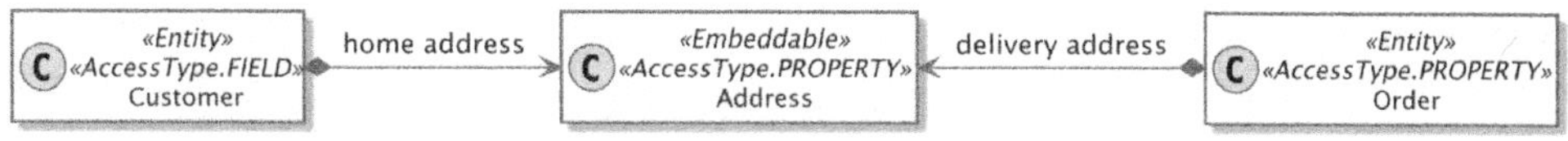

Figure 41. Address is embedded by Customer and Order

Each entity defines a different access type: `Customer` uses field access, whereas `Order` uses property access. An embeddable has its access type determined by the one of the entity class in which it is declared. If `Address` didn't set explicitly its own access type, `Address` will be mapped in two different ways, which can cause mapping problems.

Explicit access types are also very helpful in inheritance. By default, the leaf entities inherit the access type of their root entity. In a hierarchy of entities, each can be accessed differently from the other classes in the hierarchy. Including an `@Access` annotation will cause the default access mode in effect for the hierarchy to be locally overridden.

8.2. Overriding Attributes

As you've seen so far, JPA is great at dealing with default mapping, as well as being very specific and being able to customise attribute, entity, relations or inheritance mapping. But it can go even further. There are a few edge cases where you need to override the mapping when using inheritance or embedding the same embeddable multiple times. That's when `@AttributeOverride` comes into play.

8.2.1. Overriding Attributes in Inheritance

With the table-per-concrete-class strategy we've seen in Listing 83, the columns of the root class are duplicated on the leaf tables. They keep the same name. But what if a legacy database is being used and the columns have a different name? JPA uses the `@AttributeOverride` annotation to override the column mapping.

In Listing 138, we have an `Item` entity (but it could have been a mapped super-class) from which `Book` and `CD` extend.

Listing 138. Item Entity

```
@Entity
@Inheritance(strategy = TABLE_PER_CLASS)
public class Item {

  @Id
  @GeneratedValue
  protected Long id;
  protected String title;
  protected String description;
  protected Float price;

  // Constructors, getters, setters
}
```

Both the `Book` and the `CD` entities inherit from the `Item` mapping and therefore both will end-up with the same column names. This will not work, as you can't have two columns of the same name in the same table. To rename the `ID`, `TITLE`, and `DESCRIPTION` columns in the `BOOK` and `CD` tables, we use the `@AttributeOverride` annotation. The `Book` entity (see Listing 139) and `CD` entity (see Listing 140) override the attribute names.

Listing 139. Book Overrides Some Item Columns

```
@Entity
@AttributeOverride(name = "id", column = @Column(name = "book_id"))
@AttributeOverride(name = "title", column = @Column(name = "book_title"))
@AttributeOverride(name = "description", column = @Column(name = "book_description"))
public class Book extends Item {

  private String isbn;
  private String publisher;
  private Integer nbOfPages;
  private Boolean illustrations;

  // Constructors, getters, setters
}
```

Listing 140. CD Overrides Some Item Columns

```
@Entity
@AttributeOverride(name = "id", column = @Column(name = "cd_id"))
@AttributeOverride(name = "title", column = @Column(name = "cd_title"))
@AttributeOverride(name = "description", column = @Column(name = "cd_description"))
public class CD extends Item {

  private String musicCompany;
  private Integer numberOfCDs;
  private Float totalDuration;
  private String genre;

  // Constructors, getters, setters
}
```

Each `@AttributeOverride` annotation points to an attribute of the `Item` entity and redefines the mapping of the column using the `@Column` annotation. So `name = "title"` refers to the `title` attribute of the `Item` entity, and `@Column(name = "cd_title")` informs the persistence provider that the `title` attribute has to be mapped to a `CD_TITLE` column. Figure 42 shows the result.

Figure 42. BOOK and CD tables overriding ITEM columns

8.2.2. Overriding Attributes with Embeddables

The same happens with embeddables. Embeddables can be embedded several times in the same entity. When that's the case, you need to override the attributes. Listing 141 shows the `Address` embeddable.

Listing 141. Address Embeddable

```
@Embeddable
public class Address {

  private String street1;
  private String city;
  private String zipcode;
  private String country;

  // Constructors, getters, setters
}
```

Now, let's say we have a purchase order which defines two addresses: an invoice address and a delivery address. If we just add the `Address` embeddable twice into the `PurchaseOrder` entity, the mapping will not work. Remember that, with embeddables, all the attributes end-up in the same table of the entity. That means that we would have two columns `STREET1`, two columns `CITY` etc. in the `PURCHASE_ORDER` table, and this is not possible. To solve this problem, we use the `@AttributeOverride` annotation to redefine the column name on each embeddable. As you can see in Listing 142, the `street1` attribute of the invoice address will be mapped into a column called `INVOICE_STREET1` and `DELIVERY_STREET1` for the delivery address.

Listing 142. Overriding Embeddable Attributes

```
@Entity
@Table(name = "purchase_order")
public class PurchaseOrder {

  @Id
  @GeneratedValue
  private Long id;
  private LocalDateTime creationDate;
  private List<OrderLine> orderLines;

  @AttributeOverride(name = "street1", column = @Column(name = "invoice_street1"))
  @AttributeOverride(name = "city", column = @Column(name = "invoice_city"))
  @AttributeOverride(name = "zipcode", column = @Column(name = "invoice_zipcode"))
  @AttributeOverride(name = "country", column = @Column(name = "invoice_country"))
  private Address invoiceAddress;

  @AttributeOverride(name = "street1", column = @Column(name = "delivery_street1"))
  @AttributeOverride(name = "city", column = @Column(name = "delivery_city"))
  @AttributeOverride(name = "zipcode", column = @Column(name = "delivery_zipcode"))
  @AttributeOverride(name = "country", column = @Column(name = "delivery_country"))
  private Address deliveryAddress;

  // Constructors, getters, setters
}
```

The end result is described in Listing 143. The PURCHASE_ORDER table contains all the columns from the PurchaseOrder entity as well as the columns of the two Address embeddables.

Listing 143. The PURCHASE_ORDER Table with All Columns

```
CREATE TABLE PURCHASE_ORDER
(
  ID               BIGINT NOT NULL,
  CREATIONDATE     TIMESTAMP,
  DELIVERY_STREET1 VARCHAR,
  DELIVERY_CITY    VARCHAR,
  DELIVERY_ZIPCODE VARCHAR,
  DELIVERY_COUNTRY VARCHAR,
  INVOICE_STREET1  VARCHAR,
  INVOICE_CITY     VARCHAR,
  INVOICE_ZIPCODE  VARCHAR,
  INVOICE_COUNTRY  VARCHAR,
  PRIMARY KEY (ID)
)
```

8.3. Caching

Most specifications focus heavily on functional requirements, leaving non-functional ones like performance, scalability, or clustering as implementation details. Implementations have to strictly follow the specification but may also add specific features. A perfect example for JPA would be caching which was not mentioned in the specification until JPA 2.0.

The entity manager is seen as a first-level cache used to process data comprehensively for the database and to cache short-lived entities. This first-level cache is used on a per-transaction basis to reduce the number of SQL queries within a given transaction. For example, if an object is modified several times within the same transaction, the entity manager will generate only one UPDATE statement at the end of the transaction. A first-level cache is not a performance cache.

Nevertheless, all JPA implementations use a performance cache (a.k.a. a second-level cache) to optimise database access, queries, joins, and so on. As seen in Figure 43, the second-level cache sits between the entity manager and the database to reduce database traffic by keeping objects loaded in memory and available to the whole application.

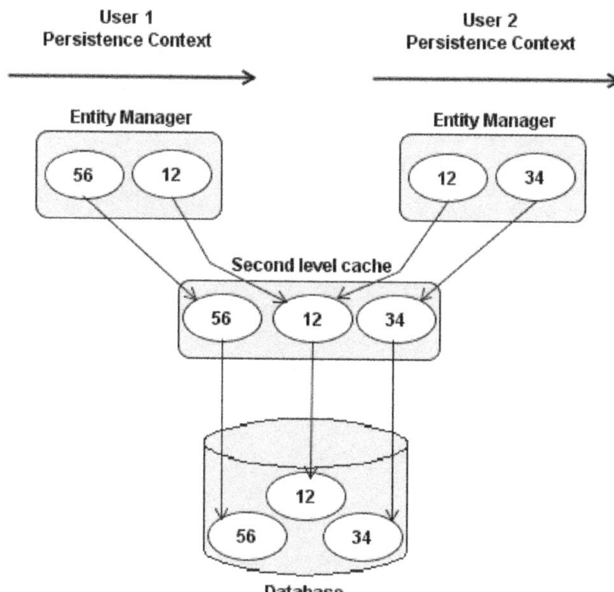

Figure 43. Second-level cache

Each implementation has its own way of caching objects, either by developing their own mechanism or by reusing existing ones (open source or commercial). Caching can even be distributed across several nodes - anything is possible when the specification ignores a topic. JPA 2.0 acknowledged that a second-level cache was needed and has added caching operations to the standard API. The API, shown in Listing 144, is very minimalist (because the goal of JPA is not to standardise a fully functional cache), but it allows code to query and remove some entities from the second-level cache in a standard manner. Like `EntityManager`, the `javax.persistence.Cache` is an interface implemented by the persistence provider caching system.

Listing 144. Cache API

```
public interface Cache {

  // Whether the cache contains data for the given entity.
  public boolean contains(Class cls, Object primaryKey);

  // Remove the data for the given entity from the cache.
  public void evict(Class cls, Object primaryKey);

  // Remove the data for entities of the specified class (and its
  public void evict(Class cls);

  // Clear the cache.
  public void evictAll();

  // Return the provider-specific cache implementation
  public <T> T unwrap(Class<T> cls);
}
```

You can use this API to check if a specific entity is in the second-level cache or not, remove it from the cache, or clear the entire cache. Combined with this API, you can explicitly inform the provider that an entity is cacheable or not by using the `@Cacheable` annotation as shown in Listing 145. If the entity has no `@Cacheable` annotation, it means that the entity and its state must not be cached by the provider.

Listing 145. The Customer Entity Is Cacheable

```
@Entity
@Cacheable(true)
public class Customer {

  @Id
  @GeneratedValue
  private Long id;
  private String firstName;
  private String lastName;
  private String email;

  // Constructors, getters, setters
}
```

The `@Cacheable` annotation takes a `Boolean` value (whose default is `true`). Once you've decided which entity should be cacheable or not, you need to inform the provider which caching mechanism to use. The way to do this with JPA is to set the `shared-cache-mode` attribute in the `persistence.xml` file. The following are the possible values:

- `ALL`: All entities and entity-related state is cached.
- `DISABLE_SELECTIVE`: Caching is enabled for all entities except those annotated with

@Cacheable(false).

- ENABLE_SELECTIVE: Caching is enabled for all entities annotated with @Cacheable(true).
- NONE: Caching is disabled for the persistence unit.
- UNSPECIFIED: Caching behaviour is undefined (the provider-specific defaults may apply).

Not setting one of these values leaves it up to the provider to decide which caching mechanism to use. The code in Listing 146 shows you how to use this caching mechanism. First, we create a Customer object and persist it. Because Customer is cacheable (see Listing 145), it should be in the second-level cache (by using the EntityManagerFactory.getCache().contains() method). Invoking the cache.evict(Customer.class) method removes the entity from the cache.

Listing 146. Dealing with Cached Entities

```
Customer customer = new Customer("Patricia", "Jane", " plecomte@mail.com ");

// Persists the object
tx.begin();
em.persist(customer);
tx.commit();

assertNotNull(customer.getId());

// Uses the EntityManagerFactory to get the Cache
Cache cache = emf.getCache();

// Customer should be in the cache
assertTrue(cache.contains(Customer.class, customer.getId()));

// Removes the Customer entity from the cache
cache.evict(Customer.class);

// After clearing the cache Customer should not be in the cache anymore
assertFalse(cache.contains(Customer.class, customer.getId()));
```

8.4. Concurrency

JPA can be used to update persistent data, and JPQL can be used to retrieve data following certain criteria. All this can happen within an application running in a cluster with multiple nodes, multiple threads, and one single database, so it is quite common for tables and rows to be accessed concurrently. When this is the case, synchronisation must be controlled by the application using a locking mechanism. Whether the application is simple or complex, chances are that you will make use of locking somewhere in your code.

To illustrate the problem of concurrent database access, let's see an example of an application with two concurrent threads, shown in Figure 44. One thread finds a book by its identifier and raises the price of the book by $2. The other does the same thing but raises the price by $5. If you execute these two threads concurrently in separate transactions and manipulate the same book, you can't predict the final price of the book. In this example, the initial price of the book is $10. Depending on which transaction finishes last, the price can be $12 or $15.

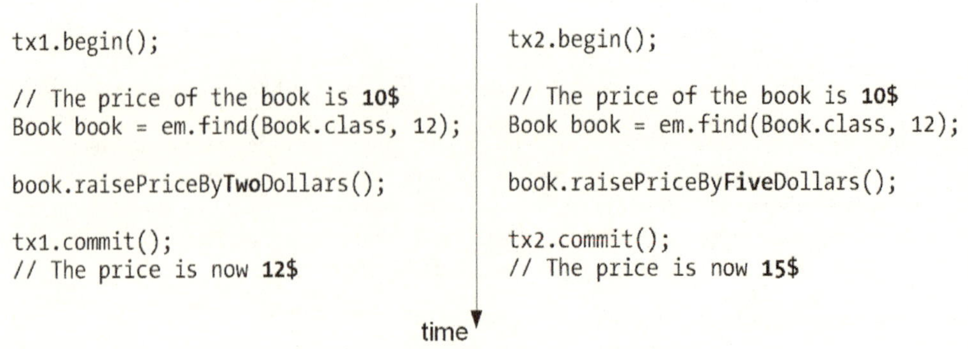

```
tx1.begin();                                  tx2.begin();

// The price of the book is 10$               // The price of the book is 10$
Book book = em.find(Book.class, 12);          Book book = em.find(Book.class, 12);

book.raisePriceByTwoDollars();                book.raisePriceByFiveDollars();

tx1.commit();                                 tx2.commit();
// The price is now 12$                       // The price is now 15$
```

time

Figure 44. Transactions one (tx1) and two (tx2) updating the price of a book concurrently

This problem of concurrency, where the "winner" is the last one to commit, is not specific to JPA. Databases have had to deal with this problem for a long time and have found different solutions to isolate one transaction from others. One common mechanism that databases use is to lock the row on which the SQL statement is being executed.

From JPA 2.1 onwards, we can use two different locking mechanisms (JPA 1.0 only had support for optimistic locking).

- *Optimistic locking* is based on the assumption that most database transactions don't conflict with other transactions, allowing concurrency to be as permissive as possible when allowing transactions to execute.
- *Pessimistic locking* is based on the opposite assumption, so a lock will be obtained on the resource before operating on it.

As an example from everyday life that reinforces these concepts, consider "optimistic and pessimistic street crossing." In an area with very light traffic, you might be able to cross the street without checking for approaching cars. But not in a busy city centre!

JPA uses different locking mechanisms at different levels of the API. Both pessimistic and optimistic locks can be obtained via the `EntityManager.find` and `EntityManager.refresh` methods (in addition to the `lock` method), as well as through JPQL queries, meaning locking can be achieved at the `EntityManager` level and at the `Query` level with the methods in Listing 90.

Each of these methods takes a `LockModeType` as a parameter that can take different values (default value is `NONE`).

- `OPTIMISTIC`: Uses optimistic locking.
- `OPTIMISTIC_FORCE_INCREMENT`: Uses optimistic locking and forces an increment to the entity's version column (see the upcoming "Versioning" section).
- `PESSIMISTIC_READ`: Uses pessimistic locking without the need to reread the data at the end of the transaction to obtain a lock.
- `PESSIMISTIC_WRITE`: Uses pessimistic locking and forces serialisation among transactions attempting to update the entity.

- PESSIMISTIC_FORCE_INCREMENT: Uses pessimistic locking and forces an increment to the entity's version column (see the upcoming "Versioning" section).
- NONE: Specifies no locking mechanism should be used.

You can use these parameters in multiple places depending on how you need to specify locks. You can read then lock.

```
// Reads the entity
Book book = em.find(Book.class, id);

// Then locks the entity
em.lock(book, LockModeType.OPTIMISTIC_FORCE_INCREMENT);

book.raisePriceByTwoDollars();
```

Or you can read and lock.

```
// Reads and locks the entity
Book book = em.find(Book.class, id, LockModeType.OPTIMISTIC_FORCE_INCREMENT);

book.raisePriceByTwoDollars();
```

Concurrency and locking are key motivators for versioning.

8.4.1. Versioning

Most software programs use versioning. In fact, even Java specifications use versioning: Java SE 7.0, Java SE 8.0, JPA 2.0, JPA 2.1, JAX-RS 1.0, and so on. When a new version of the JAX-RS specification is released, its version number is increased, and you upgrade to JAX-RS 2.0. JPA uses this exact mechanism when you need to version entities. So, when you persist an entity for the first time in the database, it will get the version number 1. Later, if you update an attribute and commit this change to the database, the entity version will get the number 2, and so on. This versioning will evolve each time a change is made to the entity.

In order for this to happen, the entity must have an attribute to store the version number, and it has to be annotated by @Version. This version number is then mapped to a column in the database. The attribute types supported for versioning can be int, Integer, short, Short, long, Long, or Timestamp. Listing 147 shows how to add a version attribute to the Book entity.

Listing 147. The Book Entity with a @Version Annotation on an Integer

```
@Entity
public class Book {

  @Id
  @GeneratedValue
  private Long id;
  @Version
  private Integer version;
  private String title;
  private Float price;
  private String description;
  private String isbn;

  public void raisePriceByTwoDollars() {
    price = price + 2;
  }

  public void raisePriceByFiveDollars() {
    price = price + 5;
  }

  // Constructors, getters, setters
}
```

The entity can access the value of its `version` property but must not modify it. Only the persistence provider is permitted to set or update the value of the `version` attribute when the object is written or updated to the database. Let's look at an example to illustrate the behaviour of this versioning. In Listing 148, a new `Book` entity is persisted to the database. Once the transaction is committed, the persistence provider sets the version to 1. Later, the price of the book is updated, and, once the data is flushed to the database, the version number is incremented to 2.

Listing 148. Entity Versioning

```
// Creates the book
Book book = new Book("H2G2", 12.5F, "Scifi book", "1-84023-742-2");
tx.begin();
em.persist(book);
tx.commit();
assertEquals(1, (int) book.getVersion());

// Updates the book
tx.begin();
book.raisePriceByTwoDollars();
tx.commit();
assertEquals(2, (int) book.getVersion());
```

The `version` attribute is not required but is recommended when the entity can be concurrently modified by more than one process or thread. Versioning is the core of optimistic locking and provides protection for infrequent concurrent entity modification. In fact, an entity is automatically enabled for optimistic locking if it has a property mapped with a `@Version` annotation.

8.4.2. Optimistic Locking

As its name indicates, optimistic locking is based on the fact that database transactions don't conflict with each other. In other words, there is a good chance that the transaction updating an entity will be the only one that actually updates the entity during that interval. Therefore, the decision to acquire a lock on the entity is actually made at the end of the transaction. This ensures that updates to an entity are consistent with the current state of the database. Transactions that would cause this constraint to be violated result in an `OptimisticLockException` being thrown and the transaction marked for rollback.

How would you throw an `OptimisticLockException`? Either by explicitly locking the entity (with the `lock` or the `find` methods that you saw, passing a `LockModeType`) or by letting the persistence provider check the attribute annotated with `@Version`. The use of a dedicated `@Version` annotation on an entity allows the `EntityManager` to implicitly perform optimistic locking simply by comparing the value of the `version` attribute in the entity instance with the value of the column in the database. Without an attribute annotated with `@Version`, the entity manager will not be able to do optimistic locking automatically (implicitly).

Let's look again at the example of increasing the price of a book. Transactions `tx1` and `tx2` both get an instance of the same `Book` entity. At that moment, the version of the `Book` entity is 1. The first transaction raises the price of the book by $2 and commits this change. When the data is flushed to the database, the persistence provider increases the version number and sets it to 2. At that moment, the second transaction raises the price by $5 and commits the change. The entity manager for `tx2` realises that the version number in the database is different from that of the entity. This means the version has been changed by a different transaction, so an `OptimisticLockException` is thrown and the transaction is rolled back, as shown in Figure 45.

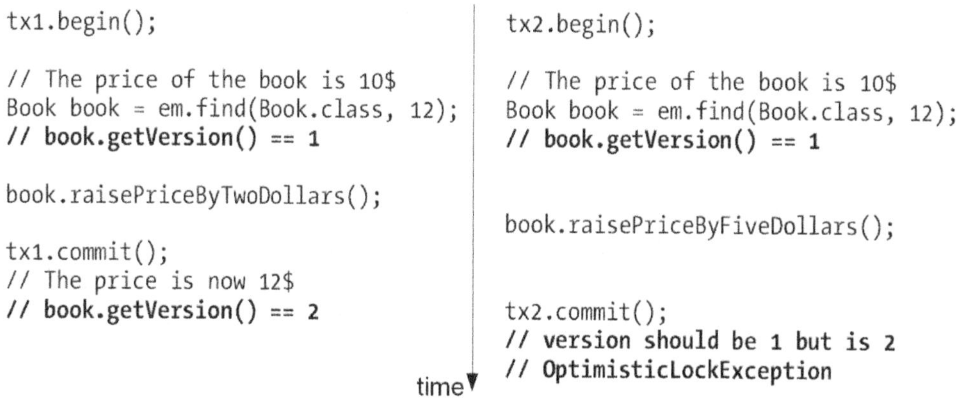

```
tx1.begin();

// The price of the book is 10$
Book book = em.find(Book.class, 12);
// book.getVersion() == 1

book.raisePriceByTwoDollars();

tx1.commit();
// The price is now 12$
// book.getVersion() == 2
```

```
tx2.begin();

// The price of the book is 10$
Book book = em.find(Book.class, 12);
// book.getVersion() == 1


book.raisePriceByFiveDollars();


tx2.commit();
// version should be 1 but is 2
// OptimisticLockException
```

time

Figure 45. OptimisticLockException thrown on transaction tx2

This is the default behaviour when the `@Version` annotation is used: an `OptimisticLockException` is thrown when the data is flushed (at commit time or by explicitly calling the `em.flush()` method).

You can also control where you want to add the optimistic lock using read then lock or read and lock. The code of read and lock, for example, would look like this:

```
Book book = em.find(Book.class, 12);
// Lock to raise the price
em.lock(book, LockModeType.OPTIMISTIC);
book.raisePriceByTwoDollars();
```

With optimistic locking, the `LockModeType` that you pass as a parameter can take two values: `OPTIMISTIC` and `OPTIMISTIC_FORCE_INCREMENT` (or `READ` and `WRITE`, respectively, but these values are deprecated). The only difference is that `OPTIMISTIC_FORCE_INCREMENT` will force an update (increment) to the entity's `VERSION` column when the transaction is committed (even if the entity's state has not been changed) while `OPTIMISTIC` only checks (and does not increment) the entity version when the transaction is committed.

Applications are strongly encouraged to enable optimistic locking for all entities that may be concurrently accessed. Failure to use a locking mechanism may lead to an inconsistent entity state, lost updates, and other state irregularities. Optimistic locking is a useful performance optimisation that offloads work that would otherwise be required of the database and is an alternative to pessimistic locking, which requires low-level database locking.

8.4.3. Pessimistic Locking

Pessimistic locking is based on the opposite assumption to optimistic locking, because a lock is eagerly obtained on the entity before operating on it. This is very resource restrictive and results in significant performance degradation, as a database lock is held using a `SELECT … FOR UPDATE` SQL statement to read/write data.

Databases typically offer a pessimistic locking service that allows the entity manager to lock a row in a table to prevent another thread from updating the same row. This is an effective mechanism to ensure that two clients do not modify the same row at the same time, but it requires expensive, low-level checks inside the database. Transactions that would cause this constraint to be violated result in a `PessimisticLockException` being thrown and the transaction marked for rollback.

Optimistic locking is appropriate in dealing with moderate contention among concurrent transactions. But in some applications with a higher risk of contentions, pessimistic locking may be more appropriate, as the database lock is immediately obtained as opposed to the often late failure of optimistic transactions. For example, in times of economic crises, stock markets receive huge numbers of selling orders. If 100 million Americans need to sell their stock options at the same time, the system needs to use pessimistic locks to ensure data consistency. Note that, at the moment, the market is rather pessimistic instead of optimistic, and that has nothing to do with JPA.

Pessimistic locking may be applied to entities that do not contain the annotated `@Version` attribute.

Chapter 9. Integrating JPA with Other Technologies

As you've seen in the previous chapters, Java Persistence API can be used as a stand-alone technology. Just embed the required dependencies in your code, add mapping annotations on your entities, and query them with the `javax.persistence.EntityManagerFactory` and `javax.persistence.EntityManager` APIs. But one beauty of JPA is its flexibility and adaptability: it integrates well with other technologies such as Bean Validation, CDI, JTA or Spring, for example.

The code in this chapter can be found at https://github.com/agoncal/agoncal-fascicle-jpa/tree/2.2/integrating

9.1. Bean Validation Integration

Validating data is a common task that developers have to do and it is spread throughout all layers of an application (from client to database). This common practice is time-consuming, error prone, and hard to maintain in the long run. Besides, some of these constraints are so frequently used that they could be considered standard (checking for a null value, size, range, etc.). It would be good to be able to centralise these constraints in one place and share them across layers. That's where Bean Validation comes into play.

Bean Validation allows you to write a constraint once and reuse it in different application layers.[55] It is layer agnostic, meaning that the same constraint can be used from the presentation to the business model layer. Bean Validation is available for server-side applications as well as rich Java client graphical interfaces (Swing, Android, JavaFX etc.).

Bean Validation allows you to apply already-defined common constraints to your application, and also to write your own validation rules in order to validate beans, attributes, constructors, method return values and parameters. The API is very easy to use and flexible as it encourages you to define your constraints using annotations or XML descriptors.

If you like the format of this fascicle and are interested in Bean Validation, check out the references for my *Understanding Bean Validation 2.0* fascicle in Appendix D.

Bean Validation has several hooks into Java EE. One of them is its integration with JPA and the entity life cycle. Entities may include Bean Validation constraints and be automatically validated. In fact, validation is performed automatically as JPA delegates entity validation to Bean Validation before insert or update.

Listing 149 shows a `Book` entity with a few Bean Validation constraints (`@NotNull`, `@Digits`, `@Size` and `@Positive`). Bean Validation annotations are quite natural to read. What the code in Listing 149 expresses is that "the title of the book cannot be null", "the size of an ISBN should be between 8 and 13 characters", or "the number of pages should be a positive number". Notice also how we can mix JPA annotations (`@Entity`, `@Id` and `@GeneratedValue`) with Bean Validation annotations.

Listing 149. Book Entity with Bean Validation Constraints

```
@Entity
public class Book {

  @Id @GeneratedValue
  private Long id;
  @NotNull
  private String title;
  @Digits(integer = 4, fraction = 2)
  private Float price;
  @Size(max = 2000)
  private String description;
  @Size(min = 8, max = 13)
  private String isbn;
  @Positive
  private Integer nbOfPages;

  // Constructors, getters, setters
}
```

In Listing 150, we create a valid book entity with a valid title, a valid price, a valid ISBN and a valid number of pages according to Bean Validation constraints. We then persist the book without explicitly calling any validation.

Listing 150. Persisting a Valid Book

```
Book book = new Book().title("H2G2").price(12.5F).isbn("1-84023-2").nbOfPages(354);

tx.begin();
em.persist(book);
tx.commit();
```

On the other hand, in Listing 151 the `title` attribute of the book is null. Once we persist the book, and without any need to programmatically use the Bean Validation `Validator` API, the JPA runtime automatically invokes Bean Validation before persisting the entity. Bean Validation will return a `Set` of `ConstraintViolation` and then, the JPA integration will throw a `RollbackException` rolling back the transaction. As the result, no data will be inserted into the database.

Listing 151. Transaction Rollbacked When a Constraint Is Violated

```
Book book = new Book().title(null).price(12.5F).isbn("1-84023-2").nbOfPages(354);
assertThrows(RollbackException.class, () -> {
  tx.begin();
  em.persist(book);
  tx.commit();
});
```

JPA entities have a specific life cycle (*Persist, Update, Remove, Load*) and Bean Validation hooks on this life cycle automatically. Data needs to be valid before persisting or updating an entity from the database.

Another interesting integration with Bean Validation is how JPA understands some constraints while generating the database schema. JPA introspects the entities and is able to generate, create and drop database scripts. If JPA finds a Bean Validation constraint that it understands, it can generate the equivalent SQL. Listing 149 is the equivalent schema that JPA might create using the entity mapping in Listing 152. `@NotNull` gives a `not null` in SQL, and `@Size(max)` has an impact on the size of the `varchar`. No need to add an extra `@Column(nullable = false)`. Just having `@NotNull` is enough to make a database field not allow null values. Of course, if the validation is too complex or doesn't have any equivalent in SQL (such as `@Positive`), it is ignored during script generation.

Listing 152. Create Table Script with Constraints

```
CREATE TABLE BOOK
(
  ID          BIGINT        NOT NULL,
  DESCRIPTION VARCHAR(2000),
  ISBN        VARCHAR(13),
  NBOFPAGES   INTEGER,
  PRICE       FLOAT,
  TITLE       VARCHAR(255) NOT NULL,
  PRIMARY KEY (ID)
)
```

9.2. CDI Integration

Context and Dependency Injection (CDI) is a central technology in Jakarta EE or in MicroProfile.[56] Its programming model turns nearly every component into an injectable, interceptable and manageable bean. CDI is built on the concept of "*loose coupling, strong typing*", meaning that beans are loosely coupled, but in a strongly-typed way. Decoupling goes further by bringing interceptors, decorators and events to the entire platform. CDI homogenises scopes among beans, as well as context and life cycle management.

But let's use CDI only for injection. So far, when we needed the `EntityManager`, we would programmatically create one giving an `EntityManagerFactory`. Once used, we would also need to close it.

```
EntityManagerFactory emf = Persistence.createEntityManagerFactory("vintageStorePU");
EntityManager em = emf.createEntityManager();
...
em.close();
```

But with CDI, we can also get the entity manager via dependency injection using the `@Inject` annotation. For that, we need to define two CDI producers: one that creates the `EntityManagerFactory` and another one to create the `EntityManager`. Listing 153 uses the JPA API to build an application-scoped entity manager factory.

Listing 153. Producing an EntityManagerFactory

```
@ApplicationScoped
public class EntityManagerFactoryProducer {

  @Inject
  private BeanManager beanManager;

  @Produces
  @ApplicationScoped
  public EntityManagerFactory produceEntityManagerFactory() {
    Map<String, Object> props = new HashMap<>();
    props.put("javax.persistence.bean.manager", beanManager);
    return Persistence.createEntityManagerFactory("cdbookstorePU", props);
  }

  public void close(@Disposes EntityManagerFactory emf) {
    emf.close();
  }
}
```

Listing 153 shows an application scoped bean that is initialised only once in the lifetime of the application. It produces and disposes an `EntityManagerFactory` so that it becomes injectable. In a similar way, we need to produce the entity manager. Listing 154 injects the produced `EntityManagerFactory` from Listing 153 so it can produce an `EntityManager`.

Listing 154. Producing an EntityManager

```
@ApplicationScoped
public class EntityManagerProducer {

  @Inject
  private EntityManagerFactory emf;

  @Produces
  @RequestScoped
  public EntityManager produceEntityManager() {
    return emf.createEntityManager();
  }

  public void close(@Disposes EntityManager em) {
    em.close();
  }
}
```

With the producers in place, we can inject an entity manager via `@Inject`. Listing 155 shows how the `AddressService` injects the `EntityManager` so it can persist an `Address` entity.

Listing 155. Injecting an EntityManager

```
@ApplicationScoped
public class AddressService {

  @Inject
  private EntityManager em;

  public Address save(Address address) {
    em.getTransaction().begin();
    em.persist(address);
    em.getTransaction().commit();
    return address;
  }
}
```

From JPA 2.1 on, CDI has also been supported within entity listeners. So, in Listing 156, we have an entity listener that checks if the zipcode is valid or not. It delegates this to a helper class called `ZipCodeChecker` that gets injected thanks to the CDI `@Inject` annotation.

Listing 156. Injecting a Helper Class

```
@ApplicationScoped
public class ZipCodeListener {

  @Inject
  private ZipCodeChecker checker;

  @PrePersist
  @PreUpdate
  private void checkZipCode(Address address) {
    if (!checker.isValid(address.getZipcode()))
      throw new IllegalArgumentException("Invalid zipcode");
  }

}
```

As you can see in Listing 157, the `ZipCodeChecker` is just a CDI bean.

Listing 157. The ZipCodeChecker Helper Class

```
@ApplicationScoped
public class ZipCodeChecker {

  private Pattern zipPattern = Pattern.compile("\\d{5}(-\\d{5})?");

  public boolean isValid(String zipcode) {
    if (zipcode == null)
      return true;

    return zipPattern.matcher(zipcode).matches();
  }

}
```

9.3. JTA Integration

In Java, transaction management is done through the *Java Transaction API* (JTA) specified by JSR 907.[57] JTA defines a set of interfaces for the application or the container in order to demarcate transaction boundaries, and it also defines APIs to deal with the transaction manager.

So far, all the examples in this fascicle have been using JPA local transactions. Resource local transactions are used in a Java SE environment, not in a managed environment (Spring or Java EE). This means that in the `persistence.xml` file we've configured the persistence unit with a `transaction-type="RESOURCE_LOCAL"`:

```
<persistence-unit name="vintageStorePU" transaction-type="RESOURCE_LOCAL">
```

Once configured, the local transactions are defined through the `EntityTransaction` API which contains basic transaction management including begin, commit and rollback:

```
entityManager.getTransaction().begin();
entityManager.getTransaction().commit();
entityManager.getTransaction().rollback();
```

Until `begin` is called, certain operations such as `persist`, `merge` or `remove` cannot be called. After a successful commit, the `EntityManager` can continue to be used, and all of the managed objects remain managed. The rollback operation will roll back the database transaction.

JTA transactions are used in managed environments such as Spring or Java EE. To use JTA transactions, the transaction-type attribute in the `persistence.xml` is set to `JTA`. If JTA transactions are used with a datasource, the `<jta-datasource>` element should be used to reference a datasource that has been configured to be JTA managed.

```
<persistence-unit name="vintageStorePU" transaction-type="JTA">
  <jta-data-source>java:jboss/datasources/MyDS</jta-data-source>
  ...
</persistence-unit>
```

When managing transactions declaratively, you delegate the demarcation policy to the container. You don't have to explicitly use the JTA transaction management to explicitly start or commit a transaction; you can leave the container to demarcate transaction boundaries by automatically beginning and committing transactions based on annotations.

Listing 159 shows a transactional service. You know this service is transactional thanks to the `javax.transaction.Transactional` annotation. This annotation will cause every method invocation to be intercepted and start a transaction if needed. That's why you don't see any explicit `tx.begin()` or `tx.commit()` in this code.

Listing 158. A Transactional Service

```
@ApplicationScoped
public class AddressService {

  @Inject
  private EntityManager em;

  @Transactional(REQUIRED)
  public Address save(Address address) {
    em.persist(address);
    return address;
  }

  @Transactional(MANDATORY)
  public String needsATransaction() {
    return "Success";
  }
}
```

You might ask how does the code in Listing 158 work? The answer is that the container is intercepting the method invocation and managing the transaction. Figure 46 shows what happens when a client invokes the `ItemService.createBook()` method. The client call is intercepted by the container, which checks immediately before invoking the method whether a transaction context is associated with the call. By default, if no transaction context is available, the container begins a new transaction before entering the method and then invokes the `createBook()` method. Once the method exits, the container automatically commits the transaction or rolls it back (if a particular type of exception is thrown).

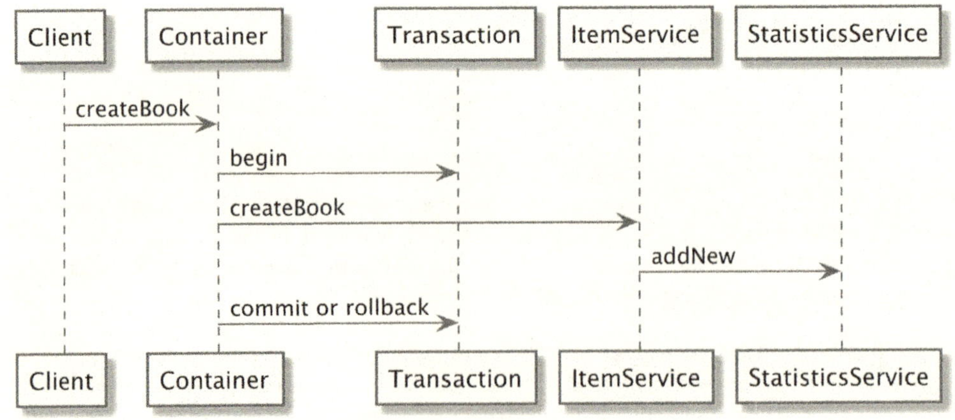

Figure 46. The container handles the transaction

The default transactional behaviour is that whatever transaction context is used for `createBook()` (from the client or created by the container), it is applied to `addItem()`. The final commit happens if both methods have returned successfully. This behaviour can be changed using metadata. Depending on the transaction attribute you choose (`REQUIRED`, `REQUIRES_NEW`, `SUPPORTS`, `MANDATORY`, `NOT_SUPPORTED`, or `NEVER`), you can affect the way the container demarcates transactions: on a client invocation of a transactional method, the container uses the client's transaction, runs the method in a new transaction, runs the method with no transaction, or throws an exception. Table 12 defines the transaction attributes of the `@Transactional` annotation.

Table 12. Transaction Types

Attribute	Description
`REQUIRED`	This attribute (default value) means that a method must always be invoked within a transaction. The container creates a new transaction if the method is invoked from a non-transactional client. If the client has a transaction context, the business method runs within the client's transaction. You should use `REQUIRED` if you are making calls that should be managed in a transaction, but you can't assume that the client is calling the method from a transaction context.
`REQUIRES_NEW`	The container always creates a new transaction before executing a method, regardless of whether the client is executed within a transaction. If the client is running within a transaction, the container suspends that transaction temporarily, creates a second one, commits or rolls it back, and then resumes the first transaction. This means that the success or failure of the second transaction has no effect on the existing client transaction. You should use `REQUIRES_NEW` when you don't want a rollback to affect the client.
`SUPPORTS`	The transactional method inherits the client's transaction context. If a transaction context is available, it is used by the method; if not, the container invokes the method with no transaction context. You should use `SUPPORTS` when you have read-only access to the database table.

Attribute	Description
MANDATORY	The container requires a transaction before invoking the business method but should not create a new one. If the client has a transaction context, it is propagated; if not, a javax.transaction.TransactionalException is thrown.
NOT_SUPPORTED	The transactional method cannot be invoked in a transaction context. If the client has no transaction context, nothing happens; if it does, the container suspends the client's transaction, invokes the method, and then resumes the transaction when the method returns.
NEVER	The transactional method must not be invoked from a transactional client. If the client is running within a transaction context, the container throws a javax.transaction.TransactionalException.

To apply one of these six demarcation attributes to your service, you have to use the @Transactional annotation. This annotation can be applied either to individual methods or to the entire bean. If applied at the bean level, all business methods will inherit the bean's transaction attribute value. Listing 159 shows how the PublisherService uses a SUPPORT transaction demarcation policy and overrides the update() method with REQUIRED.

Listing 159. A Custom Transactional Service

```
@ApplicationScoped
public class AddressService {

  @Inject
  private EntityManager em;

  @Transactional(REQUIRED)
  public Address save(Address address) {
    em.persist(address);
    return address;
  }

  @Transactional(MANDATORY)
  public String needsATransaction() {
    return "Success";
  }
}
```

So if you look at the PublisherService in Listing 159, then you'll understand that the update() method is transactional. If the caller hasn't created a transaction, then the container will create one. On the other hand, when the find methods are invoked, if it hasn't been invoked in a transactional context, then the container will not create a new one.

9.4. Spring Integration

The *Spring Framework* was created back in 2003 as an application framework and a container (based on the *Inversion of Control* principle) for Java platform.[58] The framework's core features could be used by any Java application and could be extended for building web applications on top of the Java EE platform.

Today, the term *Spring* means different things in different contexts. It can be used to refer to the Spring Framework itself, or other Spring projects that have been built over time such as Spring Boot, Spring MVC, Spring Security, Spring Data, Spring Cloud, Spring Batch, Spring WebFlux etc.

Historically, Spring added JPA support at a very early stage and JPA is still today a first-citizen integrated technology. In fact, you can integrate JPA in a Spring-based application almost everywhere, especially if you use Spring Data.[59]

Let's take a different example this time. Let's say we need a REST API to persist some addresses into a relational database. As Spring supports JPA, the code in Listing 160 will not come as a surprise to you.

Listing 160. Address Entity

```
@Entity
public class Address {

  @Id @GeneratedValue
  private Long id;
  private String street1;
  private String street2;
  private String city;
  private String state;
  private String zipcode;
  private String country;

  // Constructors, getters, setters
}
```

Listing 161 defines the REST controller that allows us to persist and query addresses thanks to a few annotations. The `createAddress()` method receives an `Address` within the HTTP request (`@RequestBody Address`) and stores it in a relational database thanks to the `AddressRepository.save()` method. All the other methods have a `@GetMapping` annotation which indicates that they return data within an HTTP response. The `countAll` method returns the number of addresses within the database thanks to the `AddressRepository.count()` method. Both the `getAddressesByCountry()` and `getAddressesLikeZip()` methods return a list of addresses based on certain parameters.

Listing 161. Spring REST Controller

```
@RestController
public class AddressEndpoint {

  private final AddressRepository addressRepository;

  @PostMapping("/addresses")
  public Address createAddress(@RequestBody Address address) {
    return addressRepository.save(address);
  }

  @GetMapping(value = "/addresses/count")
  public Long countAll() {
    return addressRepository.count();
  }

  @GetMapping(value = "/addresses/country/{country}")
  public List<Address> getAddressesByCountry(@PathVariable String country) {
    return addressRepository.findAllByCountry(country);
  }

  @GetMapping(value = "/addresses/like/{zip}")
  public List<Address> getAddressesLikeZip(@PathVariable String zip) {
    return addressRepository.findAllLikeZip(zip);
  }
}
```

What's important in Listing 161 is the use of an `AddressRepository` to store and retrieve data from the database. But if you look carefully, you won't see any `save()` or `count()` methods. That's because the `AddressRepository` extends from `JpaRepository` which is the one implementing these methods. The `findAllByCountry` method uses the naming convention of Spring Data to execute a `findAll` method with the criteria `ByCountry`. Therefore, Spring Data knows how to create a `WHERE` clause based on the country. On the other hand, the `findAllLikeZip` defines a JPQL query using the Spring Data `@Query` annotation.

Listing 162. Spring Data Repository

```
@Repository
public interface AddressRepository extends JpaRepository<Address, Long> {

  List<Address> findAllByCountry(@Param("country") String country);

  @Query("SELECT a FROM Address a WHERE a.zipcode LIKE %:zip%")
  List<Address> findAllLikeZip(@Param("zip") String zip);
}
```

[55] Bean Validation https://jcp.org/en/jsr/detail?id=380

[56] CDI https://jcp.org/en/jsr/detail?id=365

[57] JTA https://jcp.org/en/jsr/detail?id=907

[58] **Spring** https://spring.io

[59] **Spring Data** https://spring.io/projects/spring-data

Chapter 10. Putting It All Together

Now that you've read all the previous chapters on Java Persistence API, it's time to put some of these concepts all together and write a slightly more complex example. In this chapter, we will write an application that persists and queries entities from an H2 database.

The idea is to write a graph of entities (see Figure 47) that represents a book and add a `Main` class that persists a book as well as few test cases. You can then compile it with Maven and run it with EclipseLink as the JPA provider and an H2 database. To show how easy it is to integration-test an entity, I will show you how to write a test class (`BookTest`) with JUnit 5.x and use the embedded mode of H2 for persisting data using an in-memory database.

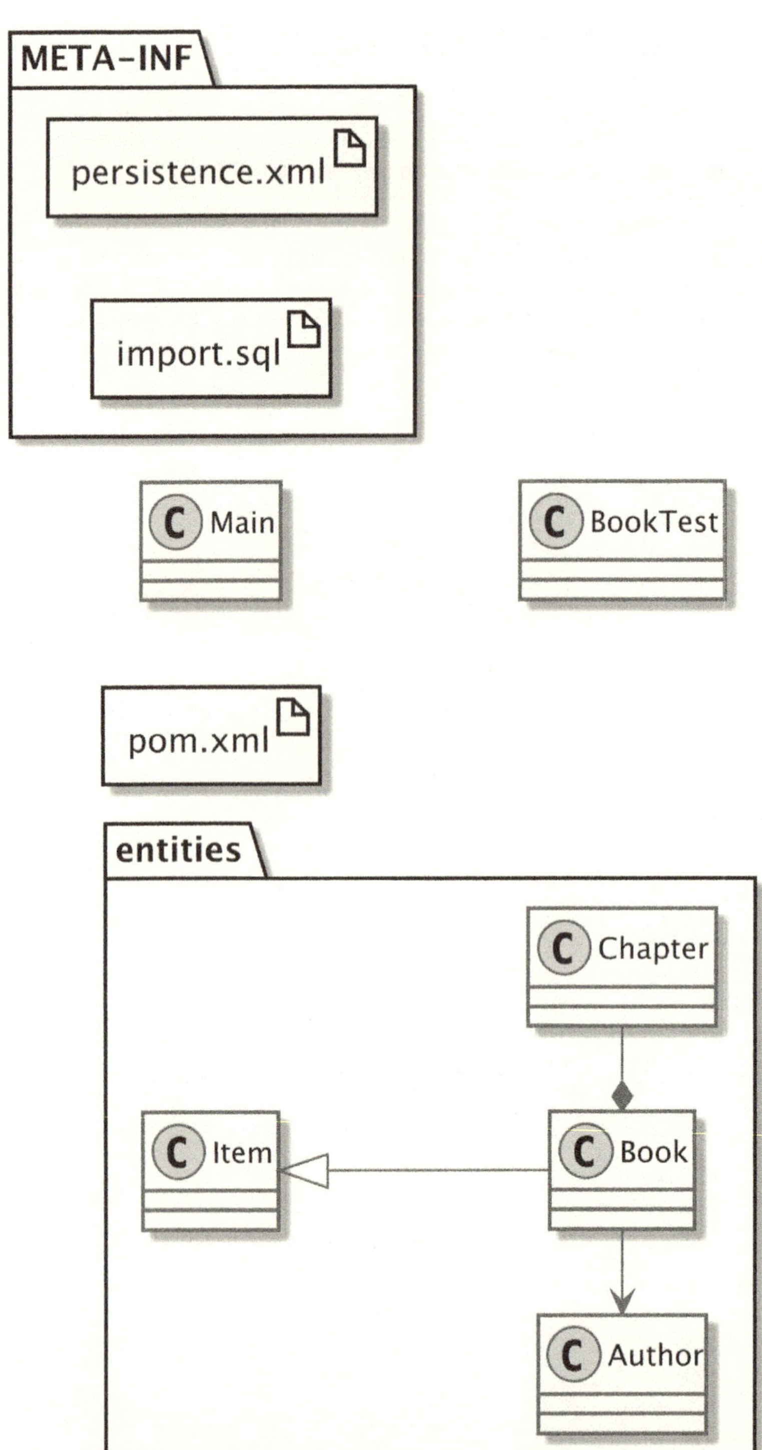

Figure 47. Putting it all together

The classes and files described in Figure 47 follow the Maven directory structure and have to be placed in the following directories:

- `src/main/java`: The directory for the `Item`, `Author`, `Book`, and `Chapter` entities as well as the `Main` class.
- `src/main/resources`: The `META-INF/persistence.xml` and `import.sql` files to describe the persistence unit and to import data into the database.
- `src/test/java`: The directory for the test cases `BookTest`.
- `pom.xml`: The Maven Project Object Model (POM) describing the project and its dependencies.

Make sure your development environment is set up to execute the code in this chapter. You can go to Appendix A to check that you have all the required tools installed, in particular JDK 11.0.10 or higher and Maven 3.6.x or higher. The code in this chapter can be found at https://github.com/agoncal/agoncal-fascicle-jpa/tree/2.2/putting-together

10.1. Writing the Entities

The class diagram in Figure 48 represents the domain model for a book. The central class in this diagram is the `Book` entity. It extends `Item` which is a mapped superclass. A book has a list of tags (Strings), a map of chapters (`Chapter` is an embeddable) and a list of many authors. Notice the bi-directional many-to-many relationship between `Book` and `Author` as a book can be written by several authors, and one author can write many books.

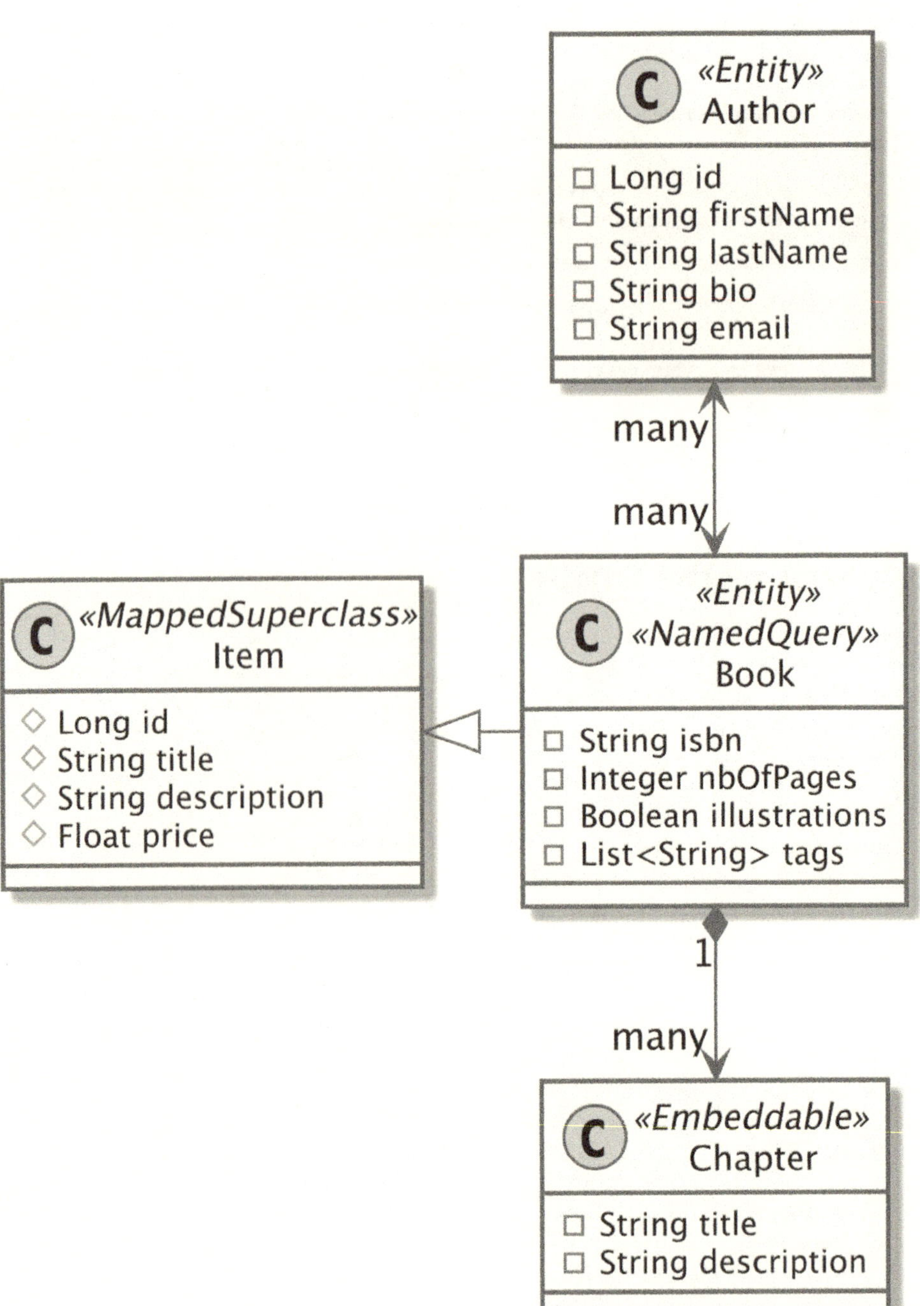

Figure 48. Domain model

10.1.1. Writing the Book Entity

Let's start with the `Book` entity. The `Book` entity (see Listing 163) needs to be developed under the src/main/java directory. It has several attributes (an isbn, a list of tags etc.) of different data types (String, Integer, Boolean and List<String>) as well as some JPA annotations:

- @Entity informs the persistence provider that this class is an entity and that it should manage it.
- The @NamedQuery annotations define two named-queries that use JPQL to retrieve all the books from the database as well as the books whose title is 'H2G2'.

Listing 163. A Book Entity with Named Queries

```
@Entity
@NamedQuery(name = "findAllBooks", query = "SELECT b FROM Book b")
@NamedQuery(name = "findBookH2G2", query = "SELECT b FROM Book b WHERE b.title
='H2G2'")
public class Book extends Item {

  @Column(nullable = false, unique = true)
  private String isbn;
  @Column(name = "nb_Of_pages")
  private Integer nbOfPages;
  private Boolean illustrations;

  @ElementCollection
  @CollectionTable(name = "tags",
    joinColumns = {@JoinColumn(name = "book_fk")}
  )
  @Column(name = "value")
  private List<String> tags = new ArrayList<>();

  @ElementCollection
  @CollectionTable(name = "book_chapters",
    joinColumns = {@JoinColumn(name = "book_fk")}
  )
  @MapKeyColumn(name = "position")
  private Map<Integer, Chapter> chapters = new HashMap<>();

  @ManyToMany
  @JoinTable(name = "books_authors",
    joinColumns = {@JoinColumn(name = "book_fk")},
    inverseJoinColumns = {@JoinColumn(name = "author_fk")}
  )
  private List<Author> authors = new ArrayList<>();

  // Constructors, getters, setters
}
```

The Book entity has several attributes and some of them use mapping annotations. The isbn attribute uses @Column to change the nullability of the columns in the database (e.g. ISBN cannot be null and its value must be unique within the entire BOOK table). @Column can also be used to map an attribute such as nbOfPages to be mapped to a database column that has a different name (NB_OF_PAGES).

A book can be described by a list of tags. The best way to map such information with JPA is by using a list of Strings. For that, the `List<String> tags` attribute needs to be annotated by `@ElementCollection`. Then we can use the optional annotations `@CollectionTable` to rename the datatable itself and `@Column` to rename the name of the datatable column.

To describe the fact that a book has a set of chapters, we could have used different strategies. `Chapter` could have been an entity, but it makes more sense for it to be an embeddable. An embeddable does not have an identity on its own. Instead, its life cycle is closely related to its embedded entity: if we remove a book, all the chapters are removed. And because a book has a set of ordered chapters, the relationship is done via a `Map` instead of a `List` or a `Set`. This way we can give a position to a chapter (e.g. the first chapter, the second chapter etc.). Notice the `@CollectionTable` annotation that indicates the name of the collection table, as well as `@JoinColumn` which redefines the name of the join column.

A book can be written by one or many authors. And an author can write one or many books. The bi-directional relationship between the `Book` entity and the `Author` entity is a `@ManyToMany`. The `@JoinTable` annotation is used to specify the name of the table joining `Book` and `Author`.

For better readability, I've omitted the constructor, getters and setters on most of the entities in this chapter.

10.1.2. Writing the Item Mapped Super-class

In our example, the `Book` inherits from `Item`. `Item` is holding the unique identifier of the book, as well as attributes such as `title`, `description` or `price`. It also uses a few JPA annotations:

- `@Id` defines the `id` attribute as being the primary key.
- The `@GeneratedValue` annotation informs the persistence provider to auto-generate the primary key, using the underlying database `id` utility.

In Listing 164, note that `Item` is not an entity but a mapped super-class. A class annotated with `@MappedSuperclass` is used to share state and behaviour, as well as mapping information which the `Book` entity inherits from. All in all, the attributes of `Item` and `Book` will get mapped into a single `BOOK` table.

Listing 164. Book Inherits from the Item Mapped Super-class

```
@MappedSuperclass
public class Item {

  @Id
  @GeneratedValue
  protected Long id;
  protected String title;
  protected String description;
  protected Float price;

  // Getters, setters
}
```

10.1.3. Writing the Chapter Embeddable

Listing 165 shows the `Chapter` embeddable. Notice that `Chapter` does not have any identifier (annotated with `@Id`), therefore it does not have any identity. But it allows the `Book` entity to have a map of chapters (the value of the map) with a position for the chapter (the key of the map): `Map<Integer, Chapter> chapters`.

Listing 165. A Book Has a Map of Chapters

```
@Embeddable
public class Chapter {

  private String title;
  private String description;

  // Constructors, getters, setters
}
```

10.1.4. Writing the Author Entity

Finally, the `Author` entity. As you can see in Listing 166, this entity just uses a set of elementary mapping annotations (`@Id`, `@Column` etc.). `Book` and `Author` engage in a many-to-many relationship. But notice that `Author` also has a list of books as an attribute. This shows that the many-to-many relationship is bi-directional (we can navigate from book to author as well as from author to book).

Listing 166. A Book Is Written by Authors

```
@Entity
public class Author {

  @Id
  @GeneratedValue
  private Long id;
  @Column(name = "first_name", length = 50)
  private String firstName;
  @Column(name = "last_name", nullable = false)
  private String lastName;
  @Column(length = 2000)
  private String bio;
  private String email;

  @ManyToMany(mappedBy = "authors")
  private List<Book> books = new ArrayList<>();

  // Constructors, getters, setters
}
```

Remember that you can download the code from https://github.com/agoncal/agoncal-fascicle-jpa/tree/2.2

10.1.5. Database Structure

One beauty of JPA is that you can leave the provider to generate the database schema of the entities we just defined. But that's not always the case. Most of the time you will have to map the persistent objects to an existing relational database, and this can be tricky. In our case, we just leave JPA to generate all the SQL code in order to create and drop our tables and constraints. Figure 49 shows the database structure the entities will get mapped to.

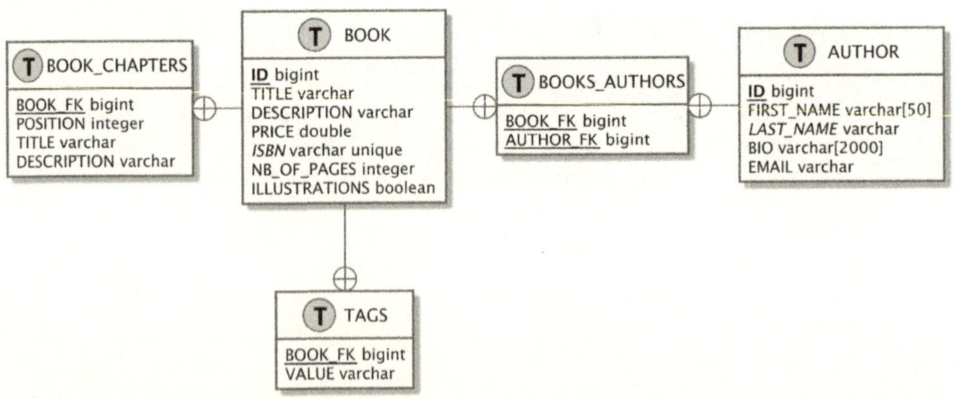

Figure 49. Database structure

In Figure 49, it is interesting to focus on the table relations. For example, `Book` inherits from `Item` and both attributes get squashed into a single `BOOK` table. `List<String> tags` gets mapped into a separate table `TAGS` using the foreign key `book_fk`. Even if `Chapter` is an embeddable with no identity, chapters have to be mapped into a separate `BOOK_CHAPTERS` table. Notice the `position` attribute which represents the key of the `Map`. As for the bi-directional many-to-many relationship between `Book` and `Author` it is represented as a join table called `BOOKS_AUTHORS`.

10.2. Writing the Persistence Units

Now that we have all our entities, we need to map them to a database. Then, a few questions arise: Which JDBC driver should we use? What is the target database? Do we need a user/password to connect to the database? This information is described in the deployment descriptor file called `persistence.xml` and is located under the `src/main/resources/META-INF` directory.

Listing 167 describes two persistence units:

- `vintageStorePU` is the persistence unit used by the `Main` class (see Listing 169), targeting an H2 server database and importing data thanks to the `import.sql` file (see below).
- `vintageStoreTestPU` is the persistence unit for testing (see `BookTest` in Listing 171), targeting an in-memory H2 database.

Listing 167. The persistence.xml File with Two Persistence Units

```
<persistence xmlns:xsi="http://www.w3.org/2001/XMLSchema-instance"
             xmlns="http://xmlns.jcp.org/xml/ns/persistence"
             xsi:schemaLocation="http://xmlns.jcp.org/xml/ns/persistence
http://xmlns.jcp.org/xml/ns/persistence/persistence_2_2.xsd"
             version="2.2">

  <persistence-unit name="cdbookstorePU" transaction-type="RESOURCE_LOCAL">
    <provider>org.eclipse.persistence.jpa.PersistenceProvider</provider>
    <exclude-unlisted-classes>false</exclude-unlisted-classes>
    <properties>
      <property name="javax.persistence.schema-generation.database.action" value=
"drop-and-create"/>
      <property name="javax.persistence.schema-generation.scripts.action" value="drop-
and-create"/>
      <property name="javax.persistence.schema-generation.scripts.create-target"
value="cdbookstoreCreate.ddl"/>
      <property name="javax.persistence.schema-generation.scripts.drop-target" value=
"cdbookstoreDrop.ddl"/>
      <property name="javax.persistence.jdbc.driver" value="org.h2.Driver"/>
      <property name="javax.persistence.jdbc.url" value=
"jdbc:h2:tcp://localhost/~/cdbookstoreDB"/>
      <property name="javax.persistence.sql-load-script-source" value="import.sql"/>
    </properties>
  </persistence-unit>

  <persistence-unit name="cdbookstoreTestPU" transaction-type="RESOURCE_LOCAL">
    <provider>org.eclipse.persistence.jpa.PersistenceProvider</provider>
    <exclude-unlisted-classes>false</exclude-unlisted-classes>
    <properties>
      <property name="javax.persistence.schema-generation.database.action" value=
"drop-and-create"/>
      <property name="javax.persistence.jdbc.driver" value="org.h2.Driver"/>
      <property name="javax.persistence.jdbc.url" value="jdbc:h2:mem:cdbookstoreDB"/>
    </properties>
  </persistence-unit>

</persistence>
```

10.2.1. Writing an SQL Script to Load Data

Notice, in the `persistence.xml` file in Listing 167, the `javax.persistence.sql-load-script-source` property. It is used by the persistence unit `vintageStorePU` to execute an SQL script before the application is loaded. In our case, we use this property to execute the script `import.sql` to insert data into the database at runtime. This means that the script in Listing 168 is executed for database initialisation and inserts three books.

Listing 168. The insert.sql File

```
INSERT INTO BOOK(ID, TITLE, DESCRIPTION, ILLUSTRATIONS, ISBN, NB_OF_PAGES, PRICE)
values (1000, 'Beginning Java EE 6', 'Best Java EE book ever', 1, '1234-5678', 450,
49)
INSERT INTO BOOK(ID, TITLE, DESCRIPTION, ILLUSTRATIONS, ISBN, NB_OF_PAGES, PRICE)
values (1001, 'Beginning Java EE 7', 'No, this is the best ', 1, '5678-9012', 550, 53)
INSERT INTO BOOK(ID, TITLE, DESCRIPTION, ILLUSTRATIONS, ISBN, NB_OF_PAGES, PRICE)
values (1010, 'The Lord of the Rings', 'One ring to rule them all', 0, '9012-3456',
222, 23)
```

10.3. Writing the Main Class

The `Main` class, shown in Listing 169, is under the same package as the `Book` entity (`src/main/java`). It creates a book, persists it into the H2 server database and executes two queries.

Listing 169. A Main Class Persisting the Book Entity

```
public class Main {

  public static void main(String[] args) {

    // 1 - Creates an instance of book with tags
    Book book = new Book().title("H2G2").price(12.5F).isbn("1-9754-742-3").nbOfPages
(354);
    book.tag("sci-fi").tag("fun").tag("geek");

    // 2 - Obtains an entity manager and a transaction
    EntityManagerFactory emf = Persistence.createEntityManagerFactory("cdbookstorePU"
);
    EntityManager em = emf.createEntityManager();

    // 3 - Persists the book to the database
    EntityTransaction tx = em.getTransaction();
    tx.begin();
    em.persist(book);
    tx.commit();

    // 4 - Queries H2G2 books
    book = em.createNamedQuery("findBookH2G2", Book.class).getSingleResult();
    System.out.println(book);

    // 4 - Queries all the books
    int books = em.createNamedQuery("findAllBooks", Book.class).getResultList().size(
);
    System.out.println("Number of books " + books);

    // 5 - Closes the entity manager and the factory
    em.close();
    emf.close();
  }
}
```

The `Main` class in Listing 169 commences by creating a new instance of `Book` (using the Java keyword `new`) and sets some values to its attributes. Up to that point, there is nothing special here, just pure Java code. But things change when the entity manager comes into play. The entity manager is the central piece of JPA in that it is able to create a transaction and persist the `book` object using the `EntityManager.persist()` method. Once the transaction is committed, the `EntityManager` is then used to create and invoke two named queries to return a book called 'H2G2' (using the `findBookH2G2` named query defined in `Book` in Listing 163) and the list of all books (`findAllBooks`).

Again, for readability, I've omitted exception handling. If a persistence exception occurs, you would have to roll back the transaction, log a message, and close the `EntityManager` in the finally block.

10.4. Writing the BookTest Integration Tests

One of the major selling points of JPA is that you can easily test entities without requiring a running application server or live database. But what can you test? Entities themselves usually don't need to be tested in isolation. Most methods on entities are simple getters or setters with only a few business methods. Verifying that a setter assigns a value to an attribute and that the corresponding getter retrieves the same value does not give any extra value (unless a side effect is detected in the getters or the setters). So, unit testing an entity has limited benefit.

What about testing the database queries? Making sure that the `findBookH2G2` query is correct? Or injecting data into the database and testing complex queries bringing multiple values? Thanks to in-memory database, CRUD operations and JPQL queries can be easily tested with JPA.

The `BookTest` class, shown in Listing 170, goes under the `src/test/java` directory. It has a set of test cases to test different interactions with the `Book` entity. Like the `Main` class, `BookTest` needs to create an `EntityManager` instance using an `EntityManagerFactory`. This is done once before testing (thanks to `@BeforeAll`) by the `init()` method which initialises the `EntityManager` (with the `vintageStoreTestPU` persistence unit) and creates a new transaction. The `close()` method releases the factory once the tests end (`@AfterAll`).

Listing 170. The BookTest Integration Test

```
public class BookTest {

  private static EntityManagerFactory emf = Persistence.createEntityManagerFactory(
"cdbookstoreTestPU");
  private static EntityManager em;
  private static EntityTransaction tx;

  @BeforeAll
  static void init() {
    em = emf.createEntityManager();
    tx = em.getTransaction();
  }

  @AfterAll
  static void close() {
    if (em != null) em.close();
    if (emf != null) emf.close();
  }

  // ...
```

The test case in Listing 171 persists a book (using the `EntityManager.persist()` method) and checks whether the `id` has been automatically generated by the JPA provider (with `assertNotNull`). If so, the `findAllBooks` named query is executed and checks whether there is more than one book in the database.

Listing 171. Persisting a Book and Retrieving from the Database

```
Book book = new Book().title("Java EE 7").price(23.5F).isbn("1-84023-742-2").
nbOfPages(354);

tx.begin();
em.persist(book);
tx.commit();
assertNotNull(book.getId(), "Id should not be null");

List<Book> allBooks = em.createNamedQuery("findAllBooks", Book.class).getResultList();
assertTrue(allBooks.size() >= 1);
```

The test case in Listing 172 persists a book with tags and chapters. First, we create the graph of entities (one book, three tags and four chapters) and then we persist the book with its relationships. The test case then checks that there are three tags and four chapters.

Listing 172. Persisting a Book with Tags and Chapters

```
Book book = new Book().title("Java EE 7").price(23.5F).isbn("1-84023-742-4").
nbOfPages(354);
book.tag("java ee").tag("java").tag("enterprise");
book.chapter(1, new Chapter("Bean Validation"));
book.chapter(2, new Chapter("CDI"));
book.chapter(3, new Chapter("JPA"));
book.chapter(4, new Chapter("EJB"));

// Persists the book to the database
tx.begin();
em.persist(book);
tx.commit();

// Checks the book
Book foundBook = em.find(Book.class, book.getId());
assertEquals(3, foundBook.getTags().size());
assertEquals(4, foundBook.getChapters().size());
```

The last test case (see Listing 173) creates a `Book` with two authors.

Listing 173. Persisting a Book with Two Authors

```
Author deepu = new Author().firstName("Deepu").lastName("Sasidharan");
Author sendil = new Author().firstName("Sendil").lastName("Kumar");
Book book = new Book().title("Full Stack Development with JHipster").price(23.5F).
isbn("5-84023-742-5").nbOfPages(354).author(deepu).author(sendil);
deepu.book(book);
sendil.book(book);

// Persists the book to the database
tx.begin();
em.persist(book);
em.persist(deepu);
em.persist(sendil);
tx.commit();

// Checks the book
Book foundBook = em.find(Book.class, book.getId());
assertEquals(2, foundBook.getAuthors().size());
```

10.5. Compiling and Testing with Maven

All the classes now need to be compiled before they get tested. The `pom.xml` in Listing 174 declares all the necessary dependencies to compile the code: EclipseLink 2.7.x (the reference implementation for JPA 2.2) and the H2 database.

Listing 174. The pom.xml File to Compile and Test the Code

```
<project xmlns:xsi="http://www.w3.org/2001/XMLSchema-instance"
         xmlns="http://maven.apache.org/POM/4.0.0"
         xsi:schemaLocation="http://maven.apache.org/POM/4.0.0
http://maven.apache.org/xsd/maven-4.0.0.xsd">
  <modelVersion>4.0.0</modelVersion>

  <groupId>org.agoncal.fascicle.jpa</groupId>
  <artifactId>putting-together</artifactId>
  <version>2.2</version>
  <dependencies>
    <dependency>
      <groupId>org.eclipse.persistence</groupId>
      <artifactId>org.eclipse.persistence.jpa</artifactId>
      <version>2.7.8</version>
    </dependency>
    <dependency>
      <groupId>com.h2database</groupId>
      <artifactId>h2</artifactId>
      <version>1.4.200</version>
    </dependency>
```

To compile the classes, open a command line in the root directory containing the `pom.xml` file and enter the following Maven command:

```
$ mvn compile
```

To test our `BookTest` class, we need a few extra dependencies in our `pom.xml`: JUnit and the Maven Surefire plugin (that allow testing).

Listing 175. The pom.xml File Dependencies to Run the Tests

```
    <dependency>
      <groupId>org.junit.jupiter</groupId>
      <artifactId>junit-jupiter-engine</artifactId>
      <version>5.7.1</version>
      <scope>test</scope>
    </dependency>
  </dependencies>

  <build>
    <plugins>
      <plugin>
        <groupId>org.apache.maven.plugins</groupId>
        <artifactId>maven-surefire-plugin</artifactId>
        <version>3.0.0-M5</version>
      </plugin>
      <plugin>
        <groupId>org.codehaus.mojo</groupId>
        <artifactId>exec-maven-plugin</artifactId>
        <version>3.0.0</version>
        <executions>
          <execution>
            <goals>
              <goal>java</goal>
            </goals>
          </execution>
        </executions>
        <configuration>
          <mainClass>org.agoncal.fascicle.jpa.puttingtogether.Main</mainClass>
        </configuration>
      </plugin>
    </plugins>
  </build>
</project>
```

Then, to execute the integration tests, it's just a matter of executing the following Maven command:

```
$ mvn test
```

The BookTest class is then executed, and a Maven report should inform you if the tests pass or not. You should see the BUILD SUCCESS message informing you that the tests were successful.

```
[INFO] Results:
[INFO]
[INFO] Tests run: 3, Failures: 0, Errors: 0, Skipped: 0
[INFO]
[INFO] ------------------------------------------------
[INFO] BUILD SUCCESS
[INFO] ------------------------------------------------
[INFO] Total time:  7.564 s
[INFO] ------------------------------------------------
```

10.6. Executing the Main Class with an H2 Server Database

Now that we know our code compiles and our tests pass, let's execute the Main class. Before that, you need to start the H2 Server Database (remember that the Main class uses the persistence unit vintageStorePU which does not use the in-memory database, but a server database instead). The easiest way to do this is to go to the $H2/bin directory and execute the h2 script. H2 starts, opens a browser and displays the login page shown in Figure 50. Make sure you set the JDBC URL to jdbc:h2:tcp://localhost/~/vintageStoreDB.

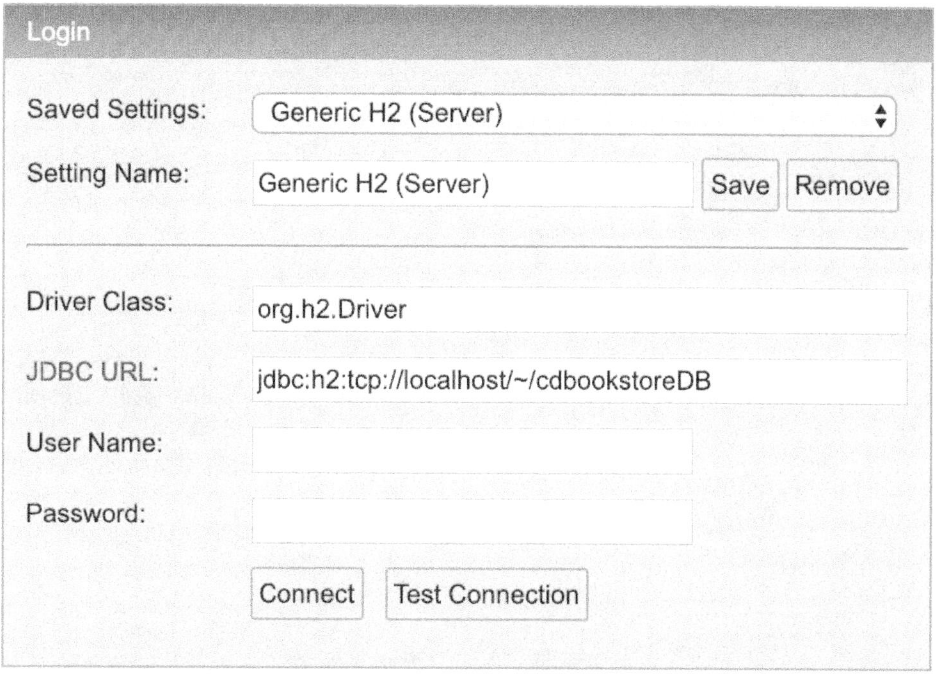

Login
Saved Settings: Generic H2 (Server)
Setting Name: Generic H2 (Server) Save Remove
Driver Class: org.h2.Driver
JDBC URL: jdbc:h2:tcp://localhost/~/cdbookstoreDB
User Name:
Password:
Connect Test Connection

Figure 50. Logging to the H2 database console

The H2 process is listening on port 8082 and waiting for the JDBC driver to send any SQL statement. To execute the `Main` class, you can use the java interpreter command or use the `exec-maven-plugin` as follows:

```
$ mvn exec:java
```

When you run the `Main` class, several things occur. First, H2 will automatically create the `vintageStoreDB` database. That's because of the `schema-generation.database.action` property defined in the `persistence.xml` which informs the JPA provider to automatically create the database schema. Thanks to the `import.sql` SQL script, the JPA provider will insert data into this newly created database.

Finally, the `Main` class is executed: a new book is created and inserted into the database and then the queries are executed. We can use the H2 console (see Figure 51) to query the database and check that the `Main` class was executed correctly. For example, enter `SELECT * FROM BOOK` in the H2 console to display the content of the table `BOOK`.

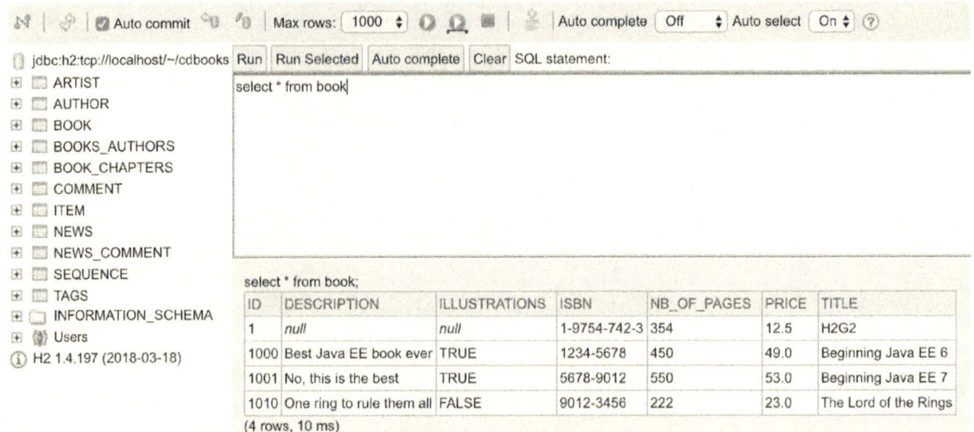

Figure 51. H2 console executing a select statement

10.7. Checking the Generated Schema

In the `persistence.xml` file described in Listing 167, we have informed the JPA provider to generate the schema database as well as creating the drop and create scripts, thanks to the following property:

```
<property name="javax.persistence.schema-generation.database.action" value="drop-and-
create"/>
<property name="javax.persistence.schema-generation.scripts.action" value="drop-and-
create"/>
<property name="javax.persistence.schema-generation.scripts.create-target" value=
"vintageStoreCreate.ddl"/>
<property name="javax.persistence.schema-generation.scripts.drop-target" value=
"vintageStoreDrop.ddl"/>
```

The JPA provider will generate two SQL scripts:

- `vintageStoreCreate.ddl` (Listing 176) with all the SQL statements to create the entire database
- and `vintageStoreDrop.ddl` to drop all the tables.

This is useful when you need to execute scripts in order to create a database in your continuous integration process.

Listing 176. The vintageStoreCreate.ddl Script

```
CREATE TABLE BOOK
(
  ID            BIGINT  NOT NULL,
  DESCRIPTION   VARCHAR,
  ILLUSTRATIONS BOOLEAN,
  ISBN          VARCHAR NOT NULL UNIQUE,
  NB_OF_PAGES   INTEGER,
  PRICE         DOUBLE,
  TITLE         VARCHAR,
  PRIMARY KEY (ID)
);

CREATE TABLE TAGS
(
  BOOK_FK BIGINT,
  VALUE   VARCHAR
);

CREATE TABLE BOOK_CHAPTERS
(
  POSITION    INTEGER,
  DESCRIPTION VARCHAR,
  TITLE       VARCHAR,
  BOOK_FK     BIGINT
);

CREATE TABLE BOOKS_AUTHORS
(
  AUTHOR_FK BIGINT NOT NULL,
  BOOK_FK   BIGINT NOT NULL,
  PRIMARY KEY (AUTHOR_FK, BOOK_FK)
);

CREATE TABLE AUTHOR
(
  ID         BIGINT  NOT NULL,
  BIO        VARCHAR(2000),
  EMAIL      VARCHAR,
  FIRST_NAME VARCHAR(50),
  LAST_NAME  VARCHAR NOT NULL,
  PRIMARY KEY (ID)
);
```

To get the structure of any table, let's say `BOOK`, you can also execute the statement `SHOW COLUMNS FROM BOOK` in the H2 console as seen in Figure 52.

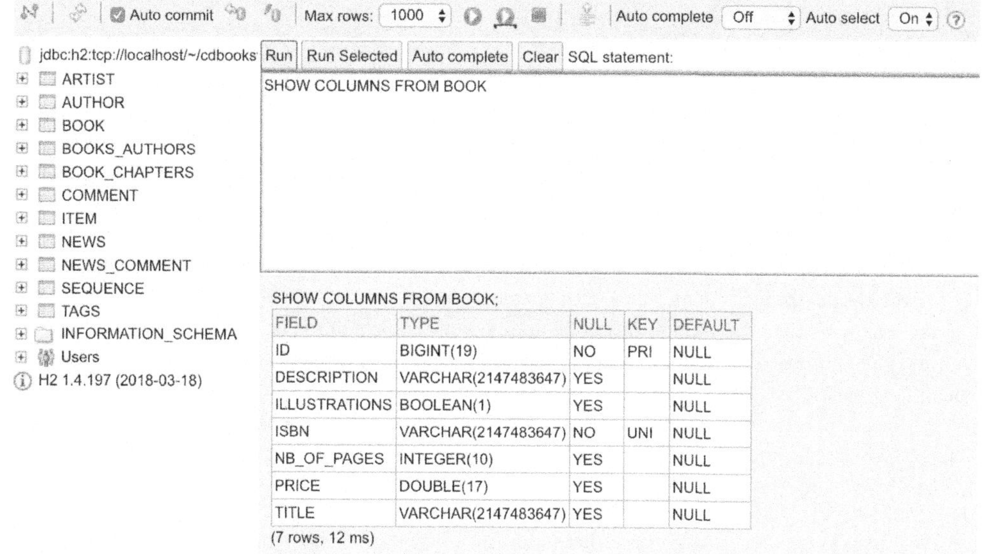

Figure 52. H2 console showing the database structure

Chapter 11. Summary

JPA has a very comprehensive approach to object-relational mapping. It focuses on a simple and easy-to-use architecture but yet has a very rich and powerful mapping and query mechanism. Thanks to configuration by exception, not much is required to map entities to tables; inform the persistence provider that a class is actually an entity (using `@Entity`) and an attribute is its identifier (using `@Id`), and JPA does the rest.

JPA has a very rich set of annotations to customise every little detail of ORM (as well as the equivalent XML mapping). Elementary annotations can be used on attributes (`@Basic`, `@Temporal` etc.) or classes to customise the mapping. You can change the table's name or the primary key type, or even avoid mapping with the `@Transient` annotation. With JPA, you can map collections of basic types or embeddables. Depending on your domain model, you can map relationships (`@OneToOne`, `@ManyToMany` etc.) of different directions and multiplicity. The same thing applies to inheritance (`@Inheritance`, `@MappedSuperclass` etc.) where you can use different strategies to map a hierarchy of entities and nonentities mixed together.

Once the mapping is done, JPA lets you query entities in an object-oriented way. The entity manager is central to articulating entities with persistence. It can create, update, find by Id, remove, and synchronise entities to the database with the help of the persistence context, which acts as a level-one cache. JPA also comes with a very powerful query language, JPQL, which is database-vendor independent. You can retrieve entities with a rich syntax using `WHERE`, `ORDER BY`, or `GROUP BY` clauses, and when concurrent access occurs with your entities, you know how to use versioning and when to use optimistic or pessimistic locking.

JPA also handles the entity life cycle and how the entity manager catches events to invoke callback methods. Callback methods can be defined on a single entity and annotated by several annotations (`@PrePersist`, `@PostPersist` etc.). The method can also be extracted to listener classes and used by several or all entities (using default entity listeners). With callback methods, you see that entities are not just anemic objects (objects with no business logic, just attributes, getters, and setters); entities can have business logic that can be invoked by other objects in the application, or invoked automatically by the entity manager, depending on the life cycle of the entity.[60]

This is the end of the *Understanding JPA 2.2* fascicle. I hope you liked it, learnt a few things, and more importantly, will be able to take this knowledge back to your projects.

Remember that you can find all the code for this fascicle at https://github.com/agoncal/agoncal-fascicle-jpa/tree/2.2. If some parts were not clear enough, or if you found something missing, a bug, or you just want to leave a note or suggestion, please use the GitHub issue tracker at https://github.com/agoncal/agoncal-fascicle-jpa/issues.

If you liked the format of this fascicle, you might want to read others that I have written. Check out Appendix D for the full list of fascicles.

[60] **Anemic Domain Model** https://www.martinfowler.com/bliki/AnemicDomainModel.html

Appendix A: Setting up the Development Environment on macOS

This appendix focuses on setting up your development environment so you can do some hands-on work by following the code snippets listed in the previous chapters. This fascicle has lots of code samples, and even has a chapter with a "*Putting It All Together*" section. This section provides a step-by-step example showing how to develop, compile, deploy, execute and test the components. To run these examples, you need to install the required software.

Bear in mind that I run all of these tools on macOS. So, this appendix gives you all of the installation guidelines for the macOS operating system. If your machine runs on Linux or Windows, check online to know how to install the following tools on your platform.

A.1. Homebrew

One of the pre-requisites is that you have *Homebrew* installed. *Homebrew* is a package manager for macOS.[61]

A.1.1. A Brief History of Homebrew

The name *Homebrew* is intended to suggest the idea of building software on the Mac depending on the user's taste. It was written by Max Howell in 2009 in Ruby.[62] On September 2016, Homebrew version 1.0.0 was released. In January 2019, Linuxbrew was merged back into Homebrew, adding beta support for Linux and the Windows Subsystem for Linux to Homebrew's feature set. On February 2, 2019, Homebrew version 2.0.0 was released.

A.1.2. Installing Homebrew on macOS

To install Homebrew, just execute the following command:

```
$ /bin/bash -c "$(curl -fsSL
https://raw.githubusercontent.com/Homebrew/install/master/install.sh)"
```

You also need *Homebrew Cask* which extends Homebrew and brings installation and management of GUI macOS applications.[63] Install it by running:

```
$ brew tap homebrew/cask
```

A.1.3. Checking for Homebrew Installation

Now you should be able to execute a few Homebrew commands:

```
$ brew --version

Homebrew 3.0.4
Homebrew/homebrew-core
Homebrew/homebrew-cask
```

A.1.4. Some Homebrew Commands

- `brew commands`: Lists the built-in and external commands.
- `brew help`: Displays help.
- `brew doctor`: Checks for potential problems.
- `brew install`: Installs a formula.
- `brew uninstall`: Uninstalls a formula.
- `brew list`: Lists all installed formulae.
- `brew upgrade`: Upgrades outdated casks and formulae.
- `brew update`: Fetches the newest version of Homebrew.
- `brew cask help`: Displays Homebrew Cask help.
- `brew cask install`: Installs a cask.
- `brew cask uninstall`: Uninstalls a cask.
- `brew cask list`: Lists installed casks.
- `brew cask upgrade`: Upgrades all outdated casks (or the specified casks).

A.2. Java 11

Essential for the development and execution of the examples in the fascicle is the *Java Development Kit* (JDK).[64] The JDK includes several tools such as a compiler (`javac`), a virtual machine, a documentation generator (`javadoc`), monitoring tools (Visual VM) and so on.[65] The code in this fascicle uses Java 11 (JDK 11.0.10).

A.2.1. Architecture

One design goal of Java is portability, which means that programs written for the Java platform must run similarly on any combination of hardware and operating system with adequate runtime support. This is achieved by compiling the Java language code to an intermediate representation called *bytecode*, instead of directly to a specific machine code. This bytecode is then analysed, interpreted and executed on the *Java Virtual Machine* (JVM).

The *Interpreter* is the one interpreting the bytecode. It does it quickly, but executes slowly. The disadvantage of the interpreter is that, when one method is called multiple times, a new interpretation is required every time. That's when the *Just In Time* (JIT) compiler kicks in. JIT is basically the component that translates the JVM bytecode (generated by your `javac` command) into machine code which is the language that your underlying execution environment (i.e. your processor) can understand—and all that happens dynamically at runtime! When the JIT finds repeated code, it compiles the bytecode and changes it to native code. This native code will then be used directly for repeated method calls, which improves the performance of the system. This JIT is also called the *Java HotSpot* (a.k.a. Java HotSpot Performance Engine, or HotSpot VM).[66] Then, the *Garbage Collector* will collect and remove unreferenced objects.

A.2.2. A Brief History of Java

James Gosling, Mike Sheridan, and Patrick Naughton initiated the Java language project in June 1991. Java was originally designed for interactive television, but it was too advanced for the digital cable television industry at the time. The language was initially called Oak after an oak tree that stood outside Gosling's office. Later, the project went by the name Green and was finally renamed Java, from Java coffee. Gosling designed Java with a C/C++-style syntax that system and application programmers would find familiar. Sun Microsystems released the first public implementation as Java 1.0 in 1996. Following Oracle Corporation's acquisition of Sun Microsystems in 2009–10, Oracle has described itself as the "*steward of Java technology*" since then.[67]

A.2.3. Installing the JDK on macOS

To install the JDK 11.0.10, go to the official website, select the appropriate platform and language, and download the distribution.[68] For example, on macOS, download the file `jdk-11.0.10_osx-x64_bin.dmg` shown in Figure 53 (you should check out the *Accept License Agreement* check box before hitting the download link to let the download start). If you are not on Mac, the download steps are still pretty similar.

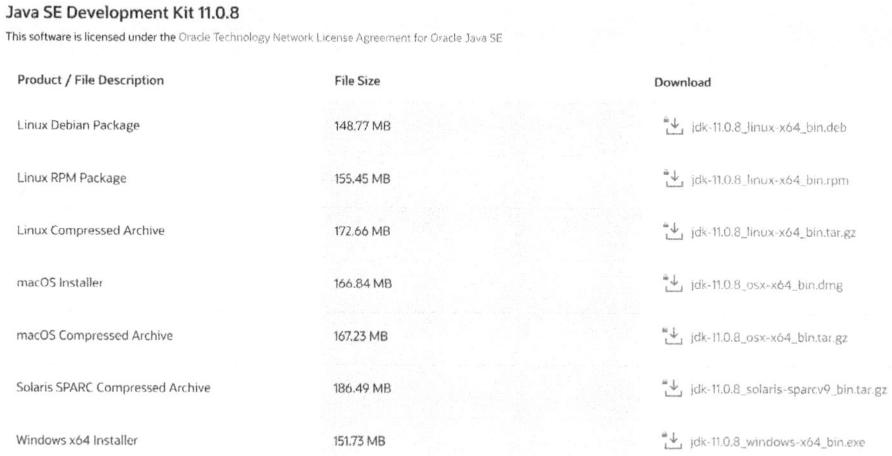

Java SE Development Kit 11.0.8

This software is licensed under the Oracle Technology Network License Agreement for Oracle Java SE

Product / File Description	File Size	Download
Linux Debian Package	148.77 MB	jdk-11.0.8_linux-x64_bin.deb
Linux RPM Package	155.45 MB	jdk-11.0.8_linux-x64_bin.rpm
Linux Compressed Archive	172.66 MB	jdk-11.0.8_linux-x64_bin.tar.gz
macOS Installer	166.84 MB	jdk-11.0.8_osx-x64_bin.dmg
macOS Compressed Archive	167.23 MB	jdk-11.0.8_osx-x64_bin.tar.gz
Solaris SPARC Compressed Archive	186.49 MB	jdk-11.0.8_solaris-sparcv9_bin.tar.gz
Windows x64 Installer	151.73 MB	jdk-11.0.8_windows-x64_bin.exe

Figure 53. Downloading the JDK distribution

Double-click on the file `jdk-11.0.10_osx-x64_bin.dmg`. This will bring up a pop-up screen (see Figure 54), asking you to start the installation.

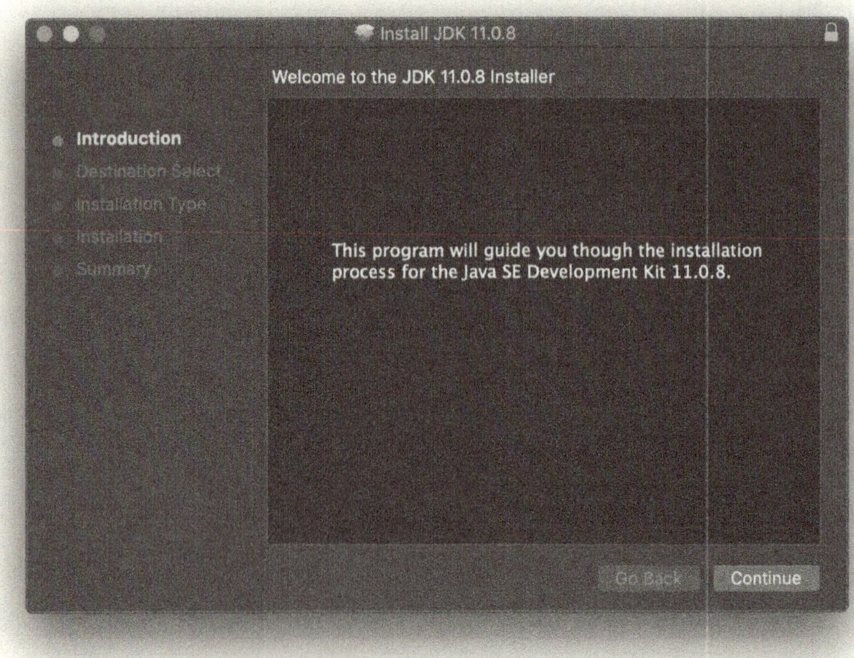

Figure 54. Installation pop-up screen

The wizard invites you to accept the licence for the software and install the JDK successfully (see Figure 55).

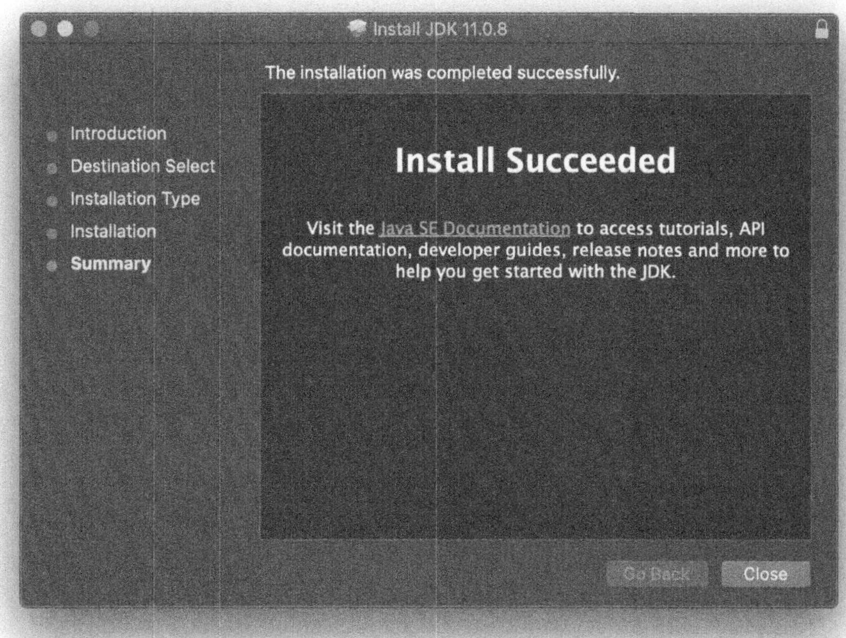

Figure 55. Successful JDK installation

There is also an easier way to install Java using Homebrew. First of all, check if you already have the Java formula installed on your machine:

```
$ brew cask list java11
Error: Cask 'java11' is not installed.
```

If the Java formula is not installed, execute the following Homebrew commands to install it:

```
$ brew tap homebrew/cask-versions
$ brew cask install java11
...
java11 was successfully installed!
```

A.2.4. Checking for Java Installation

Once the installation is complete, it is necessary to set the `JAVA_HOME` variable and the `$JAVA_HOME/bin` directory to the `PATH` variable. Check that your system recognises Java by entering `java -version` as well as the Java compiler with `javac -version`.

```
$ java -version
java version "11.0.10" 2020-07-14 LTS
Java(TM) SE Runtime Environment 18.9 (build 11.0.10+10-LTS)
Java HotSpot(TM) 64-Bit Server VM 18.9 (build 11.0.10+10-LTS, mixed mode)

$ javac -version
javac 11.0.10
```

A.3. Maven 3.6.x

All the examples of this fascicle are built and tested using Maven.[69] Maven offers a building solution, shared libraries, and a plugin platform for your projects, allowing you to do quality control, documentation, teamwork and so forth. Based on the "*convention over configuration*" principle, Maven brings a standard project description and a number of conventions such as a standard directory structure. With an extensible architecture based on plugins, Maven can offer many different services.

A.3.1. A Brief History of Maven

Maven, created by Jason van Zyl, began as a subproject of Apache Turbine in 2002. In 2003, it was voted on and accepted as a top-level Apache Software Foundation project. In July 2004, Maven's release was the critical first milestone, v1.0. Maven 2 was declared v2.0 in October 2005 after about six months in beta cycles. Maven 3.0 was released in October 2010, being mostly backwards compatible with Maven 2.[70]

A.3.2. Project Descriptor

Maven is based on the fact that a majority of Java projects face similar requirements when building applications. A Maven project needs to follow some standards as well as define specific features in a project descriptor, or *Project Object Model* (POM). The POM is an XML file (`pom.xml`) placed at the root of the project and contains all the metadata of the project. As shown in Listing 177, the minimum required information to describe the identity of a project is the `groupId`, the `artifactId`, the `version`, and the `packaging` type.

Listing 177. Header of a Maven Project Descriptor

```
<?xml version="1.0" encoding="UTF-8"?>
<project xmlns:xsi="http://www.w3.org/2001/XMLSchema-instance"
         xmlns="http://maven.apache.org/POM/4.0.0"
         xsi:schemaLocation="http://maven.apache.org/POM/4.0.0
http://maven.apache.org/xsd/maven-4.0.0.xsd">

  <modelVersion>4.0.0</modelVersion>
  <groupId>org.agoncal.fascicle</groupId>
  <artifactId>chapter01</artifactId>
  <version>1.0-SNAPSHOT</version>
  <packaging>jar</packaging>
</project>
```

A project is often divided into different artifacts. These artifacts are then grouped under the same `groupId` (similar to packages in Java) and uniquely identified by the `artifactId`. Packaging allows Maven to produce each artifact following a standard format (jar, war, ear etc.). Finally, the version allows the identifying of an artifact during its lifetime (version 1.1, 1.2, 1.2.1 etc.). Maven imposes versioning so that a team can manage the life of its project development. Maven also introduces the concept of `SNAPSHOT` versions (the version number ends with the string `-SNAPSHOT`) to identify an artifact that is being developed and is not released yet.

The POM defines much more information about your project. Some aspects are purely descriptive (name, description etc.), while others concern the application execution such as the list of external libraries used, and so on. Moreover, the `pom.xml` defines environmental information to build the project (versioning tool, continuous integration server, artifact repositories), and any other specific process to build your project.

A.3.3. Managing Artifacts

Maven goes beyond building artifacts; it also offers a genuine approach to archive and share these artifacts. Maven uses a local repository on your hard drive (by default in `~/.m2/repository`) where it stores all the artifacts that the project's descriptor references. The local repository is filled either by the local developer's artifacts (e.g. `myProject-1.1.jar`) or by external ones (e.g. `javax.annotation-api-1.2.jar`) that Maven downloads from remote repositories.

A Maven project can reference a specific artifact including the artifact's dependencies in the POM using `groupId`, `artifactId`, `version` and `scope` in a declarative way as shown in Listing 178. If necessary, Maven will download them to the local repository from remote repositories. Moreover, using the POM descriptors of these external artifacts, Maven will also download the artifacts they need (so-called "*transitive dependencies*"). Therefore, the development team doesn't have to manually add the project dependencies to the classpath. Maven automatically adds the necessary libraries.

Listing 178. Maven Dependencies

```
<dependencies>
  <dependency>
    <groupId>org.eclipse.persistence</groupId>
    <artifactId>javax.persistence</artifactId>
    <version>2.1</version>
    <scope>provided</scope>
  </dependency>
  <dependency>
    <groupId>org.glassfish</groupId>
    <artifactId>javax.ejb</artifactId>
    <version>3.2</version>
    <scope>provided</scope>
  </dependency>
</dependencies>
```

Dependencies may have limited visibility (called scope):

- `test`: The library is used to compile and run test classes but is not packaged in the produced artifact (e.g. war file).
- `provided`: The library is provided by the environment (persistence provider, application server etc.) and is only used to compile the code.
- `compile`: The library is necessary for compilation and execution. Therefore, it will be packaged as part of the produced artifact too.
- `runtime`: The library is only required for execution but is excluded from the compilation (e.g. Servlets).

A.3.4. Installing Maven on macOS

The examples of this fascicle have been developed with Apache Maven 3.6.x. Once you have installed the JDK 11.0.10, make sure the `JAVA_HOME` environment variable is set. Then, check if you already have the Maven formula installed on your machine:

```
$ brew list maven
Error: No such keg: /usr/local/Cellar/maven
```

If the Maven formula is not installed, execute the following Homebrew command to install it:

```
$ brew install maven
...
maven was successfully installed!
```

You should now see the Maven formula in Homebrew:

```
$ brew list maven
/usr/local/Cellar/maven/3.6.3_1/bin/mvn
/usr/local/Cellar/maven/3.6.3_1/bin/mvnDebug
/usr/local/Cellar/maven/3.6.3_1/bin/mvnyjp
```

A.3.5. Checking for Maven Installation

Once you've got Maven installed, open a command line and enter mvn `-version` to validate your installation. Maven should print its version and the JDK version it uses (which is handy as you might have different JDK versions installed on the same machine).

```
$ mvn -version

Apache Maven 3.6.3
Maven home: /usr/local/Cellar/maven/3.6.3_1/libexec
```

Be aware that Maven needs Internet access so it can download plugins and project dependencies from the Maven Central and/or other remote repositories.[71] If you are behind a proxy, see the documentation to configure your settings.

A.3.6. Some Maven Commands

Maven is a command line utility where you can use several parameters and options to build, test or package your code. To get some help on the commands you can type, use the following command:

```
$ mvn --help

usage: mvn [options] [<goal(s)>] [<phase(s)>]
```

Here are some commands that you will be using to run the examples in the fascicle. Each invokes a different phase of the project life cycle (clean, compile, install etc.) and uses the `pom.xml` to download libraries, customise the compilation, or extend some behaviours using plugins:

- `mvn clean`: Deletes all generated files (compiled classes, generated code, artifacts etc.).
- `mvn compile`: Compiles the main Java classes.
- `mvn test-compile`: Compiles the test classes.
- `mvn test`: Compiles the main Java classes as well as the test classes and executes the tests.
- `mvn package`: Compiles, executes the tests and packages the code into an archive (e.g. a war file).
- `mvn install`: Builds and installs the artifacts in your local repository.
- `mvn clean install`: Cleans and installs (note that you can add several commands separated by spaces, like `mvn clean compile test`).

Maven allows you to compile, run, and package the examples of this fascicle. It decouples the fact that you need to write your code (within an IDE) and build it. To develop you need an *Integrated Development Environment* (IDE). I use IntelliJ IDEA from JetBrains, but you can use any IDE you like because this fascicle only relies on Maven and not on specific IntelliJ IDEA features.

A.4. Testing Frameworks

A.4.1. JUnit 5.x

All the examples of this fascicle are tested using JUnit 5.x. JUnit is an open source framework to write and run repeatable tests.[72] JUnit features include: assertions for testing expected results, fixtures for sharing common test data, and runners for running tests.

JUnit is the de facto standard testing library for the Java language, and it stands in a single jar file that you can download from https://junit.org/junit5 (or use Maven dependency management, which we do in this fascicle). The library contains a complete API to help you write your unit tests and execute them. Unit and integration tests help your code to be more robust, bug free, and reliable. Coming up, we will go through the above features with some examples but before that, let's have a quick overview of JUnit's history.

The code in this appendix can be found at https://github.com/agoncal/agoncal-fascicle-commons/tree/master/junit

A Brief History of JUnit

JUnit was originally written by Erich Gamma and Kent Beck in 1998. It was inspired by Smalltalk's SUnit test framework, also written by Kent Beck. It quickly became one of the most popular frameworks in the Java world. JUnit took an important step in achieving test-driven development (TDD). Let's see some of the JUnit features through a simple example.

Writing Tests

Listing 179 represents a `Customer` POJO. It has some attributes, including a date of birth, constructors, getters and setters. It also provides two utility methods to clear the date of birth and to calculate the age of the customer (`calculateAge()`).

Listing 179. A Customer Class

```
public class Customer {

  private Long id;
  private String firstName;
  private String lastName;
  private String email;
  private String phoneNumber;
  private LocalDate dateOfBirth;
  private Integer age;

  // Constructors, getters, setters

  public void calculateAge() {
    if (dateOfBirth == null) {
      age = null;
      return;
    }

    age = Period.between(dateOfBirth, LocalDate.now()).getYears();
  }

  public void clear() {
    this.dateOfBirth = null;
  }
}
```

The `calculateAge()` method uses the `dateOfBirth` attribute to set the customer's age. It has some business logic and we want to make sure the algorithm calculates the age accurately. We want to test this business logic. For that, we need a test class with some JUnit test methods and assertions.

Test Class

In JUnit, test classes do not have to extend anything. To be executed as a test case, a JUnit class needs at least one method annotated with `@Test`. If you write a class without at least one `@Test` method, you will get an error when trying to execute it (`java.lang.Exception: No runnable methods`). Listing 180 shows the `CustomerTest` class that initialises the `Customer` object.

Listing 180. A Unit Test Class for Customer

```
public class CustomerTest {

  private Customer customer = new Customer();
```

Fixtures

Fixtures are methods to initialise and release any common object during tests. JUnit uses `@BeforeEach` and `@AfterEach` annotations to execute code before or after each test. These methods can be given any name (`clearCustomer()` in Listing 181), and you can have multiple methods in one test class. JUnit uses @BeforeAll and @AfterAll annotations to execute specific code only once, before or after the test suite is executed. These methods must be unique and static. @BeforeAll and @AfterAll can be very useful if you need to allocate and release expensive resources.

Listing 181. Fixture Executed Before Each Test

```
@BeforeEach
public void clearCustomer() {
  customer.clear();
}
```

Test Methods

A test method must use the @Test annotation, return void, and take no parameters. This is controlled at runtime and throws an exception if not respected. In Listing 182, the test method ageShouldBeGreaterThanZero creates a new Customer and sets a specific date of birth. Then, using the assertion mechanism of JUnit (explained in the next section), it checks that the calculated age is greater than zero.

Listing 182. Method Testing Age Calculation

```
@Test
public void ageShouldBeGreaterThanZero() {
  customer = new Customer("Rita", "Navalhas", "rnavalhas@gmail.com");
  customer.setDateOfBirth(LocalDate.of(1975, 5, 27));

  customer.calculateAge();

  assertTrue(customer.getAge() >= 0);
}
```

JUnit also allows us to check for exceptions. In Listing 183, we are trying to calculate the age of a null customer object so the call to the calculateAge() method should throw a NullPointerException. If it does, then the test succeeds. If it doesn't, or if it throws a different type of exception than the one declared, the test fails.

Listing 183. Method Testing Nullity

```
@Test
public void shouldThrowAnExceptionCauseDateOfBirtheIsNull() {

  customer = null;
  assertThrows(NullPointerException.class, () -> {
    customer.calculateAge();
  });
}
```

Listing 184 does not implement the shouldCalculateOldAge() method. However, you don't want the test to fail; you just want to ignore it. You can add the @Disable annotation next to the @Test annotation. JUnit will report the number of disabled tests, along with the number of tests that succeeded and failed. Note that `@Disable` takes an optional parameter (a `String`) in case you want to record why a test is being disabled.

Listing 184. Disabling a Method for Testing

```
@Test
@Disabled("Test is not ready yet")
public void shouldCalculateOldAge() {
  // some work to do
}
```

JUnit Assertions

Test cases must assert that objects conform to an expected result, such as in Listing 182 where we assert that the age is greater than zero. For that, JUnit has an `Assertions` class that contains several methods. In order to use different assertions, you can either use the prefixed syntax (e.g. `Assertions.assertEquals()`) or import the `Assertions` class statically. Listing 185 shows a simplified subset of the methods defined in the `Assertions` class.

Listing 185. Subset of JUnit Assertions

```
public class Assertions {

  void assertTrue(boolean condition) { }
  void assertFalse(boolean condition) { }

  void assertNull(Object actual) { }
  void assertNotNull(Object actual) { }

  void assertEquals(Object expected, Object actual) { }
  void assertNotEquals(Object unexpected, Object actual) { }

  void assertArrayEquals(Object[] expected, Object[] actual) { }
  void assertLinesMatch(List<String> expectedLines, List<String> actualLines) { }

  void assertSame(Object expected, Object actual) { }
  void assertNotSame(Object unexpected, Object actual) { }
  void assertAll(Collection<Executable> executables) { }
  void assertTimeout(Duration timeout, Executable executable) { }

  <T extends Throwable> T assertThrows(Class<T> expectedType, Executable exec) { }
}
```

Executing Tests

JUnit is very well integrated with most IDEs (IntelliJ IDEA, Eclipse, NetBeans etc.). When working with these IDEs, in most cases, JUnit highlights in green to indicate successful tests and in red to indicate failures. Most IDEs also provide facilities to create test classes.

JUnit is also integrated with Maven through the Surefire plugin used during the test phase of the build life cycle.[73] It executes the JUnit test classes of an application and generates reports in XML and text file formats. That's mostly how we will be using JUnit in this fascicle: through Maven. To integrate JUnit in Maven, you just need the JUnit dependency and make sure to declare the Surefire plugin in the `pom.xml` as shown in Listing 186.

Listing 186. JUnit Dependencies in a Maven pom.xml

```
<dependencies>
  <dependency>
    <groupId>org.junit.jupiter</groupId>
    <artifactId>junit-jupiter-engine</artifactId>
    <version>5.6.0</version>
    <scope>test</scope>
  </dependency>
</dependencies>

<build>
  <plugins>
    <plugin>
      <groupId>org.apache.maven.plugins</groupId>
      <artifactId>maven-surefire-plugin</artifactId>
      <version>2.22.2</version>
    </plugin>
  </plugins>
</build>
```

The following Maven command runs the JUnit tests through the Surefire plugin:

```
$ mvn test
```

Then JUnit executes the tests and gives the number of executed tests, the number of failures and the number of disabled tests (through warnings).

```
[INFO] ------------------------
[INFO] Building Commons :: JUnit
[INFO] ------------------------
[INFO]
[INFO] --- maven-compiler-plugin:3.7.0:compile (default-compile)
[INFO]
[INFO] --- maven-surefire-plugin:2.22.2:test (default-test)
[INFO]
[INFO] ----------
[INFO]  T E S T S
[INFO] ----------
[INFO] Running org.agoncal.fascicle.commons.junit.CustomerTest
[WARNING] Tests run: 3, Failures: 0, Errors: 0, Skipped: 1, Time elapsed: 0.032 s
[INFO]
[INFO] Results:
[INFO]
[WARNING] Tests run: 3, Failures: 0, Errors: 0, Skipped: 1
[INFO]
[INFO] -------------
[INFO] BUILD SUCCESS
[INFO] -------------
[INFO] Total time:  1.824 s
[INFO] Finished at: 2020-03-04T11:51:34+01:00
[INFO] -------------
```

A.5. H2 Database

H2 is a relational database written in Java.[74] Of small footprint (1MB), H2 is a fully functional and transactional relational database that can easily be embedded in any Java-based solution. H2 provides three different modes:

- Embedded: Refers to H2 being started by a simple single-user Java application. With this option, H2 runs in the same JVM as the application. In this fascicle, I use this mode during integration testing.
- In-Memory: Refers to multiple connections in one process but still in memory.
- Server Mode: Refers to H2 being started as a separate process and providing multi-user connectivity. I use this mode throughout the book when running applications so I can see the database structure and the data.

A.5.1. A Brief History of H2

The development of H2 started in May 2004 and was first published in December 2005. It is somewhat related to Hypersonic SQL database.[75] In 2001, the Hypersonic SQL project was stopped, and the HSQLDB Group was formed to continue working on the Hypersonic SQL code.[76] The name H2 stands for Hypersonic 2, however H2 does not share code with Hypersonic SQL or HSQLDB. H2 is built from scratch.

A.5.2. Installing H2 on macOS

Installing H2 is very easy. In fact, if you only use the embedded mode, you don't even have to install it: just let Maven download the dependency to your classpath (`com.h2database:h2`) and use H2 in memory.

When using server mode, you can download the binaries for your platform, unzip the installation file and setup your `PATH` variable.[77] Installing H2 with Homebrew is just a matter of a single command.[78] Open your terminal and execute:

```
$ brew install h2
```

A.5.3. Checking for H2 Installation

Start the H2 server mode just by launching the `h2` command.

```
$ h2
```

As seen in Figure 56, as soon as you run `h2`, a browser page opens with the URL http://localhost:8082 displaying the H2 console. This console lets you access a relational database using a browser interface. This is very handy for visualising the database structure or executing an SQL statement.

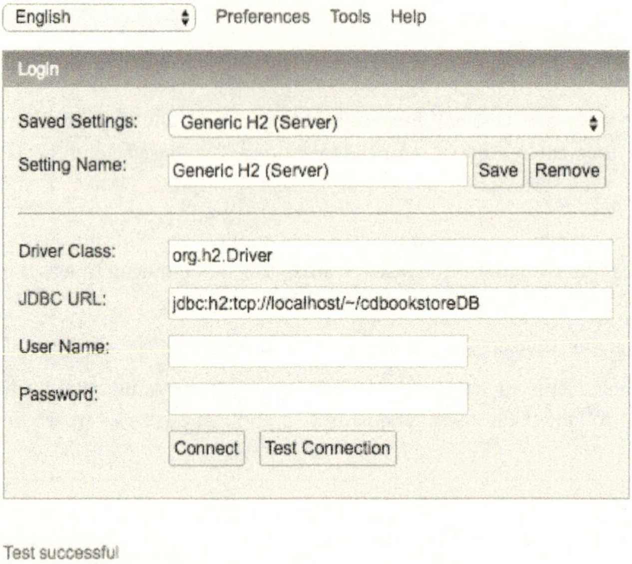

English Preferences Tools Help
Login
Saved Settings: Generic H2 (Server)
Setting Name: Generic H2 (Server) Save Remove
Driver Class: org.h2.Driver
JDBC URL: jdbc:h2:tcp://localhost/~/cdbookstoreDB
User Name:
Password:
Connect Test Connection
Test successful

Figure 56. The H2 browser console

A.5.4. The H2 Console

Make sure you've started the H2 database in server mode, and check the console on http://localhost:8082. Then, you can enter any SQL statement to create a database, a table, insert data into the table, or query the data. For example Figure 57, shows the content of the table `Artist`.

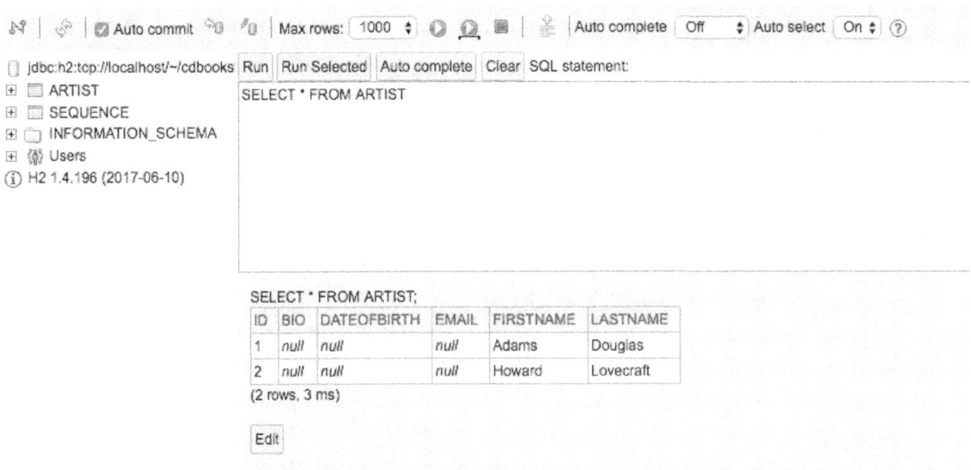

Figure 57. H2 console executing a select statement

To get the structure of the `Artist` table, execute the statement `SHOW COLUMNS FROM ARTIST` as seen in Figure 58.

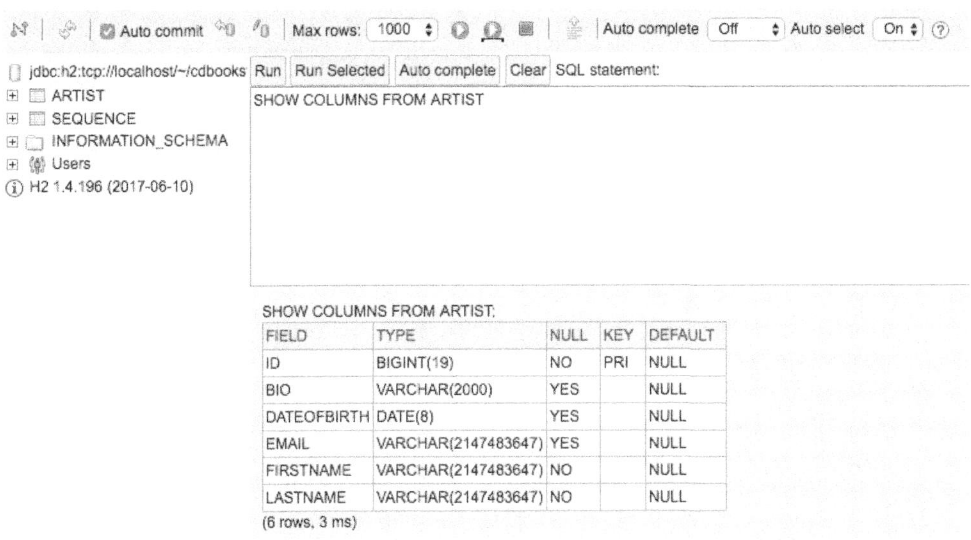

Figure 58. H2 console showing the database structure

A.5.5. Setting up the H2 JDBC Driver

Depending on the mode you want to use, you need to setup the JDBC driver accordingly. In a JPA application you will setup the JDBC driver in the `persistence.xml`. If you use H2 in a pure Java application, load the JDBC driver with `Class.forName("org.h2.Driver")`. Then, depending on the database that you target, choose the appropriate JDBC URL:

- Embedded
  - jdbc:h2:~/vintageStoreDB 'vintageStoreDB' in the user home directory
  - jdbc:h2:/data/vintageStoreDB 'vintageStoreDB' in the directory `/data`
  - jdbc:h2:vintageStoreDB in the current working directory
- In-Memory
  - jdbc:h2:mem:vintageStoreDB multiple connections in one process
  - jdbc:h2:mem: unnamed private connection
- Server Mode
  - jdbc:h2:tcp://localhost/~/vintageStoreDB user home directory

A.6. Git

Git is a free and open source distributed version control system designed for tracking changes in computer files and coordinating work on those files among multiple people.[79] It is primarily used for source code management in software development, but it can be used to keep track of changes in any set of files. Git was created by Linus Torvalds in 2005 for the development of the Linux kernel, with other kernel developers contributing to its initial development.

Git is not really needed to run the samples in this fascicle. Even if the code is hosted on a public Git repository (https://github.com/agoncal/agoncal-fascicle-jpa/tree/2.2), you can either download the code as a zip file, or clone the repository. Only if you clone the repository will you need to have Git installed.

A.6.1. A Brief History of Git

Git development began in April 2005, after many developers in the Linux kernel gave up access to BitKeeper, a proprietary source-control management (SCM). Linus Torvalds wanted a distributed system that he could use, like BitKeeper, but none of the available free systems met his needs. So, Linus started the development of Git on 3rd April 2005, announced the project on 6th April and the first merge of multiple branches took place on 18th April. On 29th April, the nascent Git was benchmarked, recording patches to the Linux kernel tree at the rate of 6.7 patches per second.[80]

A.6.2. Installing Git on macOS

On macOS, if you have installed Homebrew, then installing Git is just a matter of a single command.[81] Open your terminal and install Git with the following command:

```
$ brew install git
```

A.6.3. Checking for Git Installation

Once installed, check for Git by running `git --version` in the terminal. It should display the git version:

```
$ git --version
git version 2.30.1
```

A.6.4. Cloning Repository

Once Git is installed, you can clone the code of the repository with a `git clone` on https://github.com/agoncal/agoncal-fascicle-jpa.git.

[61] **Homebrew** https://brew.sh

[62] **Homebrew History** https://en.wikipedia.org/wiki/Homebrew_(package_manager)#History

[63] **Homebrew Cask** https://github.com/Homebrew/homebrew-cask

[64] **Java** http://www.oracle.com/technetwork/java/javase

[65] **Visual VM** https://visualvm.github.io

[66] **The Java HotSpot Performance Engine Architecture** https://www.oracle.com/technetwork/java/whitepaper-135217.html

[67] **Java History** https://en.wikipedia.org/wiki/Java_(programming_language)#History

[68] **Java Website** http://www.oracle.com/technetwork/java/javase/downloads/index.html

[69] **Maven** https://maven.apache.org

[70] **Maven History** https://en.wikipedia.org/wiki/Apache_Maven#History

[71] **Maven Central** https://search.maven.org

[72] **JUnit** https://junit.org/junit5

[73] **Maven Surefire Plugin** https://maven.apache.org/surefire/maven-surefire-plugin

[74] **H2** http://www.h2database.com

[75] **Hypersonic SQL** http://hsql.sourceforge.net/index.html

[76] **HSQLDB** http://hsqldb.org

[77] **Download H2** http://www.h2database.com/html/download.html

[78] **Homebrew** https://brew.sh

[79] **Git** https://git-scm.com

[80] **History of Git** https://en.wikipedia.org/wiki/Git#History

[81] **Homebrew** https://brew.sh

Appendix B: Java Persistence API Specification Versions

B.1. JPA 2.2

JPA 2.2 is described under the 338 and was released in 2017.[82] It was shipped with Java EE 8 but it was just a *maintenance release*, meaning that it uses the same JSR as JPA 2.1 (still the JSR 338). A maintenance release means that a specification doesn't evolve much, and therefore doesn't need a new JSR. The changes made to JPA 2.2 were mostly to support Java SE 8:

- Adds support for Java SE 8 Lambdas and Streams.
- Adds `@Repeatable` meta-annotation to JPA annotations.
- Support for CDI injection into `AttributeConverter` classes.
- Support for the mapping of the new `java.time` types (e.g. `LocalDate`, `LocalTime` etc.).[83]
- Adds default `Stream getResultStream()` method to `Query` and `TypedQuery` interfaces.

B.2. JPA 2.1

JPA 2.1 was released in 2013 under the JSR 338 and was part of Java EE 7.[84] This version brought many new features and improvements:

- Schema generation: JPA 2.1 standardised database schema generation by bringing a new API and a set of properties (defined in the `persistence.xml`).
- Converters: These are classes that convert between database and attribute representations.
- CDI support: Injection into event listeners became possible.
- Support for stored procedures: JPA 2.1 allowed dynamically-specified and named stored procedure queries.
- Bulk update and delete criteria queries: Criteria API only had select queries; from 2.1 update and delete queries were also specified.
- Downcasting: The new `TREAT` operator allowed access to the subclass-specific state in queries.

B.3. JPA 2.0

If JPA 1.0 was a completely new persistence model from its Entity CMP 2.x ancestor, JPA 2.0 was a continuation of version 1.0. JPA 2.0 was released in 2009 with Java EE 6 under the JSR 317.[85]

It kept the object-oriented approach with annotation and optional XML mapping files. This second version brought new APIs, extended JPQL, and added these new functionalities:

- Collections of simple data types (String, Integer etc.) and embeddable objects could then be mapped in separate tables. Previously, you could only map collections of entities.
- Map support was extended so that maps could have keys and values of basic types, entities, or

embeddables.

- Maintaining a persistent ordering was then possible with the `@OrderColumn` annotation.
- Orphan removal allowed child objects to be removed from a relationship if the parent object is removed.
- Optimistic locking was already supported, but pessimistic locking was finally introduced.
- A brand-new Criteria API was introduced to allow queries to be constructed in an object-oriented manner rather than using a string-based approach.
- JPQL syntax got richer (e.g. it allowed case expressions).
- Embeddable objects could be nested into other embeddable objects and have relationships to entities.
- The dot (`.`) navigation syntax was extended to handle embeddables with relationships and embeddables of embeddables.
- Support for a new caching API was added.
- Some properties in the `persistence.xml` file got standardised, increasing the portability of your application.

B.4. JPA 1.0

Before Java EE 5, the persistent component model was called *Entity Bean*, or to be more precise, Entity Bean CMP (*Container-Managed Persistence*), and was associated with *Enterprise JavaBeans* (EJBs). This model of persistence lasted from J2EE 1.3 until J2EE 1.4, but was heavyweight and finally got replaced by JPA 1.0 from Java EE 5 on. JPA 1.0 was created in 2006 under the JSR 220.[86]

[82] JSR 338 https://jcp.org/en/jsr/detail?id=338

[83] JSR 310 https://jcp.org/en/jsr/detail?id=310

[84] JSR 338 https://jcp.org/en/jsr/detail?id=338

[85] JSR 317 https://jcp.org/en/jsr/detail?id=317

[86] JSR 220 https://jcp.org/en/jsr/detail?id=220

Appendix C: References

- JPA 2.2 (JSR 338) https://jcp.org/en/jsr/detail?id=338
- JPA 2.0 (JSR 317) https://jcp.org/en/jsr/detail?id=317
- Enterprise JavaBeans 3.1 (JSR 318) https://jcp.org/en/jsr/detail?id=318
- Enterprise JavaBeans 3.0 (JSR 220) https://jcp.org/en/jsr/detail?id=220
- Eclipselink http://www.eclipse.org/eclipselink
- Hibernate ORM http://hibernate.org/orm
- OpenJPA http://openjpa.apache.org
- Testing CDI Beans and the Persistence Layer Under Java SE by Gunnar Morling http://in.relation.to/2019/01/23/testing-cdi-beans-and-persistence-layer-under-java-se

Appendix D: Resources by the Same Author

D.1. Fascicles

The *agoncal fascicle* series contains two types of fascicles. The *Understanding* collection is about fascicles that dive into a specific technology, explain it, and show different aspects of it as well as integrating it with other external technologies. On the other hand, the *Practising* collection is all about coding. So you are supposed to already know a little bit of this technology and be ready to code in order to build a specific application. Below the list of fascicles I have written.

D.1.1. Understanding Bean Validation 2.0

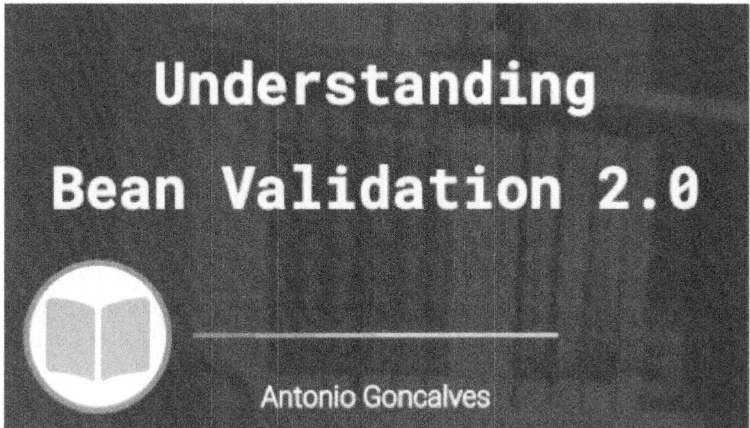

Validating data is a common task that Java developers have to do and it is spread throughout all layers (from client to database) of an application. This common practice is time-consuming, error prone, and hard to maintain in the long run. Besides, some of these constraints are so frequently used that they could be considered standard (checking for a null value, size, range, etc.). It would be good to be able to centralise these constraints in one place and share them across layers.

That's when Bean Validation comes into play.

In this fascicle, you will learn Bean Validation and use its different APIs to apply constraints on a bean, validate all sorts of constraints, write your own constraints and a few advanced topics such as integrating Bean Validation with other frameworks (JPA, JAX-RS, CDI, Spring).

You can find two different formats of this fascicle:

- eBook (PDF/EPUB): https://agoncal.teachable.com/p/ebook-understanding-bean-validation
- Paper book: http://amazon.com/Understanding-Bean-Validation-2-0-fascicle/dp/1980399026 (ISBN: 9781980399025)

D.1.2. Understanding JPA 2.2

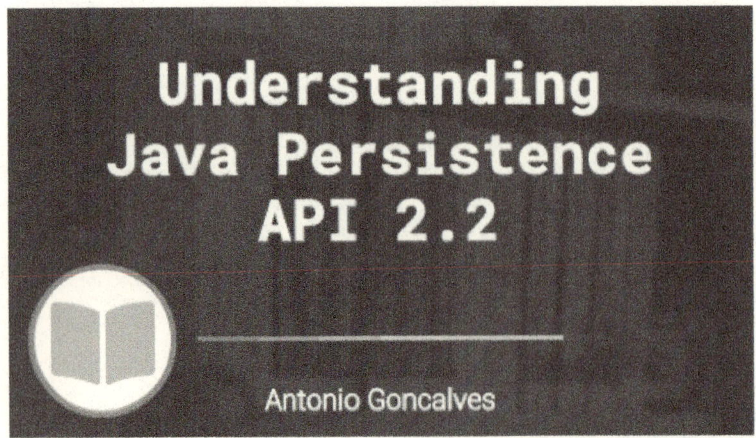

Applications are made up of business logic, interaction with other systems, user interfaces etc. and data. Most of the data that our applications manipulate have to be stored in datastores, retrieved, processed and analysed. If this datastore is a relational database and you use an object-oriented programming language such as Java, then you might want to use an Object-Relational Mapping tool.

That's when Java Persistence API comes into play.

In this fascicle, you will learn JPA, the standard ORM that maps Java objects to relational databases. You will discover its annotations for mapping entities, as well as the Java Persistence Query Language, entity life cycle and a few advanced topics such as integrating JPA with other frameworks (Bean Validation, JTA, CDI, Spring).

You can find two different formats of this fascicle:

- eBook (PDF/EPUB): https://agoncal.teachable.com/p/ebook-understanding-jpa
- Paper book: https://www.amazon.com/Understanding-JPA-2-2-Persistence-fascicle/dp/1093918977 (ISBN: 9781093918977)

D.1.3. Understanding Quarkus 2.x

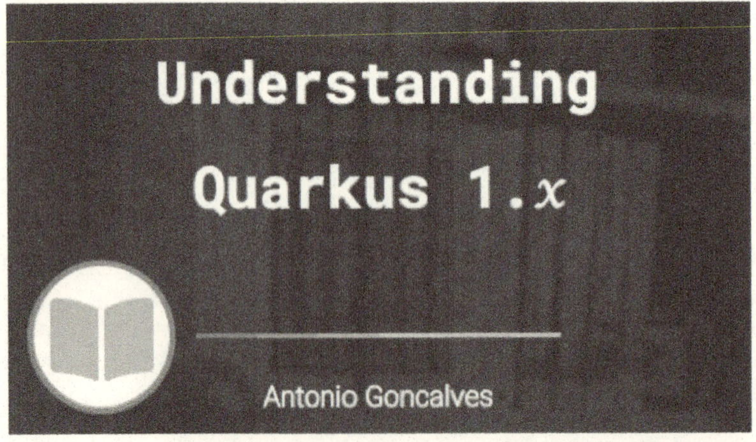

Microservices is an architectural style that structures an application as a collection of distributed services. Microservices are certainly appealing but there are many questions that should be asked prior to diving into this architectural style: How do I deal with an unreliable network in a distributed architecture? How do I test my services? How do I monitor them? How do I package and execute them?

That's when Quarkus comes into play.

In this fascicle, you will learn Quarkus but also its ecosystem. You will discover Quarkus internals and how you can use it to build REST and reactive microservices, bind and process JSON or access datastores in a transactional way. With Cloud Native and GraalVM in mind, Quarkus makes packaging and orchestrating your microservices with Docker and Kubernetes easy.

This fascicle has a good mix of theory and practical examples. It is the companion book of *Practising Quarkus 2.x* where you learn how to develop an entire microservice architecture.

You can find two different formats of this fascicle:

- eBook (PDF/EPUB): https://agoncal.teachable.com/p/ebook-understanding-quarkus
- Paper book: (ISBN: 9798689410418)

D.1.4. Practising Quarkus 2.x

Microservices is an architectural style that structures an application as a collection of distributed services. Microservices are certainly appealing but there are many questions that should be asked prior to diving into this architectural style: How do I deal with an unreliable network in a distributed architecture? How do I test my services? How do I monitor them? How do I package and execute them?

That's when Quarkus comes into play.

In this fascicle you will develop an entire microservice application using Quarkus as well as MicroProfile. You will expose REST endpoints using JAX-RS and OpenAPI, customise the JSON output thanks to JSON-B and deal with persistence and transaction with Hibernate ORM with Panache and JTA. Having distributed microservices, you will implement health checks and add some metrics so you can monitor your microservice architecture. Finally, thanks to GraalVM you will build native executables, and package and execute them with Docker.

This fascicle is very practical. It is the companion book of the more theoretical *Understanding Quarkus 2.x* where you'll learn more about Quarkus, MicroProfile, REST and reactive microservices, as well as Cloud Native and GraalVM.

You can find two different formats of this fascicle:

- eBook (PDF/EPUB): https://agoncal.teachable.com/p/ebook-practising-quarkus (PDF and EPUB format
- Paper book: (ISBN: 9798629562115)

D.2. Online Courses

Online courses are a great way to learn a new technology or dive into one that you already know. Below the list of online courses I have created.

D.2.1. Starting With Quarkus

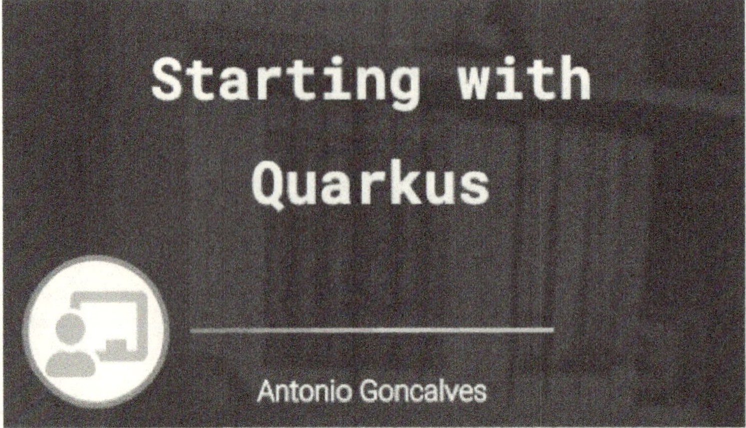

This course is for Java developers who want to discover Quarkus. It's a mixture of slides and code so you can "Understand and Practice" at the same time. This way, you learn the theory, and then put it into practice by developing an application step by step.

In this course you will go through an entire development cycle. After introducing Quarkus, you will make sure your development environment is set up, and you will go from bootstrapping a Quarkus application, to running it as a Docker container.

D.2.2. Building Microservices With Quarkus

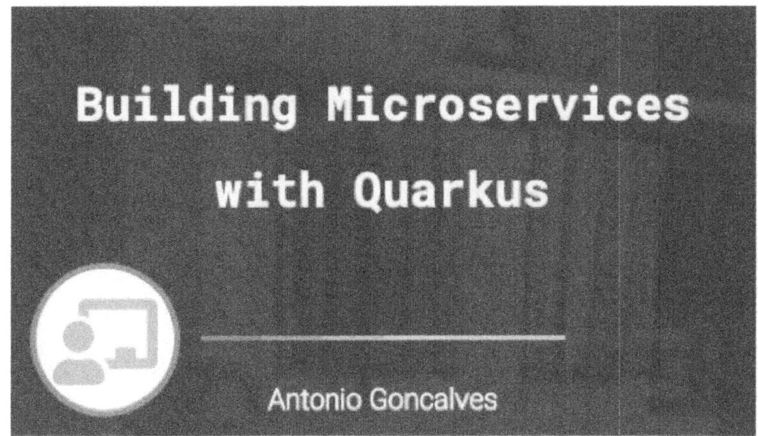

This course is for Quarkus developers who want to discover how Quarkus and MicroProfile handle microservices. It's a mixture of slides and code so you can "Understand and Practice" at the same time. This way, you learn the theory, and then put it into practice by developing a microservice architecture step by step.

In this course you will develop two microservices that talk to each other. After introducing Microservices and MicroProfile, you will make sure your development environment is set up, and you will go from bootstrapping two Quarkus microservices, to running them as Docker containers.

D.2.3. Quarkus: Fundamentals (*PluralSight*)

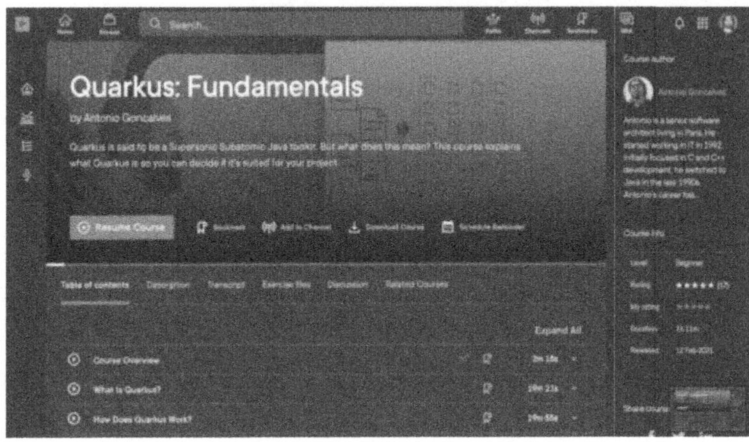

Quarkus is said to be a Supersonic Subatomic Java toolkit. But what does this mean? This course explains what Quarkus is so you can decide if it's suited for your project.[87]

D.2.4. Microservices: The Big Picture (*PluralSight*)

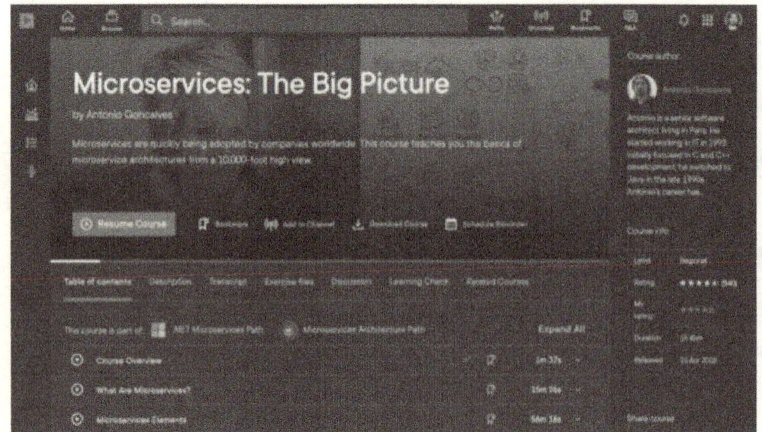

Microservices are quickly being adopted by companies worldwide. This course teaches you the basics of microservice architectures from a 10,000-foot high view.[88]

D.2.5. Java EE: The Big Picture (*PluralSight*)

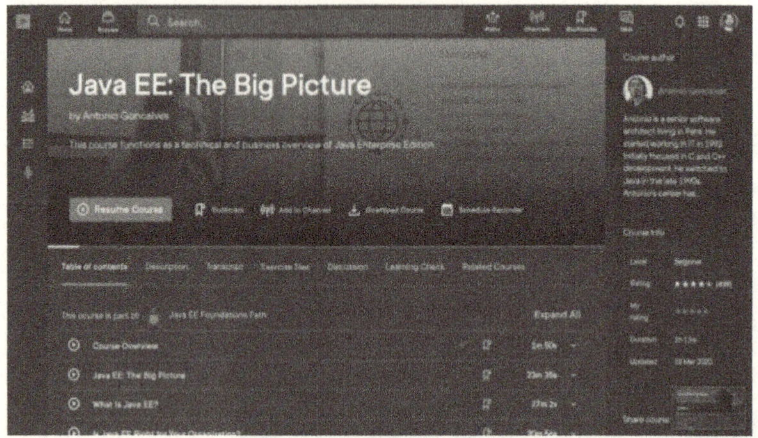

This course functions as a technical and business overview of Java Enterprise Edition.[89]

D.2.6. Java EE: Getting Started (*PluralSight*)

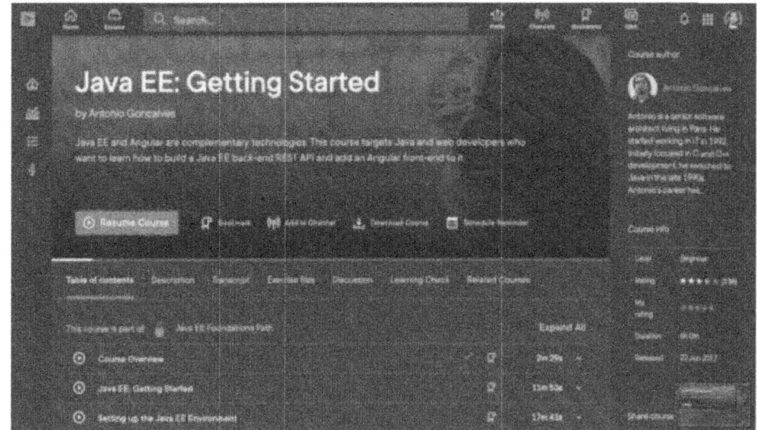

Java EE and Angular are complementary technologies. This course targets Java and web developers who want to learn how to build a Java EE back-end REST API and add an Angular front-end to it.[90]

D.2.7. Java EE 7 Fundamentals (*PluralSight*)

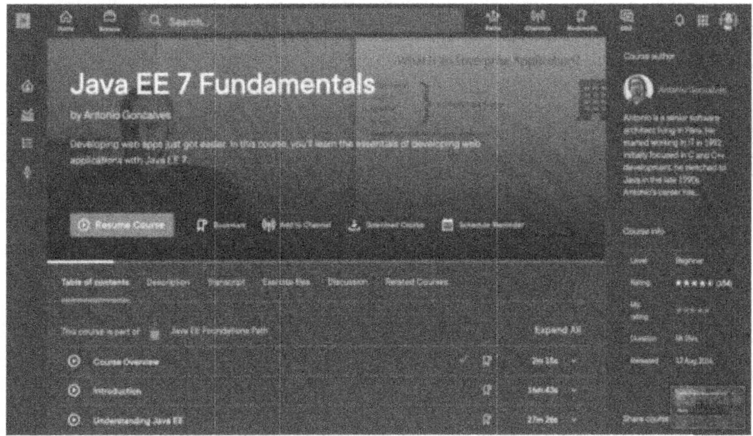

Developing web apps just got easier. In this course, you'll learn the essentials of developing web applications with Java EE 7.[91]

D.2.8. Java Persistence API 2.2 (*PluralSight*)

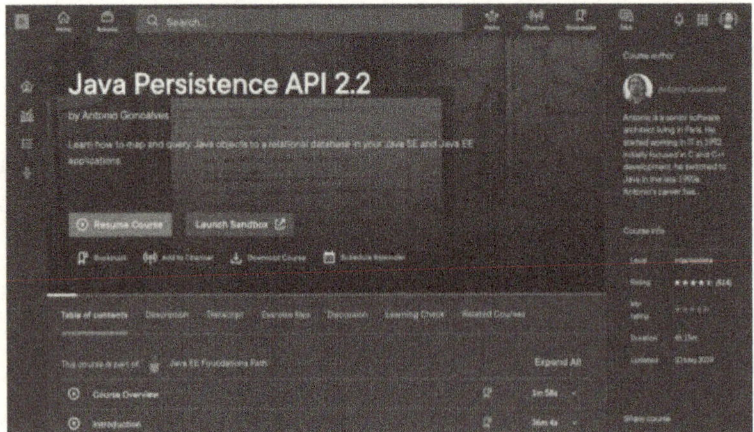

Learn how to map and query Java objects to a relational database in your Java SE and Java EE applications.[92]

D.2.9. Context and Dependency Injection 1.1 (*PluralSight*)

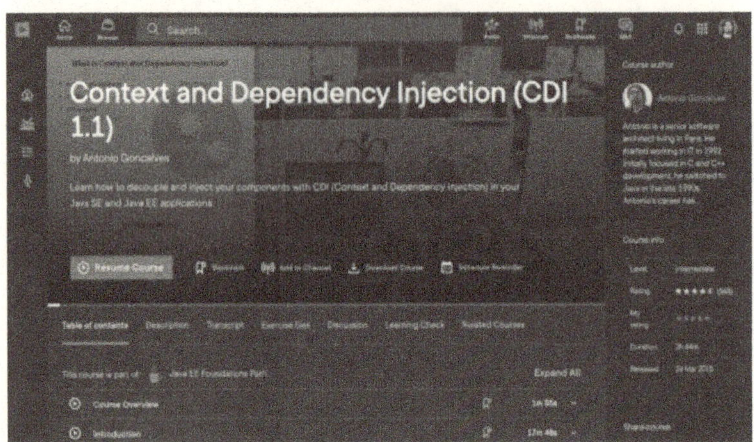

Learn how to decouple and inject your components with CDI (Context and Dependency Injection) in your Java SE and Java EE applications.[93]

D.2.10. Bean Validation 1.1 (*PluralSight*)

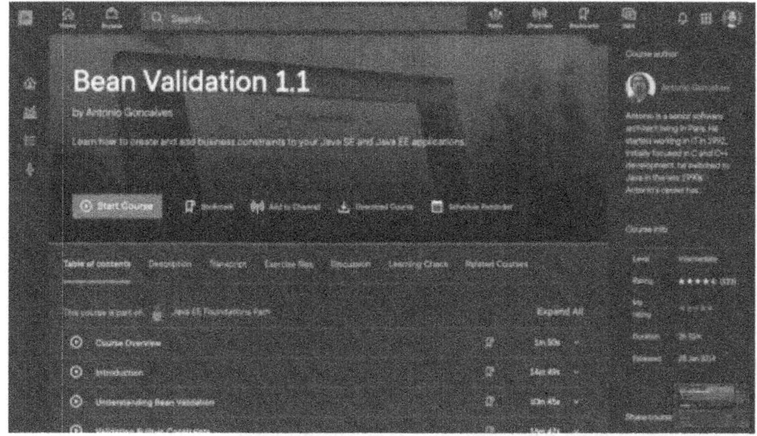

Learn how to create and add business constraints to your Java SE and Java EE applications.[94]

[87] Quarkus: Fundamentals https://app.pluralsight.com/library/courses/quarkus-fundamentals/table-of-contents

[88] Microservices: The Big Picture https://app.pluralsight.com/library/courses/microservices-big-picture/table-of-contents

[89] Java EE: The Big Picture https://app.pluralsight.com/library/courses/java-ee-big-picture/table-of-contents

[90] Java EE: Getting Started https://app.pluralsight.com/library/courses/java-ee-getting-started/table-of-contents

[91] Java EE 7 Fundamentals https://app.pluralsight.com/library/courses/java-ee-7-fundamentals/table-of-contents

[92] Java EE: The Big Picture https://app.pluralsight.com/library/courses/java-persistence-api-21/table-of-contents

[93] Context and Dependency Injection 1.1 https://app.pluralsight.com/library/courses/context-dependency-injection-1-1/table-of-contents

[94] Bean Validation 1.1 https://app.pluralsight.com/library/courses/bean-validation/table-of-contents

Appendix E: Printed Back Cover

Antonio Goncalves is a senior software architect and Java Champion. Having been focused on Java development since the late 1990s, his career has taken him to many different countries and companies. For the last few years, Antonio has given talks at international conferences, mainly on Java, distributed systems and microservices. This fascicle stems from his extensive experience in writing books, blogs and articles.

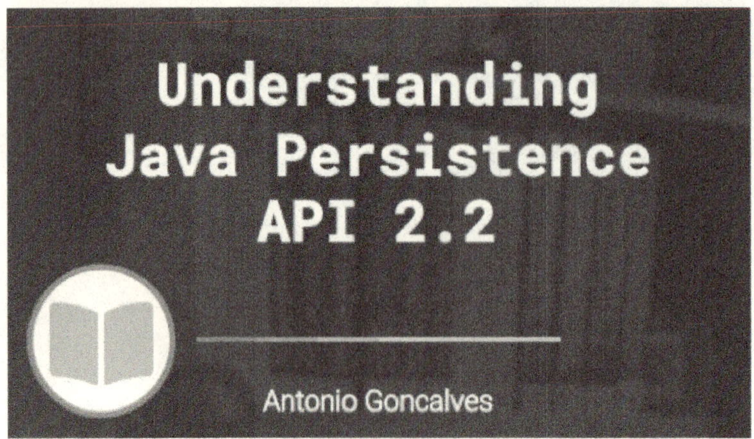

Applications are made up of business logic, interaction with other systems, user interfaces etc. and data. Most of the data that our applications manipulate have to be stored in datastores, retrieved, processed and analysed. If this datastore is a relational database and you use an object-oriented programming language such as Java, then you might want to use an Object-Relational Mapping tool.

That's when Java Persistence API comes into play.

In this fascicle, you will learn JPA, the standard ORM that maps Java objects to relational databases. You will discover its annotations for mapping entities, as well as the Java Persistence Query Language, entity life cycle and a few advanced topics such as integrating JPA with other frameworks (Bean Validation, JTA, CDI, Spring).

You can find two different formats of this fascicle:

- eBook (PDF/EPUB): https://agoncal.teachable.com/p/ebook-understanding-jpa
- Paper book: https://www.amazon.com/Understanding-JPA-2-2-Persistence-fascicle/dp/1093918977 (ISBN: 9781093918977)

Made in the USA
Coppell, TX
14 January 2022

71589381R00152